HONOR
UNTARNISHED

HONOR
UNTARNISHED

A WEST POINT GRADUATE'S MEMOIR
OF WORLD WAR II

GENERAL DONALD V. BENNETT (Retired)
with WILLIAM R. FORSTCHEN, Ph.D.

A Tom Doherty Associates Book
New York

For Bets

HONOR UNTARNISHED

Copyright © 2003 by Donald V. Bennett and William R. Forstchen

This book is printed on acid-free paper.

Book design by Michael Collica

A Forge Book
Published by Tom Doherty Associates, LLC
175 Fifth Avenue
New York, NY 10010

www.tor.com

Forge® is a registered trademark of Tom Doherty Associates, LLC.

Library of Congress Cataloging-in-Publication Data

Bennett, Donald V. (Donald Vivian), 1915–
    Honor untarnished / Donald V. Bennett and William R. Forstchen.—1st ed.
        p.   cm.
    "A Tom Doherty Associates book."
    ISBN: 0-765-30657-3 (alk. paper)
    1. Bennett, Donald V. (Donald Vivian), 1915-   2. World War, 1939-1945—
Personal narratives, American.   3. United States. Army—Officers—Biography.
4. World War, 1939-1945—Artillery operations, American.   5. Artillery,
Self-propelled.   I. Forstchen, William R.   II. Title.

D811.B4476A3 2003
940.54'8173—dc21

                                                                2003040831

First Edition: June 2003

Printed in the United States of America

0   9   8   7   6   5   4   3   2   1

Clockwise from left:
Don and Bets at Fort Sam Houston
North Africa, 1942
General Bennett around the time of his retirement
Don (*front right*) in a West Point classroom

Acknowledgments

Of course, there are so many who deserve recognition for their help and encouragement with this book. My heartfelt thanks must go to my daughter, Lynn, and her husband, Bob, who have always been there for me, in good times and bad, and were always ready with encouragement and support. The same goes for Sharon Forstchen, wife of Bill Forstchen who helped me with this book. She patiently endured two years in which her husband disappeared on weekends to spend time working with me. Brian Thomsen and the staff at Tor/Forge deserve my special thanks as well for their professionalism and patience.

Across thirty years of a military career there are so many people who remain in my memory. To name but one might imply a neglect of many others, so all I can humbly say is thank you to all of them. All that I managed to achieve—really, the simple fact that I am alive today—rests on so many comrades of old.

Of course, a special acknowledgment must go to my comrades with the 58th and 62d Mobile Armored Artillery Battalions. We who are left are old soldiers now. We, together, know so much that can never be spoken of, nor explained. The admiration and love I have for all of you, I shall cherish for the rest of my life.

Finally, a humble acknowledgment of West Point—a thousand years from now, may it continue to shape men and women to a life of sacrifice and service as it once shaped me.

Contents

1

Childhood and Early Years

I was born on May 9, 1915, in the small town of Lakeside, Ohio, located a dozen miles or so outside of Toledo. Lakeside was like a thousand other towns of the Midwest in those years, one foot still firmly planted in the nineteenth century, the other foot just beginning to edge into the twentieth.

When I was about a year old, we moved to Genoa, and then several years later to Oak Harbor.

Where I grew up had only one church, Methodist, which my family went to every Sunday. The local school had three hundred or so students, from kindergarten to twelfth grade all in one building. They were just starting to pave the streets, news came via the paper from Toledo or telegraph, and my father's job was supervising the stringing of electrical lines and the powering of the trolley that connected us to the rest of the world.

As I write this now, eighty-six years later, it seems that I was born into a far different world, and I am stunned by how quickly it changed and the role I played in creating some of that change.

When I was a boy, veterans of the Civil War were a common sight. That war was only fifty years past. The men in blue uniforms, who seemed so ancient to me then, were younger than I am now. Bull Run, Gettysburg, Shiloh, Appomattox were not just names in history books, they were memories still alive in the hearts of millions of Americans. On Decoration Day tears still flowed when flowers were laid upon graves of comrades who died in such distant places as Virginia and Georgia.

When I graduated from West Point and went to my first posting at Fort Sill, Oklahoma, I was trained in how to lead a team of horses pulling an artillery piece, riding one of the trace horses, learning the lesson all old artillerymen knew, to keep your right foot high and out of the stirrup, otherwise it might be crushed by the guide pole.

Only four years after learning that lesson I was in command of a mechanized battalion of armored artillery at Omaha Beach. That one battalion had more firepower than all the artillery pieces fired at Gettysburg. Only five years after Omaha, I witnessed the detonation of an atomic bomb in Nevada. And but ten years after that, I personally was responsible for hundreds of such weapons deployed in Germany. That is how quickly my world, our world, changed.

My family came to America from England. My father, Louis Bennett, was born in the 1890s. He never knew who his father was. Only one person knew for sure, his mother—at least we think she was my father's mother. There were some rumors that, in fact, my real grandmother, Dad's mother, had given him away to a friend, Grandmother Bennett swearing her to secrecy about who she and the father really were. For reasons we'll never know, Grandmother Bennett never once talked about it, taking the secret to her grave. It had the aura of a Victorian novel about it, and my sisters and I found it all quite mysterious and exciting. We liked to assume that our mystery grandparents, in England, were royalty. Who knows, maybe they were.

When Dad was seventeen, he went to work in the new high-tech industry of that day, wireless telegraphy, and actually apprenticed under the legendary Marconi, helping to build the first transatlantic radio station in England.

Dad's mother, Grandmother Bennett, was good friends with the Jackas, a family who had moved from England to Canada and from there to Ohio. They invited Dad and Grandmother to come over, and in 1909 they made the move.

My father, like so many others, came to America and landed at Ellis Island. I have often thought about the strange twists of history. Thirty-five years later I would go to England as part of the greatest invasion force in history, one of millions of Americans preparing for D day. If fate had been slightly different, I might have been in the British army instead, perhaps to fight and die at Dunkirk or at El Alamein.

The Jackas were an interesting family. They had a daughter who most certainly caught the interest of my father. Her name was Mary Grills Jacka, and she would be my mother.

Grandpa Jacka was born in Capetown, South Africa, long before the start of the Boer War. He became a sailor, then a minister, and finally wound up working in a limestone quarry in Lakeside, Ohio.

My mother had four brothers, all of whom went into the army during World War I. One of them was badly gassed and never really recovered.

My mother was a handsome woman, strong in character and faith. She eventually had four children, my older sister Florence, then me, and then my younger sisters, Rosemary and Margaret.

My first memories of my father were that he was an important man in town. He was, to that age, the master of a high-tech wonder, electricity, a position as mysterious to some as someone who today builds and runs complex computer systems.

Having worked for Marconi, my father quickly landed a job with the power company and was soon responsible for laying out the electrical grid to the small towns and farming communities surrounding Toledo. The power company also ran the trolley lines. I remember riding the trolleys with my father and mother as a small boy, proud that my father was responsible for the "juice" that made them run.

As I look back, I realize we were far better off than many. We actually owned an automobile, my father needing it so he could get around to the different work sites. We had a telephone, and even a radio, in fact, the first radio in town.

It was a crystal set that my father built himself, baking the crystal coil in the kitchen stove. He set up a sixty-foot-high pole in the backyard and from it strung an aerial into the house. In the evening Dad would carefully adjust the set, and if conditions were right, we might pull in WJR across the lake in Detroit or even KDKA out of Pittsburgh.

Neighbors would come over and gather around the tiny speaker, awed by this new wonder that could carry voices, news, and music from hundreds of miles away. Of course, no one was allowed to touch the set. That was my father's domain.

As I think about all that I eventually moved on to, command of a battalion in combat, the rank of a four-star general, commander of hundreds of thousands of troops, and adviser of presidents, I am grateful for that small town, and that world that I grew up in.

It was a tight-knit world. We all knew each other, knew who could be counted on in times of trouble, knew whose word was always a solemn pledge, knew who had strength and who did not.

It was a world that some today might find constricting, for it is chic and popular today to dismiss the values of small-town America of that time. But I was grateful for it and shall treasure its memories and all that it taught me.

I learned at a very early age that if a boy gave his word, he was expected to keep it. If he failed to do so, everyone knew, his teachers, the minister, the local policeman, the neighbors, and eventually his parents. As a child, if I got into some mischief or trouble, by the time I got home my parents already knew about it, and punishment awaited.

A man, even at the age of seven, was expected to be respectful of elders, look out for the welfare of his sisters, and share with those less fortunate. If told to do a job, he did it.

Recently a friend told me a story about the famous Civil War general Joshua Lawrence Chamberlain. When asked what had been the most important moment that had shaped his character, Chamberlain told a story about clearing rocks from the fields of the family farm. To a farmer in Maine, rocks in a field were simply a part of life, and before spring plowing one of the back-breaking chores was to move boulders and rocks pushed up by the spring thaw.

One day Joshua's father told him to round up his brothers and move a huge boulder from the middle of a field. Joshua and his brothers walked out to the boulder, took one look at it, and decided there and then that the job was impossible, and so they wandered off to other things.

Later in the day their father appeared and demanded to know why the rock had not been moved.

"It's impossible," Joshua argued.

"Nothing is impossible," the father replied. "Now move it, and don't come home for dinner till you do."

Eventually, late at night, the rock was finally dug out and dragged from the field.

Today Joshua's father might very well have received a visit from some government agency, ready to arrest him for child abuse, but I can relate to that story. Most of the men of my generation can relate to it. That, as much as any other reason, is why we went on to win the most bitterly fought war in history. Most of us approached that fight with a simple understanding that nothing was impossible if ever we set ourselves, as a nation, to the task of winning.

I was not a farm boy. I grew up in a small town, but that attitude, what the Romans called *gravitas,* was a daily part of our lives.

I'm not saying that the world I grew up in was one of simple drudgery and harshness. Far from it. There were wonderful times of fun, days of playing in fields and woods, lazy mornings fishing and autumn afternoons hunting. And yes, there was sadness and failures as well, as all families know and experience. But underneath it all there was always a sense of being part of a community and of a family that expected us to do our best no matter what the challenge.

Like any boy I had my share of scrapes and at times was something of a rapscallion. A movie theater finally opened in town, much to the dismay of some of our church elders, and I thought it would be a wonderful idea, on a cool fall evening, to transfer piles of leaves into the cars parked outside the theater. Another troublemaker and I were happily at work when I heard someone clearing his throat behind me. I turned to find myself staring up at the town policeman. His punishment was a simple one. He handcuffed both of us to the bumper of one of the cars and then sat back and waited for the theater to empty. With a lot of angry theatergoers standing around we were finally released, then marched from car to car with a broom to clean them all out. Needless to say, when I got home, the "stuff" really hit the fan.

I really got into it when I convinced some of my friends that school was a waste of time when compared to the prospect of seeing the Toledo Mudhens, a farm team of the Cleveland Indians, open their season. Leo Durocher was managing. So we skipped school, hopped the trolley, and headed into the big city. We had a grand time. The stands were packed with hundreds of schoolkids who also decided that a proper education included a spring day in the bleachers on opening day, stuffing their faces with hot dogs and shouting insults at the players from out of town.

Our problem was that the superintendent of schools, Mr. Waters, figured out where we were. Again, that mysterious telegraphy system of small-town America. When we hopped off the trolley, our fathers were waiting for us, and again the "stuff" hit the fan.

My school, as I mentioned, was a small one. We averaged

about thirty to thirty-five students in a class, and all of us, from kindergarten to twelfth grade, were in the same building.

It was a mile walk to school. Though I will not claim that it was uphill both ways, I do remember many a bitter winter morning, the icy wind blowing in from Lake Erie, my mother bundling us up and pushing us out the door, with me acting as the snowplow, breaking a path for my younger sisters.

From an early age I was a voracious reader. By the time I was ten or eleven I had cleaned out the small-town library of every book on its shelves. Whenever a new book came in, no matter what the subject, it could be about the animals of Africa, a book on painting, or stories of ancient history, I was eager to grab it up.

My father, being a self-trained electrical engineer, read all he could find on that subject, and I remember the delight of discovering a great pile of *Popular Mechanics* up in the attic. The issues published during the Great War were my favorites, with elaborate diagrams of fortifications, great guns, and that new marvel, airplanes. I think it was there that my interest in things military first started.

By the time I was a freshman in high school I was eager to get into varsity sports. The problem was that I weighed a hundred and twelve pounds and wasn't much more than five and a half feet tall. I never really understood the coach's logic, but he felt that my size really qualified me to be the center on the football team.

Every Friday afternoon during the fall of that year I got the crap kicked out of me, but I learned how to survive. There was no way I could meet some of those guys head on, so I simply ducked low, dodged around them, kicked back with my heels, and nailed the other guy on the legs, and either tripped him up or simply kicked him to the ground. Today penalty flags would be flying all over the place, but football back then was a lot more rough-and-tumble, and without all the padding and safety equipment. After a game I could barely walk the next day, but I hung in there. It was a matter of pride. Maybe I learned then a lesson that helped keep me alive later: When confronted with a superior foe, never get into a slugging match; figure out a way to get around him and trip him up. In war, there is no such thing as penalty flags; there is only survival.

I remember the last game of that season. We played Port Clinton for the county championship. The center for their team was huge. I heard he weighed two hundred and forty pounds. He was also the first African American I had ever met. I think back on that and realize how different the world was, that a boy could be in high school and never have met another kid from a different race. It might be nostalgia now, but I have to say that for all of us, on both teams, he was just another one of the guys, and a darn tough opponent, someone to be respected.

Somehow we won that game, and I survived getting run over by a 1930s version of "the Refrigerator."

During the winter I was on the basketball team, and in spring it was track. All the sports were coached by Bob Thayer, who had a major influence on my life. He taught us about working as a team and took a personal interest in our lives.

I also got some sports training at home. My dad loved to box, and I was his sparring partner. Mom tended to look the other way, and I often wonder what she said to Dad in private after he had given me a good drubbing. Interestingly, the boxing lessons ended the day I nailed Dad with a real haymaker and knocked him flat.

I started ninth grade in the fall of 1929. Things were looking rather good for my family. Dad was promoted to one of the top management positions with the power company, with responsibility for handling relations with the union. If there was an evening meeting during the school year, he'd throw me in the car and take me along. I watched as Dad handled meetings, negotiated, and worked with men from all sorts of backgrounds. They were hardworking guys. They strung the wires, repaired breaks in the middle of blizzards, laid and repaired track for the interurban trolley lines, and all too frequently were juiced and killed. They were a no-nonsense bunch. Dad always treated them with the utmost respect, not because it was his job to do so, but because he really felt that way, and that came across.

Yet another lesson learned. One of the great mistakes of our army is the gulf that exists, even today, between officers and enlisted men, an attitude that goes back to our origins with the British army, the tradition that officers came from the aristocracy and line infantry were the lower class.

A good army needs officers, of course, men who can lead, and enlisted men who do the dirty work, but the whole thing of class distinction, the system of privileges, especially in the field, and that sense of social distance, should not be part of an army that comes out of a true republic. Yes, I expected my men to salute (at least when we were not on the front line where German snipers were waiting to see who got saluted) and follow my orders. On the other hand, it was my duty to treat my men with respect and understanding. In many ways it was far more important for me to serve them than the other way around, and I have always held in contempt those officers who see their enlisted personnel as nothing more than lower-class servants. When I finally got the power to influence things, any officer in my command who conveyed that attitude quickly found himself sidelined or transferred with one hell of a red check mark on his fitness report.

When the stock market crashed in October 1929, it didn't take long for the wave to hit our small town on the shores of Lake Erie. Heavy industry went belly up, steel mills in Cleveland, Sandusky, and Toledo went from three shifts to two to one, and many just shut down. The vast industrial web, the barge traffic, the trains and ships loaded with the raw material that fed the auto industry in Detroit and steel mills rimming Lake Erie, all of it came to a halt.

As the wave spread out, sales dropped in the stores, landlords no longer were paid rent, pensions disappeared as stocks crashed. Overnight, it seemed, a dark cloud spread across the land.

It's a time, though, that I remember with intense pride in my family and in my town.

I remember Mr. Bauch, the owner of a small general store. His customers were friends he had known for years. He simply took IOUs, knowing that he most likely would never get paid, but he would be damned if he saw his friends and neighbors go hungry or shoeless. He finally went out of business, but he did it with his head up and a sense of pride.

To cope with the problems of the unemployed, once a week there'd be a meeting, an informal gathering of men and women, the town leaders in a way: the minister, the policeman, a couple of merchants. My dad was part of that group. They'd meet in someone's home, sit down over coffee, and go down a list. Who was in trouble? Who was about to be foreclosed? Who had a sick kid? Somehow a few bucks would be scraped up, a basket of groceries put together, pairs of shoes and clothes for the kids passed along. Sometimes the local doctor would misplace a bill and never send it.

People had a strong sense of pride, and at times it was tough to get them to accept the help. It wasn't charity; that was important for them to understand. It was just neighbors in a small town looking out for each other. No one thought much about a big government coming in to save them. They saw the problem as local and dealt with it locally.

The same routine went on inside my family. We were one of the few lucky families that knew the paychecks would continue because even in a depression the electric company had to keep the juice flowing. On payday, after dinner, all of us, Mom, Dad, Grandmother Bennett, my sisters, and I would sit down around the dining room table. Dad would lay out how much we had, and which bills had to be taken care of. If anything was left over, the debate started. There was only so much to go around, and if one of my sisters asked for something unreasonable, the rest of us would jump in against it. There was one hell of a lot of negotiating on the side between those meetings, deals struck to support a bid for a sister's new shoes if I then got backed up in a request for a football.

We were expected to throw into the pot as well. Do a chore that might pick up half a dollar and you were expected to lay it on the table. And always there'd be a reminder that, come Friday, Dad would go to that community meeting where the talk would be about how some family was literally going to lose their farm if they didn't come up with the fifty-dollar mortgage payment.

It was a sobering lesson in the harshness of life.

It stuck with me. Years later, when advancing through Sicily, war-ravaged Holland, and Germany, I'd see the pinched faces of kids, old people standing in front of the smoking ruins of homes, refugees filling the roads, all their earthly possessions packed in a wheelbarrow, and I realized how easily it could have been our country, instead, that was suffering like that. In Europe I saw the complete breakdown of civilization. During the depression there were parts of America that held together and looked out for their neighbors.

Depression or not, the daily routines went on. Years from now, when September 11, 2001, is talked about, those who lived through that day will focus on that terrible moment when they saw the twin towers getting hit on television. What might be forgotten, though, is that the following day Americans got up, went to work, stopped at the convenience store to buy gas, and maybe even went to a movie. Even in the worst of times, the daily acts of living go on.

I went to school, read books, got interested in science, and survived my first crush. Her father was the dentist in town, and they owned a cottage on Lake Erie. I thought she was the most beautiful girl ever created, and of course she had me completely wrapped around her finger. We went to the prom together and then just sort of drifted away from each other.

By my senior year I was captain of the football team, having filled out from a skinny hundred and twelve pounds to a hundred and seventy and had moved from center to left tackle, calling the signals. Another guy on my team, a fellow from Czechoslovakia, actually went on to play with the Cleveland Browns.

Even as a senior I still walked to school every day, still acting as a snowplow for my younger sisters when the blizzards came in off the lake. One of the toughest courses, chemistry, was taught by the superintendent, Mr. Walker. Miss Schloss, our social studies teacher, really had an impact on me. She was that type of teacher who was almost a stereotype—never married, totally devoted to "her students," and always pushing us. We were her kids, and by heavens she was going to make sure that we all made something of ourselves or kill us in the attempt. She was an absolute tyrant in the classroom, and all of us were a bit frightened of her. Before one of her tests I'd stay up till midnight studying. And we loved her for it. She taught a couple of generations in that town, and when she retired I think the entire community wept at the farewell ceremony.

As I went into my senior year, I wasn't quite sure where I would go next. I had my sights set on West Point, not because I was all afire to have a career in the military, but because, quite simply, if I got in, the education was free, a real plus with a depression on. My application got nowhere, and I was rejected.

Coach Thayer suggested Michigan State, and he even had a little scam that would save on tuition. His mother lived right next to the campus, so he'd arrange to have her home listed as my official residence, and at the same time pull in some contacts with friends to help with a football scholarship.

I graduated from high school in the spring of 1933 and that fall was bound for Michigan, leaving my family and that small town on the shores of Lake Erie behind.

Franklin Roosevelt had just been inaugurated as president, hundreds of thousands of farmers out in Oklahoma, Kansas, and Texas were watching their farms blow away, factory workers were selling apples on street corners, and tens of thousands of guys my age were riding the rails, looking for work. I was lucky to be going to college, and I knew it.

In Europe, however, Adolf Hitler had just become chancellor of Germany. I doubt if I thought about him at all, or contemplated how that scum of a man would change my entire life.

I left Oak Harbor, Ohio, in the fall of 1933, and America was in the middle of the worst depression in its history. Just before I graduated, both banks in town went belly up, triggering something of a panic, since a lot of people lost every dime they had stored away. I realized, even then as a fresh kid of eighteen, that I was damn lucky to have a shot at a college education.

I majored in business administration. The schedule was a long one. My football scholarship didn't mean I had a free ride, simply that I had first stab at the jobs on campus. I wound up working in the chemistry lab, doing cleanup, four hours a night, six days a week.

So it'd be classes in the morning and early afternoon, practice in the late afternoon, and lab work in the evening, and whatever time was left over went to studying.

My time at Michigan State, after all these years, doesn't stand out all that strong in my memory. I guess that's true of anyone my age. There are moments when you can recall every detail, what you ate that day, what you wore, the weather, all that was said and done, and then there can be long stretches that were simply forgettable. Michigan State was okay, but the days just sort of drifted by.

I was a fairly good student, but classwork didn't fire my imagination. There was no special girl, though I did date quite a bit. The classes were a routine that didn't stretch me or excite my passion. I had tried for West Point, didn't get in, and that kind of stung. Down deep, I was wishing I was somewhere else.

At the end of my first year at Michigan State I came back home and, thanks to my father, I landed a job with the New York Central Railroad.

A job, any kind of job, in 1934 was as precious as gold. The pay was the princely sum of forty cents an hour, and I earned every penny of it. I was a track worker on the main line that ran from Chicago to New York City.

The men on my crew were a hard-bitten lot, some of them tough old birds who had been on the job for decades. Of course, they set the "college kid" up for a hell of a lot of comments and harassment at first. If there was anything particularly difficult or nasty, "Let Bennett do it" was the standard response. I didn't buckle, though, or complain, and after a while they eased up, and I must say I was proud to be accepted by men like them.

We worked a section of track. Our job was to walk the line, repair or replace broken ties, check their alignment, replace and pack ballast, replace worn rails.

Out there, on the main line, there isn't a speck of shade: all trees, of course, are cleared far back. In Ohio, in the summer, the track, the ties, the rock ballast soak up the heat and blast it back at you. By nine in the morning the heat shimmers would already be rising off the track. Also—this was long before any regulations by the EPA—the toilets on the trains simply flushed onto the track, something a worker might experience in an unpleasant way if someone aboard a train flushed just as it went thundering past. No machinery like today, we worked the way it was done a hundred and fifty years ago, with sledgehammers, crowbars, shovels, and pry bars, and I was expected to do more than my share.

I loved it. That work peeled off my body every ounce of fat that I had gained in college. For the first couple of weeks I could barely move by the end of the day, but after that I was in shape and could swing a hammer with the rest of the gang.

Plus, we were working on "the" line of the New York Central and not some spur to a tank town or even the interurban trolleys my father had helped to build. This was the big time.

While we were working, the foreman would always have a

lookout posted. We'd be hammering away and yet be always alert so that no matter what we were doing, a train could still pass safely. When, suddenly, a cry of "Clear the track!" would go up, we'd only have seconds to react. The rule was always to run to the outside of the line, not in, for if a train came from the other way at the same time, you were dead. Second rule, hang on to your tools and make sure nothing was left lying around.

So we'd scramble out of the way and look up the line . . . and then we'd see it, the express, Chicago to New York, coming down the line at a hundred miles an hour.

The locomotives were huge, some of the greatest steam engines ever to ride the rails. We'd see the headlight glaring, smoke and steam swirling, and the rising pitch of the steam whistle as it blew a warning to get the hell out of the way because a hundred tons of locomotive were coming straight at you.

The ground would shake, the vibration rumbling through our feet, and then it'd be on us, whistle shrieking, Doppler-shifting up and down as it stormed past, steam, smoke, dust engulfing us. The power of it just got to me. It'd be years before I felt that sense of power again, and that would come in a far less innocent time, when I was part of an army going to war.

The cars would rush past in a blur. If I turned my head as they thundered past, I might catch a glimpse of someone at a window, looking out.

This was the "high rollers" train, its passengers racing from New York to Chicago in just a day, depression-wracked Ohio passing by their windows, a sweaty nineteen-year-old kid watching them roll by.

I use to wonder what it'd be like to ride as they did, eating dinner on white linen, the clicking of the track a hypnotic mantra, or playing cards in the lounge car or flirting with fine young girls of high society.

I loved it as well because the train provided a two-minute work break—a chance to gulp down some water and feel a touch of breeze (and hope I didn't get hit by something flushed out of that train), and then the foremen was yelling for us to get back at it.

And thus I spent my summer, swinging a sledge, putting my back into a pry bar as we straightened track, and watching the high rollers race by.

That fall it was back to classes. Again, there's not much to remember or talk about. The one change was that my football playing days were over. During a practice session where I was playing left end I got hammered on my left hip. They dragged me in to the doc; he did the usual tests and gave me a choice: I could continue to play ball, but if I did, I could forget about walking as I got older. So that ended my sports career at Michigan State, and with it the few perks I had as a player, one of them being the job at the chemistry lab that threw a few extra bucks a week into the budget.

And walking today is a pain, but maybe that's a result of something other than the football injury; getting picked up and thrown several times by bursting 88 shells might have contributed to the problem.

By the end of my sophomore year, I felt somewhat rudderless. I wanted to "do something" and not just go along with the flow. There was no real challenge to school. Frankly, it lacked a sense of purpose and, yes, even a touch of romance. I don't mean romance with a girl, but romance with life.

I was back on the rail gang, watching the trains roar by, hanging out with friends in the evening, wondering what was going to happen with my life when fall came. Sometimes, at night, I'd sit with my father and talk about it.

By this point Dad and I were getting a bit distant from each other. Part of it was my growing up, part of it was problems he was going through. My mother and my father were heading toward a divorce. That was still a few years off, and like most parents of that era, they were trying to hide it from the kids, though it was clear to my sisters and me that something was wrong.

Yet he was still there. Then something he did changed everything in my life.

It was the Fourth of July, 1935. Ozzie Nelson was doing a show and I went with my friends. If anyone remembers Ozzie Nelson today, it's from that absolutely boring television show in the fifties and the fact that he was the father of Ricky Nelson. But back in the midthirties he was hot; his band was one of the best dance groups in the country, though this was just before true swing music kicked in.

I went to the dance, had a good time, and got home late. My father was sitting up (another thing parents use to do when their kids were out, even college-aged kids), and as I came through the door he was grinning.

"Do you want to take another shot at West Point?"

I didn't get it. What the hell was he talking about? I had made my stab at it and hadn't got in.

"It was just on the news report," Dad continued. "Congress has authorized an increase in class size. I made a few calls and found out anyone can go for an appointment, even if you've been rejected before."

Sure. It seemed like a one-in-a-hundred shot, but anything was better than what was going on, and the Point was a dream I thought was out of reach.

Now the old system of getting into the Point might seem unfair today, but it was the simple reality of that time and typical of how political patronage works. Each congressman and senator had the power to make appointments. The spaces left over then went to those who passed competitive exams and to the sons of men who had received the Medal of Honor.

Four hundred more slots had opened up, one of the first indicators that someone upstairs was thinking about the world outside our national borders. Those four hundred slots were in the hands of congressmen. Whoever pushed the bill was thinking right on that point, allowing each of them to have a nice plum to pass out and thus win some more votes come election time.

My father didn't hesitate. It was midnight, but he started making phone calls. He knew our congressman and pulled out all the stops. The ink on the authorization bill was still wet and my father was already talking to our representative.

Eighteen days later I was at the train station, appointment letter tucked in my pocket, family and friends gathered around to see me off.

As I mentioned, there were things that would eventually divide me from my father. When the divorce hit, I stood on my mother's side. But all that was yet to come. At that moment, at the station, I was grateful. He had made a great effort to set my life in motion.

Today, I still wonder how a parent must feel when a son, or now a daughter, goes off to the Point. Years later, when I was superintendent, I'd watch parents on that first day, proudly accompanying their young man on to the Academy grounds, soaking up a last few minutes together before the army took their precious creation, the focus of the last eighteen years of their life, away.

As superintendent I watched that moment, sensing the excitement, the pride, and the fear.

I wondered how many parents, watching the child whom once they held, feared the darkness that might be ahead, a telegram in the hands of an officer at their door, their son a body rolling back and forth in the surf or frozenface down in the snow.

I saw those things. The memory of trying to pry the charred body of a comrade out of a burning tank still haunts me. I wonder if my parents, when standing with me, waiting for that train, foresaw that possibility for me.

That train, which had passed me by so many times before, approached, whistle shrieking, steam, smoke, and dust swirling, hot engine ticking and hissing as it glided to a stop, conductors, in that age-old chant shouting, "All aboard."

There was a final hug, sisters excited, Mom holding back tears, Father looking on proudly, grasping my hand. The last call from the conductor, and I went up the steps and settled into a seat.

When a train pulled by a high-powered locomotive starts forward, it is unlike anything else, far more exciting than sitting in a cushioned chair today, a flight attendant pantomiming safety instructions as you taxi off. When a train starts, you hear the whistle shrieking, smoke swirling about, the lurch as drive wheels spin, then dig into the track. Loved ones are standing outside, looking up, trying to catch a glimpse and waving. There is the deep chugging of the engine straining forward, station drifting back, speed picking up.

I don't remember whether I tried to spot my work gang. Most likely I did. If I did, they were a blur, left far behind, a world left behind, one to which I never went back again, except for a visit, and when I did, it was almost as a stranger, for so much had changed, I most of all.

2

West Point

The following day I stepped off at the small depot, down at the base of the bluffs below the Academy. The New York Central train had deposited me at Grand Central, and from there I'd crossed over to New Jersey and taken the local commuter train that ran up the west bank of the Hudson. It was a strange and wondrous new country to me: the broad open river, so fabled in our nation's history; the mountains, which were truly impressive for a kid from the flatlands of Ohio; and the excitement of embarking on an adventure that only a month earlier seemed as distant as going to China.

Now the train no longer stops at West Point, the commuter line was shut down years ago, almost all new cadets arrive surrounded by a supportive family, having driven cross-country to see their young son or daughter inducted. But for nearly a hundred years cadets arrived the way I did, alone, standing at the station, looking up at the towering, fortresslike structure of the Point, and suddenly your mouth goes a little dry.

I started up the hill, carrying my one suitcase, wide-eyed, and, yes, wondering what it was I had gotten myself into. I found out a few minutes later.

I crossed a line, an invisible one that separated the civilian world from the military, as I went up that sloping road. A cadet spotted me and came over. I guess I smiled a bit, figuring he'd offer a friendly hand, tell me where to check in, where I'd find my dorm room, the same routine I had encountered my first day at Michigan State.

Dream on.

"Come to attention!"

He was in my face, only inches away, barking orders. "Stand up straight, drop those bags when you come to attention, hands pressed against seams, who are you, why are you here, my God, is this what the army's taking now, pick up that bag, run, run, this way, move it!"

The day was a blur, and always it was run, run, run. Over here, sign this, sign that, down the hall, strip, stand up straight! Get issued a mattress and barracks bag, the old army B-bag, which was soon loaded with uniforms and equipment.

I do remember a moment of satisfaction. I was ordered to brace against the wall, shoulders back, head back, now touch the wall with your shoulders and the back of your neck.

The months of swinging a hammer on the railroad line had given me shoulders of iron. In fact, I was most likely in the best shape I've ever been in, in my entire life. I think about it now, the years having melted away that muscle; I walk with a cane now, and it's hard at times to get around. Hard to believe there was a day, now so long ago, when I could swing a ten-pound sledge for hours, and surprise an army doctor because my shoulders were so developed that my neck and the small of my back couldn't touch the wall.

I arrived at the Point on July 24, 1935. Beast Barracks, that dreaded summer orientation that all incoming cadets had to endure, was almost over. Those of us who joined through the expansion program were lucky, something the older cadets were not too enthusiastic about. If they had had to sweat blood when they were plebes, well, they would squeeze it out of us new men in the short time left.

There was one little guy in particular who decided to make my life hell. Whenever he spotted me, I had to brace. Bracing was something of a sadistic ritual, an exaggerated attention, shoulders thrown back until your shoulder blades touched, head tucked in, chin touching your Adam's apple. Try it sometime, just for a few minutes, and then imagine doing it under the boiling sun for fifteen minutes while some little Napoleon, six inches shorter than you (and, I think, damned insecure because of that fact), paces around you, screaming and hollering. Years later, I ran across him again, his rank junior to mine . . . Ah, the pleasure of seeing him come to attention when I approached!

The summer program was basically one of mental and physical conditioning, to see whether you could take it. The first half, which I all but missed, was the feared Beast Barracks, which took place right at the Point. Then as now, some cadets broke down. It was a sad thing to watch. A guy would just suddenly let go, dissolve into tears, or collapse in exhaustion. The thinking, then as now, is better to have it happen on the parade ground, or in a dorm, than have him break under the stress of a barrage or as a Tiger tank and a battalion of SS storm troopers are closing in on him and his men.

A lot of people still ask about hazing. It's basically gone today. When I became superintendent of the Point, in 1965, some of it still went on, a lot of it "unofficial," and I made a point of rooting it out, as have superintendents since. Of course, when the Academy went coed, it was reined in even more, since any type of physical harassment of a woman, especially by a young man, was way out of bounds.

The rules were, of course, that a cadet must never touch another cadet in anger. But when I started as a plebe, one hell of a lot could be done to you without actually touching you. Holding fire buckets filled with sand, endlessly running up and down stairs, bracing till you were ready to pass out, or the real sadistic act of making a famished cadet brace while trying to eat. Then there was getting dragged out of bed, hours before dawn, to clean the corridors on your hands and knees, all of it piling on till you were in a state of constant exhaustion . . . and, in truth, learning precious little.

I think part of what drove this hazing was that a lot of guys endured it, then, when they became a second-year or first-year man, well, it was payback time. "They did it to me, I survived it, now I get to have some fun."

I hated it. It was the wrong way to train men. The reputation some West Pointers had during World War II, of being assinine martinets or outright sadists who didn't give a damn about their troops, came out of Beast Barracks and the system of hazing. It was doubly true when we went from peacetime, to the greatest mobilization in the history of war. The millions of guys pouring into the ranks were civilians of a free republic. Sure, they expected discipline, but mindless hazing of new recruits simply caused contempt and hatred for officers.

In contrast, one of the upperclassmen who made a profound impression on me was a guy who was a third-year, in civilian terminology, a sophomore. He was tough, but there was always a reason behind it. He'd approach you, you'd snap to attention, and he'd ask a question. Not some bullshit question but something important, something you needed to know and understand. Get it right, there'd be a nod, a bit of encouragement, and he'd be on his way. Get it wrong, well, you might wind up getting chewed out a bit, but then he'd explain what you got wrong, how to get it right next time, and then offer a few words of encouragement. Those few words meant everything when everyone else was giving you crap. He took care of those men under him and was respectful to his superiors without brown-nosing them. You had a sense he was looking out for you as well. For so many of us, he was a role model from day one.

In terms of physical conditioning that first summer was actually a breeze. Working for the New York Central made sure of that. Our summer training camp was fairly easy. We formed into units and camped as a military force. In some ways it made me think of the Civil War, and I half-suspect some of the equipment we used, such as the tents, actually did date from the Civil War.

Sentries would be posted, guards changed during the night, and during the day we learned basic maneuvers, marksmanship, a few basic principles of tactics, again little different from what our grandfathers learned in 1861.

The academic year started in September, and that's when I finally got scared, particularly over the dreaded math courses.

Since its founding, West Point has placed a special emphasis on engineering. A field officer of a hundred years ago was expected to be able to handle life on the frontier and to build roads, fortifications, bridges, and other works. The Army Corps of Engineers was considered the "brains" outfit, followed by artillery, which required a significant mastery of math as well.

That tradition endured, and was as strong as ever when I entered. They piled the math on, and that had always been my weakest area. I had already had two years of college, so the courses in history, English composition, and literature were easy. But the math—I had stepped around that at Michigan State, taking the bare-minimum requirements. Now I was facing the real time.

When the coach at the Academy saw my athletic record in high school and first year of college, he called me in and really laid the pressure on. I have to admit, it annoyed me a bit. The last thing I needed was another injury to my leg. The doctor back in Michigan had made it clear: one more injury and I'd be crippled for life. Here, if I got hammered on the field, besides being off the team, I'd be out of the Point as well.

I had to go out for some sport, every cadet did, so I finally went for lacrosse. Dumb move, but that wouldn't hit till later.

I'll never forget the fall afternoons there at the Point. The trees were starting to turn, and nowhere is fall more beautiful than in upstate New York, in the mountains, with the river below reflecting the colors.

We'd form for afternoon parade, units falling in, orders echoing around the barracks square, and then the drumming would start, the sound of it sending a chill up and down your spine. We'd parade out onto the field in front of our barracks, drums thumping out the beat.

As you emerged onto the parade ground, the view could bring tears to your eyes, and for many an old vet going back to visit today, it still does.

Columns of cadets, dressed in full uniform, would be marching like solid phalanxes, guidons snapping in the afternoon breeze, autumn sunlight sparkling off polished brass trim.

It must have looked that way when Caesar's legions returned in triumphs of old, or when the Army of the Potomac, whose leaders marched as I now did, paraded their troops before the sad, careworn eyes of Abraham Lincoln.

Columns would deploy out, companies dressing in line. Orders would be given, we'd fall back into column, each company parading past the others under the watchful eyes of the superintendent and commandant of cadets.

The commandant in my first three years was none other than Omar Bradley. I look back on it now, and of course I can see the path ahead, how such a man as Bradley was destined to lead, but at that time, during those fall days of the late 1930s, we were at peace, the rantings of a former corporal in Germany were a strange sideshow, and the imperial dreams of Japan were yet to be taken seriously.

So we paraded and drilled, with a brief respite on Saturday afternoons in the fall if there was a home game, or that special big trip to Philadelphia for the annual Army-Navy encounter.

From day one, however, what was special for me was Sunday service.

To some that might sound strange, a twenty-year-old guy looking forward to Sunday morning church call. It required attention to my dress uniform, many of the sermons were absolutely forgettable and perhaps should be forgotten, but if you saw the church at West Point and experienced it as I did, you'd understand. I will admit that a bit of the appeal was the simple fact that I could sit for an hour and a half with no one yelling at me, and compared to being braced against a wall, the church pews were the height of luxury.

The church had been built early in the 1900s, as had most of the buildings of the modern Point, going up at that time prior to World War I when the first big expansion of the Corps occurred. The church, or more properly, the cathedral, was an inspiration of design. Gothic, but not overly ornate, with beautiful stained-glass windows admitting the morning light.

The organ, then as now, rates as the largest pipe organ in America. Combine that with the cadet choir, and you had a sound that was wonderful.

It was there that I first heard the Cadet Prayer recited.

It hit me.

It still does.

It was a call not just to faith, but to idealism, to the highest sense of nobility, that we as warriors of a free republic must pledge ourselves to something almost intangible and far beyond the scope of most men. If we were to recite that prayer, we must do so as a pledge that would become the guidepost of our lives.

A friend recently asked me how I had endured all that I saw, all that I experienced and was required to do during the war. How had I kept my sense of direction and my sanity after Omaha Beach, the frozen hell of the Bulge, or after realizing the truth of Nazism when I reached the labor and concentration camps far across the Rhine.

Quite simply, it was the Cadet Prayer. Whenever I got a chance to lie down, to catch a few hours' sleep, I'd stretch out, usually in a slit trench, sometimes with a tent over me, sometimes in the ruins of a burnt-out town, and close my eyes. I'd imagine I was back in the serenity of that church at West Point, music playing softly, and then I'd recite the prayer.

O God, our Father, Thou Searcher of human hearts, help us to draw near to Thee in sincerity and truth. May our religion be filled with gladness and may our worship of Thee be natural.

Strengthen and increase our admiration for honest dealing and clean thinking, and suffer not our hatred of hypocrisy and pretence ever to diminish. Encourage us in our endeavor to live above the common level of life. Make us to choose the harder right instead of the easier wrong, and never to be content with a half truth when the whole truth can be won. Endow us with courage that is born of loyalty to all that is noble and worthy, that scorns to compromise with vice and injustice and knows no fear when truth and right are in jeopardy. Guard us against flippancy and irreverence in the sacred things of life. Grant us new ties of friendship and new opportunities of service. Kindle our hearts in fellowship with those of a cheerful countenance, and soften our hearts with sympathy for those who sorrow and suffer. Help us to maintain the honor of the Corps untarnished and unsullied and to show forth in our lives the ideals of West Point in doing our duty to Thee and to our Country. All of which we ask in the name of the Great Friend and Master of all. Amen.

Yet again, in a modern world, which too often mocks ideals, that lets out a cynical sigh when someone speaks of honesty and truth, it is comforting to know that some of my comrades, whether they are of the class of 1940 or 2003, still recite that prayer, and believe in it.

Regardless of my belief in the Cadet Prayer, there was still a demon in my life. It was plebe-year math, and it finally caught up with me.

In all my other subjects I did rather well. I wasn't a grind, but I also wasn't the class goat. I was in-between, actually fairly well up the ladder, since a lot of what I was studying I'd been through at Michigan State.

Midyear grades were posted. The memory of that day still

haunts me. There was no sparing of sensitivities back then. At dinner that night the names of those cadets who had flunked a subject and were being washed out were read off. With a name starting with a B, I was one of the first called. It was like a knife thrust into my gut. Not my heart, my gut, for a gut wound kills you slowly.

I had flunked math.

In front of all my comrades I, along with the others who had failed, were told that we were dismissed, to turn in our gear and leave the following morning. There were no appeals, no special counseling sessions with grief therapists. We were, as well, an object lesson to those who survived. Don't screw up, because if you do, you'll be read out as well.

There was actually some sympathy extended by several of the instructors. I guess they saw something in me. I was told to go home, but—and this was the biggest of all *buts*—I could reapply at the end of the spring term. I'd have to pass a rigid exam, and not many did, and that exam included everything I had just flunked in math. If I passed that exam, the Academy would readmit me, but I would have to repeat my plebe year.

There was a moment spent mulling that over. I had ditched two years' worth of college credits at Michigan State to start over as a plebe, a freshman, at West Point. I had flunked out because of one course. Any other college in the country, as long as I held a 2.0, would have allowed me to continue, no questions asked, and I would simply take the one course over again. Now, even if I did somehow pass the readmittance exam, which very few did, I'd be back at the start, my classmates having moved on to their "yearling," or sophomore, year.

The mulling didn't last long. I turned in my uniforms, put civilian clothes on for the first time in months (they didn't fit all that well by this point), walked to the station at the bottom of the hill, and took the long train ride back to Ohio.

My dad met me at the station. There were no recriminations, just a simple question: "What do you want to do?"

"Get back in" was my reply.

Dad pulled out the stops one last time, and I give him credit for it. Hell, this was 1936, and most fathers would have informed their twenty-year-old sons who had just flunked out of school that it was time to find a job, any job, and to pitch in a bit and help the family. I guess a lot of twenty-year-olds would have said the hell with it as well.

My father made a few phone calls and came back with an answer. A retired West Point professor had a cram school, in Washington, D.C. It'd cost a bit, almost as much as a year at Michigan State. I'd go to live with this professor and his wife and follow a routine every bit as rigorous as the Point's. From the moment we rolled out at six in the morning till we collapsed at ten in the evening, we studied, took practice exams, got ripped apart, then went back and studied some more.

So I went on the train again, this time to D.C. Mr. Sullivan and his wife had a nice place, just off Connecticut Avenue, near Dupont Circle. I suspect he, or his wife, came from some wealth. There were a number of officers in the army like that, Douglas MacArthur and George Patton being two examples. But the Depression was still on, trust funds had disappeared in the big crash, so a cram school was a way to make ends meet.

Mrs. Sullivan took a liking to "her boys." Her husband worked us to death, but she always made sure we ate well, and in a motherly way offered encouragement when we needed it. On Sunday afternoons they'd actually let us free. (Partying, as it is now called, was a death sentence; we spent Friday and Saturday nights studying.)

We'd hop a trolley downtown, or sometimes just walk. Seeing Washington in that spring of 1936 was a thrill. Many of the great monuments to our history and culture were going up around the Mall at that time. The Lincoln Memorial was new, and was still being visited by people who had actually met Lincoln or served in the Union army.

Buildings like the National Gallery and the expansion of the

National Archives, where the Declaration of Independence and Constitution were stored, were going up or had just opened.

This was Washington before the war. It had gone through its first big boom back in the 1860s. World War I was too short for it to really impact the city. Roosevelt's massive expansion of the bureaucracy to manage all the federal programs was having some impact, but not too much. So in many ways Washington was more like a small Southern city than the powerhouse I would find it to be when posted to the Pentagon in the early 1960s.

Trolleys still ran, some of the streets were still cobblestoned, and on spring afternoons families would stroll along Pennsylvania Avenue, stopping in front of the White House, hoping to catch a glimpse of FDR or Eleanor.

There were twelve of us staying with the Sullivans that spring, cramming away, and those Sunday afternoons were the only respite. It was truly like living in a monastery except for that Sunday afternoon release, which was our only chance to catch sight of women. Washington, then as now, was a paradise for girl-watchers.

Watching was all we ever had the time to do. Even to contemplate a Friday night date would drive you insane, since it was impossible if you wanted to pass that exam. In fact, the only thrill we ever had was provided by a neighbor across the street. She was an attractive secretary, and she knew, absolutely knew, when we had just finished dinner and were standing around outside for a few minutes. She'd walk into her bedroom, slip off her dress, and then, in her undergarments, slowly pull the shade down. It drove us crazy. Torture like that simply wasn't fair. So after that big moment we'd return to our self-imposed monasticism, pull out the books, and go back to work.

It was, without a doubt, the toughest academic experience of my life. There was no room for failure. I had failed once, I had been given a second chance, something still rather uncommon in those days, a rare second chance, and I would be damned if I was going to blow it.

The day for the exam finally came. We were sent over to Bethesda Naval Hospital, where an army major administered the test. After all of that cramming, when I opened the exam book up, I breezed through it. I was finished in thirty minutes. That started me to worrying, for the test was supposed to last for two hours. I ran through the questions one more time, and then again. There was still an hour and fifteen minutes left. I finally stood up and handed my paper to the major.

He looked at me in surprise and whispered that I had plenty of time and should take advantage of it.

"If I go back one more time," I said, "I know I'll mess something up, sir."

He shrugged his shoulders, as if I were already doomed. I walked out.

The waiting started. It would be a couple of weeks before the Army told me if I had made it or not.

Next morning I said good-bye to the Sullivans. Across the years they have always had a spot in my heart. They helped give me my second chance. For a few months I'd been one of "their boys," and I know that they wanted all of us to make it, even though only a few of us did. I wondered, as well, what they felt as we left. Did they think about those of us who would get back into the Point, what that would mean to our futures, and how long that future might be?

Thirty years later I was indeed back at the Point, now as the superintendent. The Sullivans were still at work, just off the Academy grounds, having moved their school up to New York. It was a wonderful moment for me to walk in on them, one of their graduates now in command of the Academy.

I had no idea what was in my future as I returned home. I think everyone knows that kind of moment. A yes or no answer is coming in the mail, and day after day you go to your mailbox with a mixture of excitement and dread. After two weeks of this the letter finally arrived. I was back in.

This time around, the leave-taking wasn't as emotional. I think there was a bit of a sense from my dad that I had damned well better "return with my shield or on it."

I'd grown up a lot as well, having, by the age of twenty-one, faced a major defeat and then turned it around. I think that helped to shape a lot of what I would eventually become. I was going back in, not as a plebe of seventeen or eighteen, but as one of the "old men" of the class at twenty-one.

Failure was no longer an option, and never again would be.

This time I was ready for anything the Point could throw at me.

When I got off the train at the Point, I knew the way to go, and what to expect once I got to the top of that hill. Beast Barracks, though I had missed most of it before, was a walk in the park compared to what some of my younger companions went through. Since I was older, they also tended to look to me for leadership and help, which I gladly gave.

It was back to summer encampment for the same drill and the same introduction to basic military maneuvers. Some of my classmates of the year before were now my instructors. They tried to keep things even, but still there'd be the occasional wink and a smile; they were glad to see I had survived and come back.

Then back again to the courses I had taken the year before. In some cases this would be the third time I had studied a subject, having done it at Michigan State, then again the previous year. Needless to say, my academic record improved.

Yet again the coach came after me to play football, and again I refused, and yet again I went to lacrosse instead. Sure, it was guys waving clubs at each other, but at least there was no tackling.

Lacrosse was a mistake. I was playing goalie in an intramural game and got charged. I moved up to block, and next thing I knew I was flat on my back in the base hospital with the same damn injury I had in football—torn ligaments, bruised muscles, and a hip that was almost knocked out of joint.

A couple of weeks of missed classes, trying to keep up with assignments sent up by the instructors, and I was gradually hobbling around on crutches. For a while it looked like I might even be out altogether. The docs were not too optimistic that I could regain full use of my leg.

So it was a hell of a lot of exercising, rehab they call it today, and more than a little stretching of the truth: "No, doc, that doesn't hurt a bit."

I was finally back in the daily lineup, but for the longest time I consciously struggled not to limp, or to reveal to anyone just how much that leg hurt. It still does, by the way.

And so I finally got over the hurdle of the first year, passing the dreaded math courses and everything else. When summer came around, it was Beast Barracks again, but this time I was yearling in charge of new plebes in. Actually, we were divided into two units, half of us working with the plebes, the other half acting as infantry for the new seniors, or first-year men, who were training as company officers.

What I had learned from going through plebe year one and a half times finally began to come into play. Sure, I was hard on the plebes, but I tried to do it in a constructive way, always letting them see at least some reason for what they were going through and not just doing it for the sheer hell of it.

I'll admit, I think I was almost as scared as the plebes the first time I confronted a unit as their instructor for the day. Something a plebe rarely catches on to is the fact that the guy running him through the paces is also new at it, and is being watched every second and evaluated.

When not training plebes, we were sent to Buckner for basic combat training. The training, however, was still an anachronism, tactics still little better than those used in the Civil War. A few of our instructors were veterans of World War I and tried to impart some sense of reality, but out of the army of several million who were mobilized in 1917, only a relatively small number had actually seen combat, the war ending before our major push really hit. So there were a lot of people trained in the theory of battle, but not too many who had actually seen it for real, or truly understood what a few well-placed machine guns, backed up by a battery of artillery, could do to a thousand men advancing with bayonets fixed.

We didn't know that, of course, and so we accepted the fix-bayonets-and-charge mentality.

I settled into my third-class year, now free of some of the stress endured by plebes, and a little bit better accepted by the upperclassmen as well, who at times had some trouble dealing with a plebe who was older than they.

Class schedule was the same, five and a half days a week, Saturday afternoons off if there was a home football game, chapel on Sunday, and Sunday afternoon off to try and catch up on studies.

The course outline was rigid. Math again, a foreign language, which was French, and technical subjects. The idea of an elective, a course just for the fun of it, would have been met with incredulous disbelief.

That year stands out for several reasons, the most important one having nothing to do with my studies: I found the woman I would spend the next sixty-four years with.

Betty Deacon, or Bets as I called her from the night we met, was a student at Briarcliff. Of course, the Academy wasn't coed back then. Once you were out of your plebe year, you were allowed to attend a Saturday night social, as long as your academic reports were good and if you hadn't pulled any punishment details. That was always a killer, to get nailed by an upperclassman over some trivial issue, or simply because he didn't like you, and wind up walking a guard beat, while in the distance you could hear the music playing, and women, real women, were only a hundred yards away.

By today's standards the Saturday night socials must seem truly bizarre, like something out of Puritan times rather than the twentieth century. Women, sometimes several hundred of them, would come into town, many attending local colleges nearby solely with the intent of majoring in G.A.H.—"get a husband." Socially, catching a guy from the Point was considered a good deal. The women had to have a formal date arranged, which was usually first set up through a friend who was already dating a cadet.

Believe me, being twenty-one, in at least one sense, was no different in 1937 then it is today. You had several major obsessions on your mind. But all the rules were different then. The thought of actually being alone with a woman, of simply hopping in a car and driving off for a weekend together, doing "whatever," was absolutely beyond comprehension.

First off, we couldn't step off Academy grounds except for special events, and trying to take off with a girl was not one of them.

We were watched as well. The damn stupid movies made about West Point in the 1930s, with "flirtation walk," and dozens of couples making out and singing to each other, while moonlight glowed off the Hudson—well, go ahead and try it some time, at least try it given the restraints we were under. Besides, that walk was strictly off-limits except on Sunday afternoons, in the daylight.

The Point during those years even had a "house mother." I can't remember her name, but whenever I see *The Wizard of Oz,* the wicked witch reminds me of her somehow. She was the one who ran the dance lessons and the study of proper social behavior that we were required to take as gentlemen-in-training, and she kept a sharp eye on the Saturday socials.

You came into the reception hall and there on the other side would be hundreds of girls, decked out, all smelling so clean and fresh and some of them definitely with a lean and hungry look in their eyes; they were going to get a husband. But getting a husband did not include any "pregame recreation."

The rules were indeed different then. This was before the pill. Nice girls "didn't," and gentlemen were expected to be gentlemen. Later, during the war, I saw a lot of wild things, some of them that will never get written down because the men and women involved might still be alive, but at West Point in 1937, it was basically a nonevent.

Sure, some guys did get a girl "in trouble," as they used to say, and we would be amazed, wondering how they ever actually did get to do it, though a lot could happen during a furlough home, with a side stop along the way. But if you did, you said good-bye to West Point. As a gentleman you were expected to marry the girl, and at the same time you took that long walk back down to the train depot, bags in hand, and then served out several years as an enlisted man. Getting a girl pregnant and having to marry her resulted in an immediate discharge. If a guy got a girl pregnant, didn't have the guts to see it through, and tried to hide it from the authorities, he was an outcast in our community, someone beneath contempt. With that in the back of your mind, it acted a bit like a bucket of cold water if by some wild chance things did start to get out of control.

And for the girls who were West Point hunters, winding up with an enlisted man somewhere out in Oklahoma was a definite inhibitor as well.

So we were expected to act as gentlemen, and basically we did, attending dances that today would cause a rebellion among eighth-graders. It was indeed a different world.

For me, the fateful night was October 10, 1937. I had planned to skip the dance to study. My roommate came in, and he was truly ticked off. He had just gotten nailed, was assigned a punishment detail, and now had a problem. He had made a date with a girl. She was showing up at the dance, and he didn't want to stand her up. Would I mind going down, spend some time with her—keeping the other guys away, of course—then try to arrange a date for him the following week?

I had no ulterior motives when I walked out of the room and started for the social hall. He had described her to me. I walked in, looked around, and spotted her.

As the old saying goes, "All is fair in love and war."

She was wondrous then and for the next sixty-four years, up until that day in June 2001 when she passed on. I never lost that sense of wonder.

I've noticed how recent works about my generation, such as Tom Brokaw's *The Greatest Generation*, often deal with the bonds my generation made, marriages that survived depression, war, and long separations. It wasn't necessarily that way for all of us. I knew men who got their guts ripped out by a Dear John letter. Far worse was a letter from a parent or friend telling them to forget about their wife because she had most certainly forgotten about him.

But for so many of us it was the adversity that drew us together. We were young, we knew a war was coming, and ultimately we had to trust and depend on each other. It's almost like a bad line from a movie, but the world was about to go crazy, and all we would have would be each other.

Throughout my entire life, from the beginning as a dirt-poor second lieutenant at Fort Sill to retirement with four stars, I knew I could depend on Bets, and did.

So I met Bets at a dance. When I finally went back to the barracks, head swimming, I had to look my roommate in the eye, shrug my shoulders, and say, "Ah, gee, sorry, but . . ." The date next weekend was with me.

Bets made the weekly ritual across two years. She would come up on a Saturday afternoon. Some of the schools for women did allow their older students to actually sign off from campus, and Bets quickly made a deal with a local family, just off base, to rent a room on weekends.

She'd come up, drop off her suitcase, and then head to the dance. Don't get the wrong idea. That room of hers was strictly off limits. A lot of families living just off the base picked up a few extra dollars by renting rooms to girls with cadet boyfriends. They, too, had a reputation to maintain. If I had ever dared to show up there, I'd have been run off and immediately reported. West Point was indeed like small-town America of that time; everyone knew what everyone else was doing, and so a certain code was maintained.

For the rest of her life Bets would recall coming to the Saturday night social and sitting down patiently to wait for me. You see, she could never be 100 percent sure that I would actually show up. A last-minute detail, any number of things, could prevent me from walking that few hundred yards to meet her.

One night she was waiting patiently, sitting in a chair, back to the door, and I came into the room. I casually walked up behind her and lightly brushed my hand through her hair.

The "wicked witch" swooped in.

"Proper young ladies do not allow gentlemen to touch their hair!" the witch hissed.

I thought for a second I'd really have to grab hold of Bets to keep her from punching the old witch out.

That was another side of Bets I liked. She could be all proper and ladylike—in fact, she was stunningly beautiful; in the language of the time "classy, a real knockout"—but she had a toughness to her as well, something she would need in spades when the war came.

So now there was someone in my life, and having her gave me even more determination to succeed at the Point.

Finally, at Christmas, I was granted my first leave in nearly a year and a half. Again, there was the walk down the hill, getting on the train, and soaking up a world outside that had turned into a hazy dream while we were locked away in our monastic retreat. Seeing Bets was out of the question. Her family lived in Texas, and she had gone home before my leave started.

I remember the sense of shock of coming back to my hometown. Old friends seemed strangely distant. We now inhabited different worlds, almost spoke different languages, had different dreams and ideals.

The Point was changing me, molding me into something different.

I have two sharp memories of that leave. The first was a personal heartbreak. My parents finally admitted that they were separating and would get a divorce. My younger sisters, who were still at home, were torn apart by it. How did I react? Well, some of the feelings are still private. The closeness I had once felt for my father was gone forever.

The other shock was going to the movie theater with my kid sister. Before the main feature they ran the usual trailers, a couple of cartoons, which after a year and a half were a delight to see again, and then they ran a newsreel.

The main story was about the *Panay* incident.

It is all but forgotten today. The Japanese had started their expansion into China, invading the year before, but up to that moment the Sino-Japanese War seemed distant to me, something we didn't talk much about at the Point. Japan, in fact, had been our ally in World War I. *Panay* was the wake-up call, but damn few wanted to be bothered.

The *Panay* was a small navy boat tasked with protecting American nationals in China. Ever since the Boxer Rebellion in 1900 the United States had maintained a small military presence in China, a couple of detachments of marines, and a small flotilla of gunboats. Each was really nothing more than a riverboat with a couple of guns on board.

While the *Panay* was on patrol along the Yangtze River, a squadron of Japanese planes came in. The *Panay* was flying the American colors, but they came in and started to strafe it. The captain actually broke out a huge American flag and had his men standing on the deck, holding it up. They got gunned down. Two American sailors were killed, and nearly four dozen more wounded.

The very first Japanese reaction was almost a "So what? Now get the hell out of our way." The State Department stepped up the level of protest, and the Japanese finally came back with an outright lie, claiming it was all a mistake and they were, of course, sorry about the whole thing. So let's just forget about it.

Bull. They knew damn well what they were doing. The pilots had orders to attack, and it was a damn clear signal for us to get our butts out of China because they were taking over.

I sat in the theater watching the grainy black-and-white footage, the shot-up ship, the riddled American flag, the bodies of sailors being carried off on stretchers.

And then the movie started.

I looked around. No one was angry, no one was reacting. What the hell was going on?

After the show, while I was walking my sister home, we talked about it. She didn't see it as all that big a deal. Sure, it was tragic about the sailors, but the Japanese claimed it was a mistake, offered an apology, so let's not worry about it.

I was worried about it. I was training for the army, and maybe it would be me out there in another three years.

That's when I got interested in following what was going on. Most guys my age, even those in the military back then, tended to focus only on what was happening in their lives—how to get through the next exam, how to meet a girl at the Saturday night socials, or simply how to get through the next day. I found myself wondering about what it was I was training for.

It wasn't until a year later that I had an instructor with the answers. I think that any cadet who attended the Point in the late thirties and had any interest in what was going on in the real world will remember Professor Boekerman. He taught the social sciences. In my opinion he was one of the truly great minds in the United States military. He was something of a prophet as well. He believed that the world was heading toward the greatest conflict in history, a struggle for global hegemony. On one side would be the rising power of Nazi Germany in Europe and Japan in the Pacific. Stalin's Soviet Union would be a player as well and a force to be contended with, maybe as an ally that we really couldn't trust or, far worse, as another brutal dictatorship fighting against us. Standing against this great threat to civilization would be the western democracies, France torn by internal strife and a lack of national will, Great Britain staggering as we were with the Depression, and the United States.

We, those of us sitting in his classroom, would be the ones on the front line. He didn't pull any punches. He painted a picture that could scare the hell out of you, but he also projected a confidence that, ultimately, the free people of the world would find the means and the moral strength to win. And it would be we cadets who would have to carry the brunt of the fighting.

But America continued to sleep. I returned from Christmas furlough, traveling again across a country that was wrapped up in itself. There was already a war in China, a civil war in Spain that was killing hundreds of thousands, but for nearly everyone that conflict was remote and would never come to trouble us.

And yes, I did focus on other things, especially Bets, but now there was a lingering thought, a growing sense that the path I chose was going to eventually lead me into a very dark world.

And so my junior year passed. I was crazy about Bets, yet somehow I managed to stay focused on the work and training. We already knew that we were heading toward marriage and started to plan for the event as soon as I graduated.

That was the fall and spring of 1938 and 1939. Germany had renounced the limitations imposed upon it by the Versailles Treaty and began to rearm openly. At Munich Britain and France had caved in to Hitler's demands and let him take the Sudeten-land, and the following spring the rest of Czechoslovakia (a region I would fight through six years later). On days when I was actually allowed off base for a few hours, Bets and I would sometimes go to a movie and there I'd see newsreels of the war in Spain (1936–39), fleets of dive bombers wiping out cities, tanks charging over fortifications, crushing everything in their path, and from China the brutal images of the rape of Nanking (November 1937), where the Japanese army, in a frenzy, murdered nearly a quarter of a million innocent civilians.

Then came summer, which was the summer of 1939, and the cadets at the Point were absorbed in field exercises. One I will never forget—it shocked the hell out of me—involved Charles Lindbergh.

I was part of a special detachment sent down to Fort Monmouth, New Jersey, to participate in a four-day training exercise in air defense. Fort Monmouth was an old base on the Jersey shore, not far from lower New York harbor. The heavy coastal artillery was still in position then, huge guns that would supposedly stop any enemy attack. The exercise was to demonstrate how our new Flying Fortresses, the B-17s, might launch a long-range attack and how our up-to-date antiaircraft guns would take care of it.

The B-17 had actually been sold to a reluctant public, and to Congress, as a sort of long-range coastal artillery, capable of stopping an enemy fleet when it was still five hundred miles away. Actually, that was a bit of a stealth job by the Army Air Corps, which wanted the plane for strategic bombing, but it could only get money for production of a hundred or so Flying Fortresses by selling the plane as a defensive weapon.

The Fortresses took off from a nearby field, went out to sea, gained altitude, and then came in. It was dark, and this was before radar. What was used back then was a device that looked like a giant ear trumpet, like the kind that you see grandpa using in old movies. A couple of these huge ear trumpets were mounted on a truck, and some poor guy was hooked into them, listening intently. Once he heard the planes, he'd track on them, thus giving the first plot line. A second listener, positioned some distance away, was then supposed to hear the planes as well, and another line was drawn. They now had the planes triangulated. Estimate height, set fuses, and fire.

The damn stupid thing never worked.

The demonstration turned into a black comedy. The planes flew in, but no one could get a bearing, let alone see them. Some embarrassed staff officer who had cooked the demonstration up finally got on the radio and told the "enemy" bombers to circle around and attack again. Still no go. We could hear them. The B-17 made a hell of a racket—and even now, when one of them flies into the airport near where I live for an air show, I instantly know that sound, having heard a thousand or more of them fly overhead.

The problem was that it was cloudy, and clouds can distort acoustics. We could all hear them, but with all of us looking up, no one could get a fix so we could simulate firing on them. Searchlights were weaving back and forth, reflecting off the clouds, lighting up our position like it was broad daylight. We certainly would have made a hell of a target for someone over-head.

Finally, the planes were told to come around yet again, this time at three thousand feet, and turn on all their lights! So finally we saw them, lumbering along, throttled back, lights blazing. Whereupon we supposedly shot them down.

God, it was embarrassing, and also damned scary!

This was the summer of 1939, the Nazis had an air fleet of thousands of planes, and we had to get our guys to turn on their lights so we could make believe we shot them down.

Charles Lindbergh was there watching this farce. Lindbergh today has several different reputations. Some only remember him for his famous flight across the Atlantic, which had taken place but twelve years earlier. How things had changed in those twelve years!

Tragically, Lindbergh had got himself mixed up in what some people felt was a pro-Nazi movement in America. I don't necessarily buy that. Yes, he did say some positive things about the Nazis, a lot of people did before the war, but I think he was also offering a warning, that America had better wake up to the military buildup that was going on in Germany.

When war finally did hit, there was no question about his patriotism. He worked in the U.S. aviation industry. His role during the war is still not recognized because of some of the bad choices he made just prior to the start.

Lindbergh was there that summer night of tragicomic maneuvers just outside of New York, its skyscrapers glowing. Once the circus was over, he climbed atop the breech of one of those huge and thoroughly antiquated coastal guns and asked us to gather round.

He then gave us a short talk. This was the guy who was the hero of my generation. Of course we listened.

He told us about visiting Germany, about the power of their air force and their new weapons that were as wondrous, and as fearsome, as lasers, stealth bombers, and nukes are to us today.

Something that is forgotten now are some of the prophecies about air warfare back in 1939. Men like Giulio Douhet and Billy Mitchell believed that air fleets would indeed be the weapon that could not be stopped, especially if poison gas was used. Images were painted of fleets of thousands of bombers blackening the sky over cities, unleashing deadly nerve-gas bombs. Gas had been used during World War I, and nearly all of us knew someone, an uncle, an older brother, a neighbor, who had taken a dose of it. One of my uncles was nailed by mustard gas, and it tortured him every day for the rest of his life.

Nerve gas is not something new. It was around in the 1930s, and a single droplet could kill you. Imagine, then, the fear of watching those B-17s overhead, with us unable to do a damn thing to stop them, and filled with the thought that a thousand such planes could kill every man, woman, and child in New York City in a single night.

Visions of the apocalypse did not start on September 11, 2001, or on August 6, 1945. They were with us on that night back in 1939.

Lindbergh told us we had to rearm, to train, and to be ready, that only by presenting a strong front could we hope to avert war. If we did not, war would come. Too bad no one who could do something about it truly listened. We did, because we knew we'd be the first ones to go.

It was a sober bunch that rode the train back to the Point the following day. It was only going to get worse.

Just before Labor Day of 1939 I was told I had qualified for the ultimate pleasure, a true weekend pass. No one would follow me, no one would track my every step, I was free to walk down that hill and go wherever I wanted.

There were half a dozen of us, a couple with girlfriends. Bets, having graduated from college, was back home in Texas so I had to go it alone. It was a Friday, and we got sprung, running to the station. The girls were to meet us at the station in Jersey. From there we took a ferry to Manhattan and checked into a hotel—actually, two hotels. The girls went to one, and we went to the other. And believe me, that is the truth. The old rules still applied.

So we had three glorious days ahead of us in Manhattan, on the first weekend of September 1939. There was the World's Fair over in Flushing Meadows, the chance to walk with girls along Fifth Avenue, and if we budgeted things just right, maybe even a Broadway show. There were other hot acts to catch as well, for swing was in. Jimmy Dorsey, Benny Goodman, Glenn Miller, they might be in town . . . and that was the weekend World War II started.

Germany had invaded Poland, and Britain, steeling herself at last, presented an ultimatum. Twenty-four hours later, France and England declared war on Germany.

It was one sober bunch of guys that weekend in that hotel room in New York. We spent the weekend picking up the latest extra edition of the *New York Times*, or we stood in the hotel lobby and listened to the radio and broadcasts from London with the latest bulletins.

At the end of the weekend I took the train back up the Hudson and walked back up the hill to get ready for what was to come.

That fall some of us, at least, were focused. We were barely back in class when Poland, with an army of over forty divisions, was gone, to be divided up by Nazi Germany and the Soviet Union.

It's all but forgotten today, but from September 1939 until June 21, 1941, the Soviet Union and Germany were allies. The specter thus presented to the West was indeed terrifying, a combination of two goliath dictatorships capable of marshaling tens of millions of soldiers.

There was a strong sentiment, as well, with some of our so-called intellectuals that it was time to choose between one or the other. Socialism, whether it was the racist nationalism of the right or the struggle of the working class against capitalism on the left, was chic in many circles. More than a few believed that our system of democracy in a free capitalistic republic was an anachronism and that Germany or the Soviet Union represented the new wave of the twentieth century.

It was a view not held by anyone I knew at the Point. Some might argue that our military establishment has always been conservative in its politics, but I don't see it as being that simple. In fact, in the army I knew in my youth, there was a strong tradition that officers must be apolitical. Voicing support for Democrats or Republicans was bad form. We believed that we took our orders from those who held power under the Constitution, so we saluted, went out to do our duty, and, if need be, died.

I think there is the key to the view we held—"to do our duty, and if need be die." We were rooted in the Constitution. That and the Declaration of Independence were our sacred texts. We had taken a solemn vow to defend the United States and all that those documents stood for. If the Republic did die, the bodies of all those who had gone through West Point would be on that funeral pyre with it.

That might seem naive today, and some might even say that

what I've just written is the sentimental memories of an old man. It's not. The beliefs that the Point inculcates in its cadets, and all those who teach and work there, is one of idealism, and above all else a reverent respect for the principles that our Founding Fathers fought and died for at Lexington, Valley Forge, Yorktown, and even on the very ground where we paraded every day.

The problem was, America was not ready for war. Our resolve to fight did not mean we were going to win. In fact, our fear was that we could very well lose what Lincoln once called "the last best hope of mankind."

It is frustrating at times, today, to convey what it felt like between September 1, 1939, and December 7, 1941.

To younger generations today the war, "grandpa's war," is a known event. We won.

Dad or Grandpa is here. He's honored as being of that "Greatest Generation," and then the conversation shifts to something else.

Those who actually lived through it? For us there is always something else when this time is spoken of, remembered, or written down as I am now doing. We remember the ghosts, all the lives that were never lived, and, from that, all the children and grandchildren who would never be born to ask "What did you do in the war, grandpa?"

Many of those ghosts were my classmates in the fall of 1939.

There was a certain gallows humor among us that year. Someone would talk about plans, getting married, promotions to come, and then the ice water would be dumped: "We'll be dead in a year, so what the hell are you talking about." Being at the Point is what separated us from nearly all the other guys our age.

Most of our generation, and our parent's generation, in the fall of 1939, ignored what was going on in the world, or dreamed we were so far away we'd never get into it, or if we did get into it, the navy, and the guys already in the army, would handle it.

Of course, we were the guys who were going to be in that army, so we thought about it and talked and worried.

We knew that the army was pathetically ill prepared.

We'd watch newsreels of German tanks racing across Poland, and then we'd participate in maneuvers using equipment from World War I.

We'd see film of endless columns of German troops on the march, and we knew that even Portugal or Argentina had more men under arms than America.

The Army Air Corps did have a few modern planes, like the B-17, but most of the planes, such as the P-36 and P-39, would be nothing more than target practice when a ME-109 got on their tail.

So we tried to get ready. For many, there was an increasing awareness, a buckling down, because what was coming would put us in the front lines.

Bets was back with her family in Texas, and in one sense that might have been for the best. My second year, or junior year, well, I let things slip. I lived for the Saturday night socials, the rare chance for a Sunday afternoon walk with Bets, and then thought about it the whole rest of the week. My grades slipped a bit, my efficiency was down, and I lost out on the plum assignment I had been aiming for, cadet brigade commander. In fact, I didn't even make it as a cadet company commander, something I had too rashly assumed was mine for the taking. Instead, I was simply cadet lieutenant of Company A. A good assignment, it meant I was seen as being in the top twenty-five of my class, but still, it was something of a letdown.

Of course, there was no such thing as phone calls to Texas in 1939 for a cadet, so there was a daily letter and then study and attending to the duties of being second in command of a company. There were plebes and yearlings to look out for, help to be offered, someone to talk to when it was needed. The responsibility added hours each day to an already full schedule.

The year without Bets was a tough one, but nearly every day there was a letter, even if it was nothing more than a brief sentence telling me that she loved me.

The winter passed. In Europe it was the winter of the Phony War, a surreal situation. England and France mobilized, put well over a hundred divisions in the field, and then—did nothing, absolutely nothing. History would later show that if they had attacked immediately, they would have faced less than a dozen second-rate German divisions.

That contemptible little corporal had his opponents figured. He knew they wouldn't attack. They were terrified by the memories of World War I and the millions of casualties everyone expected. Yet he was planning a new kind of war, the blitzkrieg, the rapid movement of combined arms, of armor, mobile artillery, and motorized infantry, directly supported by hundreds of airplanes.

In April 1940 there was the first indicator that things were about to let go. The Nazis hit Norway, taking it in a brilliant combined operation of naval support and airborne assault.

At that point I was only six weeks from graduation and seven weeks from getting married. And yes, like any guy my age, even though the world was obviously going to hell, I was hoping for at least a final brief moment of peace and a chance to marry the girl I loved.

Just four weeks before graduating and five weeks before marrying Bets, the hammer came down. In an operation that one must admit was absolutely brilliant, the German army sliced into France. Attacking first in Holland and Belgium, to lure the Brits and French in, they then came racing out of the Ardennes with nearly two thousand tanks. Within a week they were at the Channel, cutting off the bulk of the British and French armies.

We weren't allowed to have radios in our rooms, but we could still get the daily news. All the New York City papers were available, and in common areas radios were constantly on. If conditions were right, live broadcasts would even come in on CBS from Paris, London, and, yes, even Berlin.

The valiant British and French armies, which had fought Germany to a standstill in 1914, collapsed in 1940. During the week that led up to graduation we started to hear of a place called Dunkirk. We listened, awestruck, to descriptions of the British attempting to evacuate half a million men out of the encircled pocket.

The Germans, as well, were putting out their propaganda. Eventually, newsreel footage reached us showing the stunning airborne assault on the Dutch fortress of Eben Emael. The Germans literally crash-landed gliders on top of the fort with a hundred men on board and took it. A position that was supposed to be able to hold out against a hundred thousand men for weeks fell in less than a day. Late in 1944 I fought within a mile or two of that fort.

How in God's name were we supposed to fight something like that? It made some people wonder about all the German talk of creating a nation of supermen. Maybe they had really done it.

At the exact moment I stepped up to the stage and accepted my diploma from West Point, German tanks rolled into the suburbs of Paris, three thousand miles away.

The next day my mother and I left the Point and drove to Dallas, where Bets and I were to be married on June 24.

Yes, we were happy. We were crazy about each other, the years of waiting were at an end. No longer would there be curfews, a few hours perhaps on a Sunday afternoon for a walk, or letters quickly scribbled off. We would be together, and then as now, that is a remarkable moment for any guy in his midtwenties, or woman in her early twenties.

And yet, throughout the final week, news was there in the background, on the radar or in a newspaper on a table.

"Paris Declared Open City" . . . "Paris Surrenders" . . . "Germans Advance Unchecked" . . . "France Surrenders" . . . and then, that one voice in the darkness . . . "Britain Vows to Fight On."

Winston Churchill's voice, that remarkable, unforgettable voice, was heard at last.

For years he had warned all of us of the darkness to come. He was, at best, ignored, and by many denounced as a warmonger bent on provoking the Nazis, who only wanted peace. That has usually been the treatment given to those who attempt to speak out against the threat of war.

In those early weeks of June 1940, I at last heard a defiant voice, and one even of hope, when he vowed that England would fight on to the end, no matter what the cost. Then, prophetically, he declared, "the New World" would at last come to the rescue of the Old.

I knew he was speaking about me, though that almost did not happen.

My orders had been cut. I was assigned to the Philippines. Bets and I were delighted. It was considered a great assignment. General MacArthur had been sent over five years earlier to organize and train a Filipino national army. In 1940 the Philippine Islands were officially a protectorate, a fancy term which actually meant it was a colony ceded by Spain to the United States in 1898.

Our strategy for dealing with Japan was centered on the Philippines and outlined in secret plans referred to as Plan Orange and Plan Rainbow.

If war started with Japan our assumption was they'd move first to knock out our base in the Philippines. Therefore, the mission of the Filipino army, and the small contingent of American troops there, was to dig in and hold on. Meanwhile, the powerful American fleet would sortie from our major base in the Pacific, yes, Pearl Harbor. Our battlewagons would tear the Japanese fleet to shreds, and the war would be over before it had even started.

So Bets and I were heading to a danger zone, but if we were thinking about a serious war in the spring of 1940, it was in

Europe. Besides, the assignment had a certain romantic side to it. Young couple gets married, newly commissioned lieutenant out of West Point, long cruise to a beautiful tropical region. Even a chance for a leave to visit Hong Kong or Singapore. The summer tropical uniforms looked great. In a way it was supposed to be our honeymoon trip, taking the train to San Francisco and then a nice slow ship to Manila.

And then the army changed my orders. Somewhere somebody decided, "No, Bennett would be better with the artillery here in the States."

I had to break the news to Bets that there was to be no honeymoon aboard a ship bound for Manila. We were going to Fort Sill, Oklahoma.

Fort Sill? If there is a base that has darn little appeal, especially in the heat of summer, or in the cold of winter, it is Fort Sill, the main training facility for artillery. There I was to learn the drill of how to run a battery. Hundreds of thousands of men would go through the old "forts" in the plains states for training during the war, the forts dating back to before the Civil War. For many it was at times interesting, and even exciting, but if you ask the wives who went with them, that's a whole different story . . . dust, heat, more dust, wind, and then more dust.

It was the first of a hundred times I would have to tell Bets, "Well, our plans are changed." And then, as always, she took it with grace. She knew from day one that when she decided to marry me it meant the army would control her life as well.

And so we were married, on June 24, 1940, without a doubt one of the happiest days of my life. A couple of days later we were on the road to Fort Sill.

Thus closed my first tour of duty at West Point.

And I should add this: Five of my comrades in the class of 1940 went to the Philippines. None came back. They died at Bataan or were brutally murdered on the Death March.

3

Fort Sill / Fort Sam Houston / Fort Knox

Bets and I arrived at Fort Sill, Oklahoma, late in June 1941, driving up from Dallas after our wedding. Honeymoon plans of a long slow cruise to Manila had been replaced with a hot dusty trip across the plains, the tropical white uniforms and dresses packed away, never to be retrieved.

We settled into an apartment on the second floor of a widow's home, and I was immediately sent into training—with horses. While at the Point I'd been on the equestrian team and did rather well, representing West Point at a number of events, but this was different. I was now working with horse-drawn artillery.

In some ways the drill was changed little from the Civil War. A gun, a surplus French 75mm from World War I, and caisson filled with ammunition were pulled by a team of six horses. In short order I was up on a trace horse, learning to guide the team as we first walked and, by the end of the day, galloped across the plains.

I'll admit it was exhilarating—horses racing, gun and caisson bouncing along behind me, and downright dangerous, too. You had to keep your right foot out of the stirrup and up on the limber pole, otherwise it'd get crushed. And God save you if you ever fell off. I had fallen off horses plenty of times before, but falling was decidedly unhealthy with the wheels of a one-ton field piece only a couple of feet behind you. It was a common death for gunners.

Our training officers were definitely of the old school, convinced that if we ever did get into a tangle with Germany, horse-drawn artillery would win the day. They had little use for mechanization. A horse got its fuel from the nearest field, while a mechanized piece needed gas and oil, and if things ever got really bad, you could at least eat the horse. Their logic did not impress me. Nevertheless, every morning we led our horses out, harnessed them up, a process that could take quite a bit of time, mounted up, and went trotting off, just as it was done at the battle of Gettysburg.

The training program was designed for newly minted officers, a quick orientation for second lieutenants who would then go on to field commands. In our group of fifty about a dozen of the men were not West Point, but ROTC.

There was some tension in that. After four years at the Point we who graduated—well, we had something of an elevated opinion of ourselves. We had endured four years of draconian conditions and at times outright hell, and there, standing along-side of us, wearing the same gold bar of a second lieutenant, was some guy who showed up for drill once a week, most likely on a coed campus, did a couple of summers of training camp, and drew the same pay we did.

I know now that, on the other side of the coin, we were viewed as too often arrogant, uptight, and were far too "by the book."

In retrospect, we were both right and both wrong. The whole idea of ROTC is in the first word, "reserve." Our army, in that summer of 1940, was woefully ill prepared for all that was about to come down on us. West Point only produced several hundred officers a year. If we didn't get a hell of a lot of reserve officers, and quick, we were sunk.

I should add that many of the ROTC guys were running

circles around me when it came to artillery. Artillery isn't just run-the-guns-up-and-shoot. Even two hundred years ago it was a branch that required a lot of math. In 1940 it required a hell of a lot of math. Many of the young lieutenants around me had been engineering majors in state universities, and they had drilled extensively in artillery with their ROTC training. Since I was from the Point, a lot of eyes were on me, so what I thought would be something of a honeymoon turned into an intense nine weeks of trying to stay even.

And while we were out there galloping around the plains of Oklahoma, the Luftwaffe launched the greatest air campaign in history, attempting to pound England into submission. I was mesmerized by the reports of hundreds of German planes sweeping the English coast and finally turning on London in massive night-long raids.

During the Gulf War in 1991 there was a lot of talk about how sci-fi our war effort looked, with high-tech weapons, "smart bombs," and laser-guided weaponry. The German attack on England in that summer of 1940 looked just as futuristic. We soon learned the relative merits of the ME-109 versus the Spitfire and Hurricane, knew the range of the German bombers and their maximum loads, and wondered how England would hold out for even a month against the onslaught of over two thousand Nazi aircraft.

Throughout it all the voice of Churchill was heard, growling defiance, and all the time hinting as well that eventually America had to face reality if western civilization was to survive. At times, when the conditions were right, CBS radio even had live broadcasts from London, complete with air-raid sirens wailing and Edward R. Murrow describing the action. That was just as startling to us in 1940 as CNN broadcasting from Baghdad in 1991.

Yet it is hard to grasp that time now, over sixty years later. In 1940 there were many who still said that the European war was none of our business, that even to start to prepare militarily was simply an act of warmongering and provocation. Even in the

White House there were some who questioned which side we should be on, especially during the time when Nazi Germany and the Soviet Union were allies.

With all that in mind our training exercises were inane. If a single ME-109 or one of the new German Mark IV tanks caught our horse-drawn battery out in the open, we were dead meat.

When we did study larger operations, involving battalion and division-level firing missions, it was pure World War I thinking. Dig your guns in, pile up the ammunition, carefully lay out a firing plan, calculate how many shells are required to flatten a particular section of front, hook everything in with miles upon miles of phone wire, then gear up for the big moment and let everything loose in a sustained barrage. Once you've finished, the infantry climbs out of its trenches and moves forward, you pick up your gear, advance with them, dig in, and start all over again.

No one ever seriously talked about what to do if the enemy should be so discourteous as to actually move just before we started shooting, or worse yet, if it moved straight into us at twenty miles an hour or suddenly came in from behind after cutting through at a weak point fifty miles away while Stukas circled overhead like vultures.

Always there was the obsession with laying out plenty of phone lines. We were supposed to carry miles of the stuff, laboriously string it out, and then of course roll it back up when finished, since this was a peacetime army. Radios? There were a few around, but the old-timers placed no trust in them and told us to do the same.

On weekends Bets and I managed to get a little time off together and actually travel around a bit like a married couple. I might not put Oklahoma on the top of a list of scenic attractions, but in 1940 it was certainly unusual at times and also something of a depressing shock as well.

Only fifty-two years had passed since the great land rush of 1888, which was nothing more than an outright grab of what was supposed to be Indian territory forever. There were still Indians alive at that time who could remember fighting the U.S. cavalry. For both Bets and me it was all rather exotic. A number of people still got around on horseback, and in many ways Fort Sill had more the look of a frontier outpost than what would become the primary training center for the vast buildup to come.

The depressing part was that the base sat at the center of the great Dust Bowl. All around us were signs of the devastation and poverty left in its wake, abandoned farms, trucks filled with a few meager possessions, and entire families heading toward California. America in 1940 was still reeling from the depression. A quarter of the men coming into the army that year were rejected because of the effects of malnourishment, childhood diseases, and decayed teeth. When you saw newsreels of triumphant German troops marching in the victory parades through Berlin, it made you wonder.

After nine weeks of training at Sill I was assigned to a battery with the 2d Infantry Division at Fort Sam Houston. So there was another drive across the prairie, with Bets attempting to settle into another town, though at least this was San Antonio, which did have its appeal, then and now.

The training at Sill had been oriented to breaking in new officers. At Fort Sam Houston it was the real thing. I was taking my first command, and I thank God I was greeted by Sergeant Sullivan, the top NCO of the unit. Sullivan was first sergeant of the recruit training camp.

He was classic old army, a genuine sergeant with enough enlistment hash marks to intimidate even a captain or a major.

In a way it's strange how western armies are organized. A tough old sarge who has been in the army longer than his commanding officer has been alive must snap to attention and salute as you approach for the first time, and if you tell him to jump into a latrine he'd darn well better do it. Of course, it was far more subtle than that, and a good officer had better learn it, and damn quick. Treat an old sergeant without the proper degree of respect, deference even, or try to point at the single bar on your shoulder and yell that he had better salute it; well, he'll salute it, and then all sorts of things will go to hell behind your back.

Tragically, far too many officers never figure out that it's the old NCOs who truly make the army run. Yes, they salute you, but you also return the salute. Treat them with respect and you'll earn some respect as well. I sensed from day one that the important thing was to earn the respect of men like Sergeant Sullivan so that when they did have to salute, they did so because they wanted to and not because they had to.

I made it clear to Sullivan that I knew there was still a lot for me to learn. Once that was clear, if I was about to stumble and make an idiot out of myself, Sullivan would all so carefully step in, set things right, and in the process show me how to avoid making the same mistake again.

Sullivan was always immaculate, pressed khakis with pleats, the uniform fitting him like a glove. He never seemed to sweat. Everything he did seemed effortless. I knew I was running a "grace period" with him. If I met his expectations, there would be mutual respect; if not, there could be a lot of subtle ways he could make things difficult.

Ever so gradually he began to step back, satisfied that he had nursed another lieutenant into shape. Before long I was running my unit with just an occasional sidelong glance from him as a quiet signal to try a different approach.

I clearly remember one day when nothing seemed to go right with the men I was training. Several of them were outright pains in the neck, always pushing things to the edge, but not quite stepping over the line. That evening Sullivan showed up at my tent and politely asked, "Will the lieutenant be staying in his tent for the next fifteen minutes?"

An interesting question. It was in fact, a firm suggestion. I was not to step outside no matter what I heard. Sullivan saluted and walked off. I thought I heard a ruckus but knew it was best to ignore what was going on. After my allotted time I stepped out and wandered over to the mess tent. My three troublemakers were sitting within, faces a bit puffy, nursing black eyes. Sullivan sat at the other side of the tent, cup of coffee in hand. He greeted me with a blank, innocent stare. The issue was settled. To the sensibilities of today's army that might seem extreme. If we are ever facing a global war again, I don't think it will seem extreme at all.

I clearly remember a day, as well, when we were out on a field exercise. A decision had to be made, and I gave a sidelong glance at Sullivan and his sidekick, a classic old corporal who had been with Sullivan for years. Both were silent. They broke eye contact and looked the other way. It was time, they were saying, for this second lieutenant to do his job. Fortunately, I made the right moves. From then on they stepped back and I did my job.

Sergeant Sullivan was the transition man who took me from the theories of West Point into the practical realities of a peacetime army that was just beginning to stir. He was one of the best trainers I ever had, and I will always be grateful to him. One of the ironies of history is that the names of generals are remembered, and they are given the credit for this campaign or that battle, but behind every general stands a legion of sergeants going back to that first sergeant who quietly nursed him along.

Late in the fall of 1940 our first wave of new recruits began to pour in. The draft bill was about to pass and the army was offering a choice of branches of service for those who enlisted before their number was drawn.

The system that would be used later, of a standardized basic training at places like Fort Dix, was yet to be instituted, so raw recruits were literally dropped in our laps, still in their civvies. We had eight weeks to bring them on line before their assignment to a unit within the 2d Infantry Division, and I was assigned to help out.

As a new officer, it was a great experience and one that would put me in a good position two years in the future. The men came from all over the country and not just Texas or the Southwest. I had recruits from New York with several years of college, and standing next to them would be a kid straight off a farm in Alabama who could barely read or write.

I had to learn how to communicate with all kinds of men, from every possible background and every kind of attitude, from patriotic idealist to "What the hell am I doing here, and by the way, lieutenant, I hate your guts."

Then as now I believe that simply browbeating a man into doing something is assinine. Yes, at times Sergeant Sullivan had to step in with those who had a "failure to communicate," but that was a last resort. If you explain to a man why it is necessary to do something and try to cut out as much of the B.S. as possible, ninety-nine times out of a hundred you can get him on your side.

Late in 1940 the big wave started to hit. Hundreds of thousands of men were being called up by the draft. In a way, the draft was a miracle. The selective service bill passed just before the presidential election and usually no politician in his right mind would have voted for it. But there was a growing sense, at last, that the United States was facing a national emergency. If that bill had failed to pass, chances are I never would have lived long enough to write this book, and you might not be alive to read it.

The draft gave us the core of an army that, though still woefully inadequate on December 7, 1941, was at least beginning to become something.

A lot of men who were "caught in the draft" were not at all pleased with their situation. They were going along with their lives and then the letter from the draft board arrived. A couple of weeks later, girlfriends, parents, buddies, all were gone, and they were in the hands of a new second lieutenant like me and men like Sergeant Sullivan.

Training was not a pleasant experience, and I doubt that many of the draftees liked it. If anyone from that Class of 1940 is reading this, I bet he has a few choice words to say about the whole thing that don't quite fit an idealistic image of the Greatest Generation.

The army was my chosen profession. For the men lining up in front of me, it was a year to be endured, and then it would be back to the civilian world. There was even an acronym for it: O.H.I.O., "Over the hill in October." The draft bill, as originally passed, was served up to a still reluctant country as a half measure. The men who went in would serve only a year and then be discharged back to moms, dads, and girlfriends in October 1941. And by God, if anyone tried to stop them or extend that year of service, a lot of men avowed they were over the hill, no matter what.

I had a job to do, to try to turn them into soldiers of a free republic. Perhaps this is the key definer, and ultimately why we won. The men might not like it, in fact, very few of them did, but down deep there was an innate sense in the vast majority of draftees that our country was threatened and that we, as free citizens, had to rise to that challenge. We were not seeking conquest, we were not out to purify a race, or force the solidarity of the working class at gunpoint; we were defenders of a sacred trust passed down to us across a hundred and sixty years of freedom.

I think there's a very interesting trait that is unique to the American soldiers of that war. Nearly all of us were professional grumblers. I was part of the system, a West Point man, so I had to keep my grumbling to myself most of the time. The average soldier, though, was free to speak his mind. Every other word when he discussed the army started with F. He didn't look much like a soldier, he made it clear he didn't want to be one, and yet, when the crisis came, he proved to be about the best damned soldier on the face of the earth.

A year into the war, a general took a look at some of my men after our first action and said, in words I'll never forget, "There isn't a damn soldier in the entire outfit, but by God they sure can shoot."

As time fades and we tend to remember with nostalgia our past, or the past of our parents and grandparents, we see it through a soft, golden glow. All men were heroes, all stood heroic and were without fear, and all went forth to battle without hesitation. That's ridiculous. We were scared. Many didn't want to be there, and yet, when the time came to pitch in, by and large they did it. Professional soldier or draftee, they refused to turn back. I think the same was true of the men who staggered through the sleet and mud with Washington, marched behind Stonewall Jackson, and went into the forests of the Argonne. They didn't like it, they most likely soundly cursed everything about it, but nevertheless, as free men, they stuck with it to the end, no matter what. They constituted a true citizen army.

The things my men said would have gotten them shot or beheaded in the Japanese army or sent to a labor battalion in Germany. In Russia a commissar would have executed them on the spot. That is the difference between them and us. That is why we won and they didn't, both in World War II and in the long twilight struggle that came afterward. The grumbling, the cursing, the reluctance, the disdain that they kept to themselves when I and other officers were around, was all part of an inner game, to remind everyone that ultimately we were free men, not part of some dictator's machine.

That's not to say that I, or Sergeant Sullivan, ignored military procedure and protocol. If you tried to "go along with the guys," as some officers did, your unit went to hell. A good sergeant played a dual role, part S.O.B. and strangely, at times, part old uncle or father, giving just the right encouragement at the right moment.

An army does not run by consensus. No one says, "Let's have a meeting and talk this over." Try that when someone is trying to kill you. And try it when that terrible moment comes and you know you are ordering men to what might be certain death. You cannot hesitate, and they in turn cannot hesitate or wonder for a second whether you know what you are doing. There must be discipline, top to bottom, if an outfit is to survive.

So we trained throughout the winter and spring of 1940–1941. We watched with admiration and awe as the "chosen few" of the Royal Air Force turned back the Nazi horde, truly one of the greatest triumphs of freedom over tyranny in the history of arms. The victory in the Battle of Britain did not mean by any stretch that the tide had turned, it simply looked as if the inevitable had been postponed.

The German U-boat campaign started to gear up, a war by no means as riveting or even as glamorous as the air war, but one just as deadly, especially when you contemplated the fate of a crew dumped into the North Atlantic on a dark night in January. England was slowly starving, even as it tried to kick back in North Africa.

On the other side of the world things were heating up as well. Japan, bent on imperial conquest, was expanding its operations in China and eventually jumped into French Indochina, a place that would haunt us across forty years. That move triggered Roosevelt's decision to place an oil embargo on Japan (July 26, 1941), the turning point on the path to war with the United States and Great Britain.

I was now the S-3 for the 37th Artillery attached to the 2d Infantry Division. That summer our unit loaded up and went to Louisiana to participate in the now famous war games of 1941. They turned out to be an equal measure of vision and farce.

There was absolutely no integration of training between artillery and infantry. The infantry went off and did their thing while we did ours. Liaison, which is absolutely crucial when artillery is in support of infantry, was all but nonexistent. There wasn't enough of the precious phone wire to go around, and the few radios we had were antiques even by the standards of 1941.

Entire units got lost and floundered around in the bayous and heat-scorched flatlands of western Louisiana and east Texas. Old trucks were used to mimic tanks, with the word "Tank" painted on their sides. The airplanes were lumbering old relics, since the few good aircraft that had been produced had all been shipped to England.

The vision was primarily that of one man, George Patton, the commander of the 2d Armored Division. His team won when he scrapped the plan and went off on a mad dash with his ersatz tanks, swinging fifty miles behind the lines and then cutting into the rear of the opposing force. Higher-ups and umpires for the game screamed bloody murder, but he had proved his point, and shortly thereafter he appeared on the cover of *Life* magazine. I know he loved that, even though Patton did look a bit foolish in the photo wearing a uniform he had designed, complete with football helmet rather than the standard-issue World War I surplus tin pot.

While we were exercising, the Wehrmacht, with over a hundred divisions, a dozen of them armored, cut into the Soviet Union. In one sense it was a relief. The invasion switched the alliance overnight. No longer was there the specter that we might have to fight a combination of the two great dictatorships. It meant as well that some of the pressure was off England.

On the other side, though, it looked as if Russia would be wiped out before Christmas, its limitless resources in Nazi hands. It was the level of violence and scope of battle, though, that was truly appalling. In a single battle the Russians lost close to a million men. Entire divisions, entire armies, were annihilated in a single day. The Germans claimed over ten thousand aircraft destroyed in the first month, and a territory as vast as the entire eastern United States fell under the Nazi yoke. Cities the size of Chicago were under siege, and tens of millions of refugees staggered toward the Urals, uprooted in a war unlike any ever seen.

I think that was one of the real wake-up calls. In spite of the horrors of Stalinism there had been a lot of sentiment in some circles for the Soviet Union during the 1930s. That meant an instant turn around within their circles and now an endorsement of our own buildup. Beyond that type of politics, though, the average American simply woke up and started to realize that Hitler and his goons would not stop until someone made them stop. That someone would, in the end, have to be us.

We returned to our barracks after the war games in Louisiana and really dug into our jobs. There was still some grumbling about O.H.I.O., especially when Congress, showing some backbone, extended the draft for another year and ordered all those in the army to stay in the ranks, a decision that passed by a one-vote majority. The talk about desertion, however, died. It was okay to grumble about it earlier, but everyone started to realize that we were getting ready for the real thing, like it or not. If not us, who?

In September 1941 orders came through transferring me to the newly forming 5th Armored Division at Fort Knox, Kentucky. Again I would be in artillery, this time a supposedly mechanized artillery battalion. So Bets and I packed up again and drove across the country.

It was early autumn, and the Kentucky hills are beautiful at that time of year. Not quite as good as the Hudson River Valley, but a darn sight better than the scorched flatlands of Fort Sam Houston.

We found a small three-room house, bedroom, kitchen, and living room with a potbellied stove. It was fifteen miles from the base, which meant I was up at five in the morning to get ready and usually not home till nine at night. We did get Sundays together, and Louisville was not that far away.

Bets really liked our time there, and so did I. I recall that time as a happy one. I was madly in love with my wife. We had survived our first year of marriage and my first year as an officer with both our relationship and our career intact. You'll notice I refer to the career as "our" career. In those days it truly was. A wife was considered to be a part of the team. Twenty-first-century thinking might chafe at some of these requirements, but in 1941 an officer's wife was expected to be supportive of her husband, a lady as he was expected to be a gentleman.

It was also our final autumn of peace, a last chance to live something of a normal life. Sometimes I'd even be home for a late dinner or have a Sunday off to lounge around, go for a drive, watch the leaves turn, and dream about a future together, even though, deep down, we both feared the future together might be a short one.

That made it even more poignant and rich in my memories now. Most newlyweds our age, at least today, can dream of things to come, talking quietly about them late at night, and live with the assurance that a week from now, when they awake in the morning, the person they love will be asleep by their side.

We didn't have that. We play-acted at it, but there were nights when Bets was asleep, I'd look at her and wonder where we would be in six months. When I slept, she would look at me and think the same.

The fall season drifted past, and finally there was a beautiful Sunday morning. The sky was crystal clear, the weather pleasant, with just a touch of frost in the air and a promise of warmth by midday. We decided to get off base for the day, go for a ride, and have dinner.

We drove around for a while, and it is a bit curious to me now that, though we had a radio in the car, we didn't turn it on that day. That, at least, gave us a few more minutes alone together.

As we headed back home, I decided to pull into the battalion area, stop at the office, and pick up the mail. As soon as we hit the gate, I knew something was wrong, but there was no panic, no one running around, just a sense that something had changed. I got out of the car and walked into battalion HQ. Someone, I don't remember who, looked at me and said, "Lieutenant, we're at war."

That moment, of course, is etched in my memory forever. And yet it didn't come as all that great a shock, as it would for many. In comparison, September 11, 2001, was far more stunning, for it was so unexpected, so utterly out of the realm of contemplation. Only a few days before September 11, I had talked with a historian friend of mine, and we had discussed the prospect of a terrorist strike on America, but it seemed abstract. Yes, it would happen someday, but on the morning of September 11, when I got up, I did not think "it might be today that we are hit."

December 7 was a day we had long dreaded but knew would come, and come soon. The shock, when it did hit, was in the level of devastation and the number of lives lost, not just at Pearl Harbor, but across the entire Pacific region, from the Philippines to China to the Dutch East Indies. As the reports began to flood in, there was the cold realization as well that I might very well have been in the middle of it in the Philippines, rather than driving my wife home at Fort Knox, Kentucky.

There was no panic on the base. The troops were assembled, the word was passed. Most of us spent the evening gathered round radios. Next morning we awoke and listened to President Roosevelt's speech, in which he asked for a declaration of war on Japan.

We were in it now.

Three days later Germany, and then Italy, declared war on us, something we had expected. From that moment I sensed that in short order our unit would wind up somewhere in Europe.

A flood of leaves hit the base for Christmas. It showed that in spite of the grumbling about the army on the part of many, there was a human side to it as well. Leaves were granted with the unspoken message that we should grab a few final moments of happiness. It would be the last Christmas we would spend at home, and for many the last Christmas we'd spend with family, ever again.

Bets and I drove to Chicago, where her mom and dad were visiting. Uniforms were everywhere. The entire country was shifting from the bright new rayons and nylon colors to khaki and navy blue. We had one night with her parents and then headed east to Ohio, driving along the edge of Lake Michigan and across Indiana into the industrial belt of Ohio.

The steel factories, silent for so long, were back in production. I could sense that the shock of Pearl Harbor had awakened a deep resolve and anger in spite of fears of the price that might have to be paid. It was no longer a time of doubt and appeasement. If we were going to go down, we'd go down fighting.

I had two nights with my family, and it was tough. Mom and Dad were now divorced and living apart. I stayed with Mother and spent a little time with Dad, though that time was strained.

Both Mom and Dad, you might recall, were English by birth, and a bit of them was still tied to that proud motherland. They were more in touch with the struggle over there, and their attitude was classic "stiff upper lip." I knew for my grandmother, Jacka, it was going to be tough. Eventually eight of her grandsons would go off to the war.

I said good-bye to my sisters, parents, and grandmother. Bets and I then turned around and drove back to Fort Knox.

That would be our last Christmas together for four long years of war.

Shortly after I returned to Fort Knox, my unit shipped out.

4

1942 Stateside

In the days after that Christmas leave the training was intense. Everyone, from the newest recruit to the division commander, knew that the game was real. All the news that was coming in was bad. In spite of what the press was saying about the fighting in the Philippines, those who knew anything about warfare and our plans for contending with Japan knew the men of the Philippine army were dead.

The old Plan Orange was built around the concept that our fleet in the Pacific would sail for the Philippines at the onset of hostilities. All that the garrison on Luzon had to do was hold out, digging in on the Bataan Peninsula.

The problem? There was no fleet. It rested on the bottom of Pearl Harbor.

It was chilling for me to read the news and know that, but for a twist of fate, I'd have been out there, perhaps with Bets trapped in Manila rather than safe in our small home just outside the base. Hundreds of wives and families had stayed on in Manila even after the army urged evacuation in the summer of 1941. Many of them spent the war in hellish internment camps.

Singapore was surrounded, the Dutch East Indies fell, and isolated American and British garrisons across the Pacific fell to the Japanese onslaught.

Though the news was pretty well blacked out, there were also indications that things were going badly in the Atlantic. The Germans, with less than a dozen submarines, were running amok along the East Coast and Gulf Coast, sinking hundreds of ships. Fires burned at night off the coast near New York City, and bodies washed up on the beaches.

Our training and equipment were beginning to take on some semblance of reality. We were issued a weird hybrid attempt at mobile artillery, a 75mm gun welded on top of a half-track. It was an ungainly monster. It had a silhouette damn near ten-feet high, which was a royal pain when we had to reload, the men having to hoist shells up over their heads. The driver had to lock brakes when the gun fired; otherwise, the recoil slammed the whole vehicle backward. On the battlefield it was a sitting duck just begging to be shot at. It could be aimed by slowly shifting the entire half-track back and forth, but at least it was a start. The division was starting to get Grant tanks. They were a weird concoction as well, with two guns, a turret that could not fully traverse, and armor so thin a 20mm shell could punch through it at close range, but again, it was a start. I just prayed we didn't have to face off with a panzer division armed with such weapons.

For a while, though, it looked like we wouldn't face the Germans at all.

A couple of months after the attack on Pearl Harbor we got orders to turn in most of our gear and be ready to ship out. We were now the 58th Mobile Armored Artillery and became a "detached" battalion, meaning we were intended to support whatever unit might need us at the moment. Nearly all of us saw that as a great assignment. A detached battalion has a lot more independence. It gets sent where it is needed most, and, in general, it gets better equipment as well.

I was tipped off that the deployment was to California, so yet again it was time to uproot Bets. The trip took nearly a week, all the way out to California to Fort Cook (now Vandenberg Air Force Base), between Los Angeles and San Francisco.

As I think about it now, it was a strange move, pulling our division out of Kentucky and hauling it all the way across the country to California, but at the time the great fear was that the Japanese might actually attempt an invasion.

In retrospect, the idea seems ludicrous. The Japanese didn't have the sea-lift capability to cover all their fronts and open a new one in America, and they were already stretched to the limit trying to devour the vast domain conquered in the opening moves of the war, but in 1942 the threat seemed all too real. To add urgency to the move, on the day we detrained at our base, one or more Japanese submarines actually appeared off the coast of California and lobbed some shells, hitting several locations between Los Angeles and our base. Los Angeles was darn near in a panic. An armada was expected to be off Long Beach within a day or two.

The shelling helped trigger one of the darker moments of the war, the rounding up and imprisoning of all American citizens of Japanese descent. President Roosevelt issued an executive order endorsing the move. I witnessed the deportation of these citizens to internment camps. It was a frightful and confusing time, and I was ashamed of what was being done. The only defense I can offer now, years later, is that at least we did not sink to the depths of what nearly every other country did in that time.

With that kind of paranoia running loose, you can imagine the state of alarm in the country, but particularly the West Coast. It hit a climax late in May. After consolidating their hold on the Dutch East Indies, the Philippines, and Singapore, the Japanese turned their attention back toward Hawaii. The first move in their new campaign would be the taking of Midway. It was their intent that an attack there would lure what was left of our fleet into a final encounter.

Admiral Chester Nimitz's intelligence team had surmised that

Midway was the target, but there was fear that a secondary strike might hit somewhere else. Someone somewhere in the War Department figured it would be Los Angeles.

We were pulled out of our base up the coast and rushed down to the city. The mere sight of us rolling through the streets in our hybrid M-3 mobile field pieces, the old 75mm guns welded to a half-track, might have contributed more to a sense of panic than to reassurance. Most people were excited by the sight of our equipment, not realizing just how shoddy it was. It was hysterical watching our column of vehicles weaving in and out of traffic, terrified drivers pulling over to gawk. Of course, my men were delighted with the show, for this was Los Angeles, Hollywood. We were treated like heroes. It was the American army to the rescue. I think about it now, and if it wasn't for the gravity of the position we were in, the entire action has a certain comic aspect to it. For many there were visions of thousands of Japanese Imperial Marines swarming ashore on Venice Beach, tearing through Hollywood, and shooting up the movie studios. Then again, perhaps a dose of military reality would have been helpful for the movie industry and stopped them from churning out some of the absolutely dreadful films made during the war.

The Hollywood crowd that actually got into the fight, men like Jimmy Stewart, Clark Gable, and John Ford, did a tremendous service to their country, along with people like Bob Hope, Dinah Shore, and the hundreds of others who got up on the front line to boost morale. A lot of the stay-behinds, however, maybe could have used a day or two at the front as a lesson on the truth of just how ghastly the war really is, and the folly of not being prepared for it. Many American citizens could definitely use that lesson today.

The invasion, of course, never came. There was only a diversionary attack thousands of miles away at Dutch Harbor, Alaska. Eventually we learned that our gallant navy, in a defiant stand, had torn the guts out of the Japanese navy at Midway. With that victory the tide in the Pacific began to turn, though it would take three more bitter years and hundreds of thousands of casualties to end it.

With the invasion scare over, we packed up and went straight out to the Mojave Desert.

The moment we hit that desert and started intensive maneuvers and training in desert warfare, we pretty well figured out where we would wind up. For the next couple of months it was truly hot work. All of us, today, have become used to an air-conditioned environment. I remember during the buildup to Desert Storm how there were entire news articles devoted to the efforts to keep our troops "hydrated," with the men consuming five gallons of water a day. Our tanks even had air-conditioning. In 1942 I'd have given anything for a gallon of the precious stuff and an old-fashioned electric fan during that summer of training.

Down inside the driver's position in a half-track, with the heat of the engine blowing back on you, the temperature damn near got to the boiling point. Men inside a tank would go nearly insane after half an hour in the midday heat. In fact, the heat killed more than one man. You could quite literally crack an egg and cook it on the tank's armored skin. At night the temperature would plummet, so that by two in the morning you were freezing your butt off. Sunrise would be a welcome relief, and then by nine you'd be cursing the heat again. It was, quite simply, a toughening-up session; either you adapted, physically and mentally, or you collapsed and got hauled away.

Every once in a while I'd get a chance for a shower. I actually took some of them without even peeling my clothes off. I just jumped under the stream of water, clothes on, and let the cool soak in. Then I stood in the back of a truck to air-dry as we headed back to our encampment. By the end of that short run every drop of moisture would have been sucked away and my uniform would be as dry as a bone.

We were still running around out there with hybrids and equipment designed in the early to midthirties. Meanwhile, in North Africa the Afrika Korps had overrun Tobruk, and Rommel was driving on Alexandria. In Russia, a million or more Germans, backed up by thousands of tanks, were overrunning the Ukraine and slicing toward the Volga and the oil fields on the Caspian Sea. When we ran orientation sessions on German equipment, I'd get a knot in my stomach. Their dreaded 88mm pieces (which I would become very familiar with at close range) could blow our tanks away at a range of a mile. Our puny 75mm equipment was little better than a BB gun against an elephant if their armor ever broke through. It was all very sobering as we tried to figure just what to hell to do once we got on the front line.

After more than two months of this hell, my battalion got orders to head back to the East Coast. That was a very clear indicator that our time stateside was getting short.

Leaving our equipment behind, we loaded into packed trains and took the long, slow ride across the country. What a transition it was. Only seven years earlier I had taken the train from Ohio to the Point through a landscape mired in the Depression. Now the country was bursting with activity. The tracks were loaded with trains roaring in both directions, the first wave of the biggest industrial buildup in the history of humanity. You could sense it: the "Sleeping Dragon" was stirring.

A week later we got off the train at Fort A. P. Hill in northern Virginia. My battalion was understrength, with only two hundred enlisted personnel and officers for a unit that was supposed to have close to eight hundred. As quickly as we'd start to build up a cadre, men would be pulled off and reassigned to new units that were forming up. That was a major problem for the first couple of years of the war. It was a fundamental question of how to create the army. Do you train guys together, get them built up as a unit, and send them into battle? Or do you then tear the unit apart and scatter those trained men to half a dozen new units just forming up? We tended toward the latter approach, which would mean that, when battle came, in spite of all the months of training, 80 percent of the men in my unit would be green. We had no guns and no equipment, yet even an idiot could figure out that we were staging for a move overseas.

Bets, who had followed me out to California, had somehow gotten ahead of me this time and found a place for us about an hour away from the base. She was already settled in, but the time we'd actually get together would be brief.

That was another part of the war, especially that first year, that is forgotten today, the mass migration of hundreds of thousands of wives, trying to steal a few minutes or hours with their husbands before they shipped out. With gas rationing, driving was out of the question, unless four or five girls managed to pool their stamps. So it was onto the trains, packed so tight that passengers had to stand in the aisles, sometimes for days, and in the summer heat the air-conditioning was an open window with cinders from the steam engine flying in.

Then the mad scramble for a place to live, any place to live, with the landlord gouging every dime he could get. Then there was the waiting, perhaps for weeks, before the soldier was granted a precious leave of a day.

Quite frankly, it's no surprise that there was such a baby boom after the war was over; everyone had one hell of a lot of catching up to do. And I'm not just talking about catching up in the physical sense. Lost to all our youths were the lazy days of waking up together, going for drives, seeing a movie, and ever so slowly growing older together.

Oliver Wendell Holmes Jr., the Supreme Court justice, who was on the bench when I was a boy, once spoke of his Civil War experiences, saying, "In our youth our hearts were touched with fire." Yes, and our youths were also touched by loneliness unfathomable, endless nights of staring at the ceiling or at the sagging bunk above you, dreaming you were somewhere else, going all but insane with the memory of what it was like to hold your wife for a minute or to hear her voice in the morning, the smell of coffee, eggs, and bacon filling the house.

Our youth, the springtime of my entire generation, was spent on slow trains, baking in desert heat, dying on beaches, or watching in horror as comrades fell in flames from twenty thousand feet. For the women of my generation it always seemed to be waiting, waiting for a letter, praying for a glimpse, dreaming of a night together, and terrified of a telegram declaring "We regret to inform you . . ."

It was now early fall of 1942. There was no official word out, but I could sense that my time stateside was short. Something was building up, the summer training in the desert of California, our getting shipped back east rather than overseas to Australia or Hawaii. We were bound for the war against Germany. The only question was when.

The news was bad from all fronts. The marines had put a single division ashore at Guadalcanal, but the navy, lacking the strength to support them, left the division to its fate, nightly bombardments from Japanese ships lying off shore. In Africa the Brits were backed up nearly to Alexandria, and the pessimists were saying Rommel would soon be across the Suez Canal. In Russia the Nazis were on the Volga, near Stalingrad, and racing toward the oil fields on the Caspian Sea while Leningrad, besieged, continued to starve.

We were waiting at A. P. Hill, located between Richmond and Fredericksburg. There were no facilities. We camped in pup tents along a stream where the armies of Lee and Grant had once camped.

One day, I believe it was in mid-September, I was told to get the men ready to receive our new equipment. When our "gift" arrived, courtesy of Uncle Sam and Detroit, I must admit it felt something like love at first sight.

I know that might sound strange, but I suspect more than one old soldier reading this will understand. You get handed a weapon, and the moment you see it, the moment you use it for the first time, you have this gut feeling that this thing, this tool, will make the difference between your living and dying, the difference between your country's winning and losing. There's a bond between you and it. I know old pilots who, when they hear the throb of a Merlin engine and look up to see a P-51 Mustang tearing through the skies, get a lump in their throats. An artilleryman's tool might be a lot more prosaic, but it still hits you.

It was that way for me with the M-7, 105mm, mobile armored field piece. I remember every detail of it, the way a pilot remembers the feel of a cockpit, or a kid grown old remembers the first car that was really his.

It was a brilliant piece of "cobbling" design work, created by a team working with Detroit and most likely produced on an assembly line that had been cranking out sedans ten months earlier.

Eighteen of them arrived at a railroad siding on the base, covered with heavy tarps for security, everything still packed in protective grease. They were quite literally the first production run. Serial number 1 had been shipped somewhere else, but we had eighteen of the first twenty-one off the line.

It was actually quite a heady experience to realize that our unit was getting the first of them. There were no manuals yet, no concept of how to properly use them, no doctrine, no training schedules. They came into the siding, we carefully off-loaded them, and like kids at a car lot, we walked around them and gaped.

I'll bless to my final day the people who came up with the idea and ran it through.

The M-7 was built on the chassis of the M-3 tank. That in itself was classic American thinking. Take a basic design, such as a chassis that you know works, then use it for half a dozen other machines.

Too many people believe that the Germans had the edge on this. They didn't. They tended to design nearly every weapon from the ground up and from scratch, and rival companies rarely cooperated with one another. The German army was a quartermaster's nightmare, since each different machine needed its own supply of parts.

The United States, throughout the war, basically had one truck. Whether it was made by Studebaker, Ford, or Chevrolet, it was the same deuce-and-a-half. A mechanic, once trained, could work on any of them, in fact, a lot of GIs, trained or not, could strip one down and put it back together again. The jeep, the best all-around light vehicle of the war, was designed by the Bantam Company and then contracted to other companies (such as Willys and Ford) that, before the war, were its rivals.

The M-7 was built around the chassis of the proven M-3 tank. Once that chassis was completed, however, the body, rather than being fitted with a turret, was left open, with thin armor siding built up. In the center a modern 105mm howitzer was laid in. Behind the gun were racks for ammunition. Inside their storage bins the rounds were still in their cardboard shipping containers, but six rounds were already set in their brass cartridges and ready to be fired instantly. That was brilliant as well. All the loader had to do was turn, pull a shell out, slam it into the breach, and fire within seconds. It gave us a tremendous rate of fire, far faster than the standard towed-105 with separate ammunition containers.

A two-wheeled armored trailer was designed to be towed at the rear, hauling extra ammunition. The complete system was self-contained, carried close to a hundred twenty rounds with it, and was fast and reliable. In addition, ten two-and-a-half-ton trucks loaded with ammo were assigned to each battery.

Something that was apparent from the first look was the fact that if need be in a crunch, a crew could open fire in a matter of seconds, compared to the several minutes it took to swing a towed piece around, unlimber, set up, load, and fire. In the type of warfare we were going into, that hundred and twenty seconds or so would be the difference between living and dying.

Storage racks built along the sides stored personal gear for the crew, tools, extra oil, grease, and some spare parts.

The driver and assistant driver sat up front, the barrel of the gun projecting between them. It was a tight squeeze. This wasn't a luxury car, but it worked. The gun had some traverse to left or right, but if you needed to make a major adjustment, all you did was start up the engine, shift the entire unit in a matter of seconds, and you were on target.

One nice touch was the armored side turret. It looked a bit like a pulpit, which resulted in the nickname "Priest" being given to the M-7 by the Brits. The pulpit was ideal for preaching to Germans soldiers since it mounted a .50 caliber machine gun for close-in defense. It was a great idea. I know. It saved my life more than once.

It was what some people call an elegantly simple machine. Elegant in that it was well thought out and functional at every level. Simple because it was just that, nothing overly complex, yet rugged and dependable. I think it stands as one of the finer examples of what America can produce when it faces a crisis and good minds are brought in, the bureaucratic bull is pushed aside, and people start thinking about what is best for the fighting men rather than about personal gain or whose congressional district gets the best deal on a contract.

Years later I would work, at times, in the development of new systems for the army, and the process drove me to distraction. I still do not accept the argument that with weapons being more complex, it must take eight to ten years to go from initial design to an in-the-field system. What causes that delay is the self-serving attitude of far too many, both in uniform and out, in Congress, in the army, and in industry. The current debate about the Crusader Challenger mobile field gun is but one example. Fortunately, in 1942 there were enough people who were putting their country and the survival of our soldiers first. Equipment like the M-7, Higgins boats, P-51s, and Essex-class carriers was the result.

This is not to say that the crisis that had preoccupied me for so many years had passed and that America was on its way to certain victory. Far from it. It's just that the M-7, to me, seemed to indicate that at least we were starting to move in the right direction. It was one hell of a leap by the way. Remember that little more than a year earlier I had been in maneuvers with old trucks simulating tanks.

Another indicator that we were far from what needed to be achieved was the assignment given to us with these precious new M-7s. Along with the eighteen guns we received a grand total of one hundred rounds to test them—about five rounds for each piece. Once those rounds were fired off as a test of the new equipment, we were to pack them up and ship them off. So my understrength battalion labored for days cleaning the pieces, going over every detail, learning how to drive them, and then carefully loading a round.

The first time you fire a 105 in the confines of an M-7 you are in for an experience. The recoil of the barrel can kill a man. At least with a standard field piece you can step back and away. On an M-7 the entire crew is packed in, with only inches to spare. It's like learning how to juggle rattlesnakes. You only have to grab the wrong end once to be out of business. Bend over at the wrong second and you wind up with a broken back. The noise is incredible. It's not just the volume, it's the sharp crack of the shock wave. If you're behind the gun, it isn't so bad, but get in front of it, or to the side, and it will stagger you. Most civilians, if they've ever heard a 105 firing, have experienced a blank charge, which contains only a fraction of a full load. A full load pushes out a shell weighing up to forty pounds at a couple of times the speed of sound. That's why most old artillerymen today wear hearing aids.

Five rounds was absurd for any kind of training, especially the training needed to get a crew up to a sustained maximum rate of fire. We did endless hours of dry firing, simulating loading, standing clear, firing and reloading, but without that real punch at the end, the strain of hefting the weight of the shell and the powder charge, it wasn't the same.

Realize that an artillery crew is, at a basic level, a team of moving men. What they are moving are forty-pound shells, sometimes up to half a dozen every sixty seconds, with a shock wave washing over them every ten seconds. A couple of years later my battalion fired close to five thousand rounds in six hours. That's roughly three hundred rounds per tube. We never got the training on how to do that stateside; it was something we'd learn on the job, with someone shooting back at us.

So we fired our five rounds, packed the M-7s back up, and watched them roll away, shipped ahead of us to wherever it was we were going. I'd fallen in love with the darn things. I trusted their design. If I was going to war as an artilleryman they were the tool I wanted. It was a major compliment as well that we were the first unit to get them.

Bets and I managed to get two days off that fall. We went down to Richmond, which back then was still a town that seemed more rooted in the Civil War than the twentieth century. We visited an uncle who gave me a sleeping bag. It was not the standard army issue, but it was warm and durable. I used it for the next three years.

We seemed to be loitering, still understrength, with only a quarter of the men needed for a battalion of artillery. And then everything hit at once.

Orders came in that we were shipping out. Our ultimate destination was a secret, but when we got word to report to Camp Kilmer, New Jersey, we knew this was it. Kilmer was the staging camp from which troops were loaded up in New York Harbor. My battalion commander called me and several other officers in, told us the news, and gave each of us a four-hour leave to say good-bye to our wives.

It was a mad dash down to where Bets lived. An hour each way. So we had two hours together, hours I will never forget.

How can I write about it?

I can't.

If you have lived through a moment like that, you know what

I mean. If you haven't, well, you might think you understand, but no words can ever fully convey it. I had to be brave, to reassure her, even when I was aching inside. And she, of course, had to do the same for me.

As I walked out that door, and turned to look back one last time, all I could wonder was what all soldiers leaving for war must wonder: Will I ever see her again?

After saying good-bye I returned to camp. A couple days later the base was in chaos as we loaded up, for the rest of our battalion had arrived, six hundred brand-new draftees who only two days before had been civilians. The army dragged them in, stuck a couple of dozen needles into both arms and both cheeks, piled uniforms and gear into barracks bags, then dumped them at A. P. Hill. No basic training, no drill instructors running them around for eight weeks to get them into some semblance of shape or to teach them how to salute or tell a breech from a muzzle. Six hundred GIs fresh from the farm, the factory floor, or the college classroom. There were no barracks, and we didn't even have enough tents, so we had them spread out a sleeping bag wherever they could find a comfortable spot.

Next morning we piled them all into a sealed train and roared north, rolling through Washington and Philadelphia and finally coming to a stop just outside New York.

Kilmer was established during World War I as a base for embarking overseas. The old barracks were still there and the place was bursting at the seams as we off-loaded from the train. It was obvious that something damn big was afoot. I was ready for it, as were the men who had been with the battalion in California. The draftees, however, were babes in the woods. Some of them were scared stiff, and I couldn't blame them.

In today's world of interstate highways, jet travel, and casual wanderings to Europe or Asia, it's hard to realize that for the generation growing up in the Depression a trip out of one's home state was a big deal. Quite a few Americans never left the

county or the city where they were born and raised. The army
had just uprooted eight hundred young men, and without any
preliminaries, without any hand-holding or "orientation and
counseling sessions," it had tossed them onto a train that was
obviously taking them to a ship that was undoubtedly taking
them to war.

Several months later, when we were overseas, someone in the
unit had a copy of a magazine, maybe it was *Time*. In it there
was a comment from FDR solemnly declaring that no American
boy was going into a combat zone without a minimum of six
months of training. How we laughed at that one.

It might have been true later, but at that time and that place,
we needed bodies, and any body would do, trained or not.

We stayed at Kilmer for two weeks. Most of the men even
got a two-day furlough, and every last one of them reported
back as ordered, which was a testament to how dedicated we
were as a nation. The talk about O.H.I.O. was gone, at least
until victory had been won. We were then loaded aboard trains
that made the short run down to Jersey City. There we off-
loaded again, dragging our barracks bags loaded with gear, and
staggered down to the ferryboats that were to take us across the
harbor to the Brooklyn Navy Yard.

The harbor was swarming with ships, old ocean liners, beat-
up transports, and destroyers and cruisers. I thought of how, less
than three years before, I had spent the weekend in New York,
the first weekend of the war, pondering what would happen in
my life. Now it was coming full circle. I was part of a ragtag
bunch, the first GIs going overseas to the front lines. And I was
thrilled.

That is always a paradox in my profession. If anyone learns to
be a realist about war, it is the trained soldier. He knows the
price far better than anyone else. It is not uncommon to hear
some civilians shouting for war at the slightest provocation, or
on the other side to hear some whining that war will never solve
anything. The trained soldier knows the truth, for he must live

with it. Never get into a fight unless you have to, but never avoid one if running away from it will only provoke a far worse fight in the end.

You train for it, and when it does come, there is a strange feeling that you will now be tested, and you want to see whether you will meet that test. My country had invested a fortune in me with four years, actually four and a half, of training at West Point. I was thrilled, because now I would get the chance to do the job I was trained for.

I figured our destination was North Africa, and that meant we would face the Afrika Korps, the most famed of German formations, led by their most famous general, Erwin Rommel. If we could stand up to him, maybe, just maybe, we could pull the entire thing off when the time came to fight our way into the heart of the Nazi empire.

There was another factor at play, too. It had been a couple of weeks since I had said good-bye to Bets, and already there was an agony in not knowing how long it might be before I would see her again. The sooner we got over there, the sooner the job would be done, and the sooner we could get on with our lives if we survived it.

The ferry took us across the harbor, swinging around Battery Park to the Brooklyn Navy Yard. Throughout the war that base was a madhouse of activity twenty-four hours a day. Convoys coming in from the deadly run across the North Atlantic would tie off there. Casualties were taken off, damage was repaired, and then a new convoy was formed up to go back out. It was America's front door to the war in Europe. And during that year, I'm told, if you went up to the Atlantic Highlands along the coast of New Jersey, you could see the glow on the horizon of ships burning in the night.

I drew a small room aboard the *Santa Rosa*, a converted ocean liner, with seven other officers, all our gear piled up from floor to ceiling. It was cramped, but then again it was a luxury compared to how so many GIs would cross, jammed belowdecks, with bunks stacked six high, with barely enough room to turn over.

Once we were loaded aboard, the ship was sealed, and we waited in the harbor for the convoy to get underway. I realize now that it was one hell of a security operation. Over a hundred and fifty ships from several ports would be heading out, transporting well over a hundred thousand men and their weapons. All it would have taken was one German spy, sitting in an office in lower Manhattan, to blow the entire operation wide open. And that is something we thought about, looking out toward the Narrows, between Brooklyn and Staten Island, where the Verrazano Bridge now stands. Half a dozen U-boats sitting out there could have killed thousands of us before we ever had a chance to fire a shot back.

Whoever handled security and counterintelligence for that operation did a hell of a job. Not a single word leaked out.

The following morning we could feel the engines starting up, the vibration running through the ship. Tugs pushed us out, and as we turned, lower Manhattan was almost within reach. I guess that those standing on shore, watching us leave, knew we were heading into harm's way, and I know their prayers were with us.

There was no ceremony, no speeches, no fireboats spraying a salute, just a quiet departure, taking us off to a faraway mystery from which so many would never return.

I stood on the deck, watching as first Ellis Island, and then that blessed statue drifted by on our starboard side. Like so many Americans who see those two places, I thought of how I had come to be an American, my father sailing into this same harbor, catching sight of the Statue of Liberty for the first time, wandering wide-eyed into Ellis Island, and coming out of it with that treasured pass to a boat that would take them across the harbor to America.

America had given them a home, a chance to succeed far beyond the dreams of their parents and for me to grow up in freedom. Now I would have to pay the price for that, and it was a price I was willing to pay. Like so many Americans, I took pride, and still do, in the country that my parents came from. That country, England, was under siege, and I felt that my going would somehow help to save it.

So I stood on the deck, watching the statue as it drifted by. And then, leaning over the rail, I continued to watch until it was lost in the morning mist.

I was on my way to war.

5

Casablanca

We were at sea. The *Santa Rosa*, a former Grace Line ship on the old South American run, had a fairly shallow draft and rolled like a tub. Gone were the bright colors. Everything was slapped over with a dull camouflage gray, every porthole and window covered with blackout drapes. It was my first time at sea. A strange feeling was present as I watched the coast of America recede and finally disappear, knowing that already I was in a war zone. For the war was literally on America's doorstep at this time, unseen and unknown back on land, but still the ocean was a killing zone.

The crew on board ship ran us through the drill if we were attacked, which was basically to get the hell out of the way. If hit, well, it was obvious it would be frightful, with green troops trying to get to the lifeboats and rafts. We were all cautioned that even striking a match, at night out on the deck, might give us away.

The convoy, herded by a small fleet of destroyers and cruisers, slowly weaved back and forth, our speed pegged to that of the slowest ship. We had one sub alert, and a destroyer escort came shooting through the convoy at flank speed. Needless to say, we were all edgy. We were infantry and artillerymen, ground fight-

ers. There's a terrible helpless feeling to being aboard a ship. If
we got hit there was not a thing we could do except stay out of
the way of the sailors and sit it out. Get hit badly enough and
we were in the sea, in November, drowning like a rat before we
could even fire a shot.

There's the old saying that rank has its privileges. I've never
really liked it, for there are far too many officers ready to exploit
the division, flaunting their extra perks in front of men who have
to do the fighting. I knew from the very start of my career that
a good officer lives the life of his men. If they're stuck out in
the rain or snow, you damn well better be out there with them.
If they've been eating K rations for two weeks straight, you
better be on the same diet, and that doesn't mean sneaking back
to your tent to indulge in some hidden treat. The men always
find out.

I will admit, though, that on that passage I was darn grateful
to be up in a cabin with only seven bunkmates. The scene down
below, at times, was like something out of Dante's *Inferno,* especially when we hit rough seas. The bunks were rough built,
stacked floor to ceiling. The facilities, the heads and dining
rooms, were way overtaxed. Most of the men spent a fair part
of each day just standing in line to get a sandwich, if they could
keep it down, or waiting to get to the head, if there was still
anything inside to bring up. Most of them were sick, and at
times damn sick, lying in their bunks, vomiting their guts out.
The ship stank of vomit, no matter how hard the few well men
or the numbed sailors on board struggled to keep things clean.
I at least could retreat at times to my little bunk, with only a
couple of men around me retching into a bucket as we rode the
roller coaster of the Atlantic.

Samuel Johnson once said that life aboard ship was like being
in prison, with the added prospect of drowning. He should have
added that, for a lot of men, the prospect of drowning would
have been a welcome relief.

As the training officer for the battalion, I tried to organize some activity, if for no other reason than to divert the men. It was so crowded that the thought of trying to conduct classes, with men packed together like sardines and throwing up, was absurd. I finally settled on a little orientation with small arms. All the men had been issued Garand rifles, but only a few had ever actually fired a weapon, any kind of weapon. So I cleaned out the galley of tin cans, sealed them, then threw the cans overboard (on the convoy's outward side, of course; we didn't want rounds skipping into the rest of the fleet). It might not have helped much with marksmanship, but at least it served as a bit of a diversion. We sealed the cans up and tossed them overboard, and some of the men got a chance to do target practice. For more than one it was the first time he had ever handled a rifle. And here we were, going into a war zone that might be hot.

As soon as we were at sea the word became official, our destination was Casablanca, French Morocco, North Africa. This was all part of America's first tentative step against Nazi Germany. We were opening a secondary front to the rear of the Afrika Korps, which at that same moment was about to get nailed by the British Eighth Army at El Alamein, all the way over on the other side of the continent.

The goal was to make landings in French Morocco and Algeria, then launch a rapid drive into Tunisia and Libya and cut the Afrika Korps off in the rear. All very optimistic, but all SNAFU once set in motion.

The landing areas were a thousand miles or more from the final goal of cutting Rommel off. The planners wanted to play it safe, bringing our troops in outside the range of German aircraft, which is understandable, but the distance gave Rommel and his successor months to react.

Second, and far more complex, was the issue of which side the French were on. When France collapsed in June 1940, the month I graduated from the Point, it signed an armistice with the Germans. About half of France, the region along the coast, Paris, and the border area with Germany, became a zone of military occupation. The rest of France, however, was allowed to form a new government, under the pro-fascist Pierre Laval and, surprisingly, the old World War I hero Philippe Pétain. This government, the Vichy government, was then allied with Germany.

That is yet another fact of the early years of the war that is all but forgotten or ignored, today. The Vichy government was Hitler's lapdog, and for that matter the lapdog of the Japanese as well. Vichy French troops were already fighting against the British in Lebanon and Syria. It was in combat against these units that the famous Israeli general Moshe Dayan lost his eye while serving with the Jewish Brigade of the British army.

In the Pacific, in Indochina, the Vichy government openly collaborated with the Japanese, a fact that would eventually come to roost on our doorstep when we backed France's attempt to regain control of Indochina in the postwar period after first promising the Vietnamese that if they fought against Japan, we'd back their effort to gain independence.

When our first wave came in at Casablanca, some hoped that the sight of an old ally would immediately cause the local French garrison to turn their weapons on the few Germans stationed there. A bright idea was cooked up to outfit an American ship with loudspeakers, have it come into the harbor and start playing a speech by FDR, in French, appealing to our old comrades in arms to welcome us as liberators.

It was a fiasco.

The French shot the boat apart, the first wave of troops in were ambushed, and around five hundred GIs and sailors were killed before the local French rulers, seeing they were about to be overwhelmed, suddenly announced that it was all a tragic mistake and they were on our side after all.

Eisenhower, in his first field command, came very close to losing it and spending the rest of the war stationed in Alaska when he allowed himself to get sucked into negotiations with Admiral Jean Darlan, one of the Vichy leaders, making promises he had no authority to offer. It caused a hell of a stink and required a lot of backfilling to get Ike extracted. The crisis was resolved in part when someone assassinated Darlan.

After more than two weeks our convoy finally came within sight of the North African coast, pulling in three days after the initial landings. For the men who had been seasick for most of the crossing it was a blessed relief. A man in that condition would be happy to land in hell if it meant getting a few minutes on firm ground, no matter how hot it was.

We steamed into a port that was a junkyard, some of it still smoking from the fight. Our new allies had made a thorough job of sabotaging most of the port facilities, and what was left had got torn up in the fighting. Half-sunken ships with blackened stacks littered the harbor. We tied off alongside one of these wrecks and started to off-load, and the battalion took its first casualty, a man, fully burdened with gear, going over the railing. He sank like a stone. There wasn't a damn thing I or anyone else could do about it.

That's a sickening feeling, the first time you lose someone in wartime. In peacetime, when a man dies, be he civilian or soldier, the whole world seems to stop. In a war zone, if you have time, you try to do what you can, and then there's the cold realization, "He's dead. Now who is going to take his place?" And then you move on.

On this day there was no ceremony, no moment of silent reflection by the battalion. We simply loaded the men up and got them moving. Later on, if the body came up, someone else would bury him, and the battalion CO, when he had some time, would write a letter home, though the dead man was a stranger, one of the draftees whom no one really knew. A stranger for us, but the end of the world for a family back in the States.

We passed through Casablanca on a twelve-mile march to our bivouac location. It was a wild, exotic place. (The movie of the same name, staring Humphrey Bogart and Ingrid Bergman, came out the week we landed, but I didn't see it until after the war.) The Casablanca I saw in 1942 bore no relationship to the movie.

It was exotic, to be sure, a strange mixture of French colonialism and Moorish Africa, but it also stank, with raw sewage in the streets and fly-covered beggars. For all of us, literally fresh off the boat from America, it was an eye-opener.

We set up our base camp in a quarry twelve miles out of town. Here we truly began a crash course on becoming soldiers first and then artillerymen in a mechanized armored battalion.

Our six hundred draftees had to be run through the basics—taught how to march without causing embarrassment, to salute, to take care of themselves in the field, to keep clean. As we started to figure out who knew what, who had worked as mechanics, who had fooled around with radios, who could type, who could cook, who showed some ability at leading, we began to slot men into their various assignments within the battalion.

This was a rush job of the first order. It was almost Christmas, 1942. Rommel was retreating westward across Africa toward Tunisia, and our assignment would be to rush in and slam the back door shut as soon as possible.

To make matters worse, a lot of our gear never showed up. The army had managed to off-load our precious M-7s and some auxiliary equipment when a scare went through the fleet. A German wolfpack was closing in. The ships scrambled, running out to sea. One of the most important components for a battalion of artillery, our fire control center, was still aboard one of the ships.

So we had to make do.

I fell on the simple idea of issuing each man a three-by-five-inch index card. Printed on the card was a priority list of his responsibilities. As we tried to sort out a brand-new battalion of eight hundred men the system allowed the few old NCOs and officers (I was now an "old" officer of the battalion) to figure out who was assigned to what. The men were required to carry the cards with them at all times.

Remember, we were something entirely new in 1942, a mobile, armored battalion, with equipment so new that no one knew exactly how to use it in combat. So we simply learned to make up procedures and tactics as we went along.

Right then and there I saw my chance. It set me on to an attitude that stayed with me throughout my nearly forty years in the military. I started to ask why.

Why is it that we do things the way we do? Is it because it's always been done that way? Is there a logical reason for doing it? Why should we continue doing it this way if we can perhaps find a better system?

The "by the book" method for a battalion of artillery to go into action is to receive orders from division or the appropriate commander for the battalion to deploy and engage a target. The battalion then deploys, fire control is set up, each gun is aligned on the target, range is set, and communications are established. The chain of command goes from gun to battery to battalion fire control and from battalion to division. Meanwhile, forward observers are deployed to gain a visual on the target, and communications are established with them. Most of the communications are via phone line. Once all is in place, a ranging shot is fired from each gun to register it on target. The final adjustments are made, and then it is fired for effect.

Absolutely ridiculous. If your opponent has any sense, he'll do one of two things, either tear you apart before you open fire, or get the hell out of the way so you waste tens of thousands of dollars' worth of shells blowing up trees, goats, or bare rock.

One of the big weaknesses I saw was the communications. The army was still dependent on telephone line. Miles of wiring had to be strung every time we went into a new position. That just might be okay in a static battle or siege, but even then enemy shells had a way of landing on a wire and shutting everything down until a couple of poor GIs crawled around under fire and found the break. And given that we were supposedly mobile, we might very well move twenty or thirty miles in a day and deal with half a dozen firing missions. Just to string the wire for those missions would take forever. And where the hell were we supposed to get all that wire?

We had just been issued new FM radios, yet another example of America turning its industrial power around from peacetime to war. This "500" series radio had a relatively short range, but it was fairly rugged and reliable. I felt this was the key to speeding us up. I became obsessed with making sure that every single man, from the cook to the battalion commander, knew the basics of the radio and how to make fundamental repairs on the spot if one of the units failed. Maybe it goes back to my father being with Marconi and his building of that first crystal radio when I was a kid. Regardless of the source, I saw that we needed to dump the whole arcane system of wires and go to wireless ASAP.

I made it a point to overstock on radios and to have spares in reserve, an activity the quartermasters in the rear always took a dim view of. We ignored it (as we came to ignore a lot of other things).

Radio operators received a high degree of training. Before long I had men who could strip a radio down, find out what was wrong, and have it running in short order. Radios became our method of communicating inside the battalion and to division.

As for registering our guns on target, the whole idea struck me as absurd. Sending lone shells over was like knocking on the door and announcing you were going to come around in fifteen minutes or so to take care of business. We seized on the idea of a mass firing of all guns at once. Sure, some of them might be off, but some would definitely be on. If the bulk of the ranging salvo fell short by several hundred yards, call it in, adjust on the spot, and fire for effect. We used six guns of a battery to fire a salvo, then the entire battalion opened up. Six shells impacting at once could be spotted; one round could many times be missed. Visually, you could spot six impacts. You knew immediately if you were long or short, left or right. No warning. Just pour it in, in bulk, every available tube firing.

Using this, and the advantages of the M-7's design, we felt that in fairly short order we'd be able to deliver, on target, the equivalent fire of several battalions. The whole idea here was to make up for our faults in overall training and battle experience with a massive response, and to do it as quickly as possible. All was tied in by the one thing Americans are almost always superior in, communications technology.

Here was one of the core issues of the war, and our response to the Germans.

We as Americans are damn reluctant to get into a war; we see war as a waste, an aberration that at times we avoid, much to our peril. Our key to winning is to be flexible in our thinking. If need be, throw out "the book," don't get hung up on doctrine, figure out those things we do best, and then pour it on. Nine times out of ten, doctrine is based on previous experience. We are a technological society. Imagine basing a computer system on technology that is ten years old, or making cars from 1985 designs. The same is true of our military, but, unfortunately, too often we are guided by the past rather than experimenting efficiently with the technology we have now. That has always been one of the keys to our winning in a crisis, our ability to rapidly adapt where more rigid societies see any change as a fundamental threat. Those times that we become inflexible, when we get tangled in our bureaucracy and too much top-down management, that is when we lose.

Maybe one of the advantages of our men being raw draftees was that no one had yet indoctrinated them to a routine. Second, they knew with a grim certainty that this was not play-acting. It was all too real. There was no room for games. We were going up against the Afrika Korps, and we had damn well better get it right the first time or we were all dead.

It turned out, though, that for a moment it looked as if I might not be going into action with my battalion, and that scared the daylights out of me. The scare came from the most unlikely of sources.

Casablanca was overrun with prostitutes. There were thousands of them, native born, French, Italian, Spanish, Moroccan, Arab, you name it.

Tens of thousands of still wet-behind-the-ears American boys were pouring off the troopships, leaving the USA behind and stepping right into the middle of all that. You can imagine the results.

The America of 1942 was a hell of a lot different than it is today when it came to sex and what teenagers were told was acceptable. Only weeks before, most of the young men pouring into Casablanca had been living with all the constraints of civilian life, taking their dates to see movies staring Mickey Rooney and Judy Garland, who just might share a chaste kiss at the end of the film. They were boys from small towns, kids fresh from farms, going to church every Sunday, and just maybe having had a little experimentation in the backseat of a car, which usually never got very far because she was saving herself for marriage.

Take a bunch of healthy nineteen- and twenty-year-old guys like that, with most of them convinced they were going to be dead within six months, and you can imagine what it was like when they saw the temptations of the back alleys of Casablanca. They went nuts.

Within weeks after the landing we had more men going into the hospital with venereal disease than combat wounds. Of course, this is stuff the folks back home were not being told about. Newsreels back in the States were showing our fresh-faced lads going to USO shows and spending a Saturday night with their buddies singing around a piano. Anyhow, a lot of grandfathers out there today have a lot of stories that will never be told to the grandkids when it comes to what they really did in World War II.

Back in 1942 syphilis was still a killer. To my generation, it was far more terrifying than AIDs, and it was far more deadly.

The only thing that could take it out for certain was a new miracle drug, penicillin, and that was still rare and incredibly expensive. A single regimen of treatment cost thousands of dollars—in 1940s' money. Penicillin was literally worth its weight in gold, and the sentiment was that such a miracle should be reserved for combating infection from battle wounds, and not for curing a dose some idiot caught while engaging in horizontal recreation. The army, however, still had to treat the soldier, since he was under their control; no one wanted him going back home in that condition, and the soldier was a valuable commodity that was needed in combat.

The bottom line was that the army had to figure out a way to keep the guys from getting sick, and so a lot of things were done overseas that rarely got talked about back home.

Frightening training films that graphically showed what happened had little impact on some men. When they hit downtown Casablanca, they had only one thing on their minds, and it was causing chaos. I don't know if that shows that the training films were a bust or that the urge is strong in a nineteen-year-old soldier who figures he's going to buy it anyway in his first battle.

Then, on top of it all, fights were breaking out. You had a lot of bad feelings when soldiers, sailors, merchant marines, French troops (many of them black, which bothered the racists in our ranks), and local civilians got tangled up trying to find a young lovely.

High command got fed up and screamed bloody murder. The way stuff always rolls downhill, the problem finally landed on some young captain, which just happened to be me.

West Point prepared me for a lot of things, but not this one.

The chain of command had kicked the job down the ladder, and for some unknown reason it rolled into my battalion, and since I was still the training officer, it stopped with me. I was to become responsible for straightening out the problem with the prostitutes of Casablanca.

I must admit that when I found out about my new job, I was

actually afraid that somehow the war would go on without me. I'd get stuck in Casablanca running a bordello till everything was over and then have to go back home and try to explain to my wife what I did to help save the world from Fascism.

I went downtown to take a look around. I knew right off there was no way in hell I was going to shut down prostitution in Casablanca. Try that and I'd just drive it underground, and then it would get worse. Besides, there would have been riots for certain, not just of the soldiers and locals, but of hundreds of prostitutes as well, something I didn't want to deal with. This might sound strange, but I had to look at it from their side, too. There was a war on, it was a booming business for some of them, and a lot of them were pathetic girls trying to stay alive in a world gone crazy. There is that other side, and it was heartbreaking to see. I saw it not just in Casablanca, but all the way through to the end of the war, girls who in another time or place would have gone on to school, got married, and settled down to raise a family. Now they were out selling themselves for a couple of cans of C rations or a pack of cigarettes that they could trade for food. You'd look at them and just feel sick at times, imagining your own family trapped in a war and having to do unthinkable things to stay alive.

I had to put thoughts like that aside, though, and try to figure out the best way to keep things relatively safe and sane. After looking around, I sat down with several of the men who got assigned with me, and we figured out a plan.

There was already a walled-off compound for the red-light district. We turned it into a fortress. The top of the wall was covered with barbed wire and broken wine bottles. We had two gates, one going in and one going out. A soldier, looking for some recreation that he certainly wasn't going to write home about, came to the front gate. A head man up front took the soldier's dog tags, ID card, and pass, then issued out the antivenereal kit, which was an army condom and some antiseptic ointment. Once all that was taken care of, the GI was free to wander into the land of sin.

The officer I assigned to run the front gate was a divinity student from Yale. He was a good soldier, one that I knew would keep things straight—there were a lot of opportunities here for bribes and such—but I'll admit the irony of it all was appealing as well. I heard he dropped out of school after the war and went into the contracting business. I hope I didn't have something to do with that.

Once the soldier inside the compound was finished with his business transactions, he headed to the back gate and then straight into the Pro-Clinic. That was a grim place. If you ever wandered in there during business hours, it was something you didn't forget, even though you wanted to.

A bunch of medics had to oversee the guys getting part of their anatomy scrubbed down with antiseptic, having some vile medication poured into them, and then checked for any sores. Yet again, a "What did you do in the Great War, Daddy?" type moment.

Once all that was taken care of, the GI got his dog tags, ID card, and pass returned. It amazed me, but I'd see some of them back on line again an hour later at the front gate. I guess they figured they'd never again see something like the Casablanca bordello if they ever made it back to Toledo or Sacramento, and besides, chances were they weren't getting back home anyhow.

I did that for a little less than month. It was a hell of a way to get into the war. When my orders came through to head to the front with my unit, I was one happy man, in spite of what I knew was waiting up there.

Some people have asked me if I ever went inside that place. No, I wasn't crazy! Besides, I was from the old school of those who really did believe in those vows we made on the day we got married. I think about that place now, and I still find it amazing. It was the strangest job of my military career, but one

I never put down on a vitae. Just how the hell was I supposed to describe something like that?

After my stint in that madhouse almost any other assignment would have been a pleasure, but my next assignment doubled the knots in my stomach. I became part of the team providing security for FDR and Winston Churchill. The two great leaders were coming to Casablanca for a conference. Choosing that place was, in part, a public relations statement. They were meeting on territory that until recently was part of the fascist empire, the first stage on the long road to Berlin.

All claims to the contrary, there was serious doubt as to whether Casablanca was really secure. Sleeper agents, perhaps even assassins, might still be lurking in the city and in the surrounding countryside.

Just before New Year's we were hit with an air raid. It wasn't effective, but it still told us that we were inside a war zone.

The two great leaders met, reviewed some troops, and then decided to move to Marrakesh to continue their meetings. The two of them rode in a small convoy of six or seven vehicles.

The 58th was directed to secure the road ahead of the convoy and to insure that no vehicles or people approached. Two firing batteries were used to preceed the convoy with a third battery following in the rear. Finally we put up our two spotter planes, light Piper Cubs, and I hitched a ride with one of the planes, figuring it'd be the best place to keep an eye on things and direct action if something went wrong while my CO rode with the column. So there I floated, above the two most important men in the world, filled with nightmare images of Nazi commandoes waiting out there ready to pounce, or a suicide strike of fighters coming in to hit us. The whole world knew that FDR and Churchill were in Casablanca and the town was most likely still swarming with enemy spies; it didn't take much of an imagination to think about the possible results. If the Nazis could take out one of the great fortresses of the world by crash-landing gliders on top of it, getting Churchill and Roosevelt out in the middle of the desert was a prize they just might figure out a way to snatch.

I was flying up at the front of the column watching the road ahead, swooping down on anything that looked suspicious when an announcement came over the radio that our "wards" had stopped out in the middle of nowhere. There was a moment of panic and I ordered my pilot to pour it on and head back down the road. There'd been no order to stop, no communications and I, of course, imagined the worst, that security had been breached and the convoy had been attacked by surprise. As I circled in, I saw, to my utter amazement, the Big Two just loitering by the side of the road, indulging in a picnic.

I now realize that too often someone of importance might just lose touch with how nervous he can make others. We were a bunch of young soldiers, we held these two men in revered awe, and frankly they scared the crap out of all of us with that little stop, all of us imagining the worst. So we hung around, waiting, until the picnic finished and the convoy moved on.

This move took place on a Sunday, the worst day of the week to do something like this. Since Sunday is market day in Islamic countries, the streets in every village along the way were packed with shoppers. We raced across the open countryside but once we entered into a village we were in a jam. The convoy stalled, and all of us were horrified that a second-story window might pop open to reveal an ambush. There were no roads around the villages that the cars containing our leaders and their staff could negotiate. One of my men finally seized on a brilliantly simple idea.

Just before reaching a village he pulled his half-track off the road, pointed the .50 caliber machine gun toward some barren stretch of desert, and then opened up. In an instant the main street in the village was cleared. Everyone was running . . . not to take cover, but swarming out to gather around the half-track to watch the "fight." With the street empty our convoy roared on through, finally arriving at Marrakesh without a hitch.

It was a great honor to serve them as a young captain, to actually see two of the greatest men of the twentieth century together . . . and I was damn glad when they were no longer my responsibility.

Charles de Gaulle was also in Casablanca, and I saw him as well. He was an imposing figure, and already overbearing and arrogant. Regardless of his personal qualities, we trained with French Goum troops (Native North Africans), and they were truly frightful and proficient killers. I pitied the Nazi that had to face them, especially at night when they infiltrated the line armed with knives. They were living proof, as well, of the absurdity of the Nazi belief in racial superiority. Pit a Goum against an SS trooper, and I know who I would have bet on to win.

After a couple of months in Casablanca we started to look like a unit that just might make it into combat. We finally got our orders to head to the front.

The invasion of Algeria, which was supposed to have immediately driven overland to Tunisia and then cut into Libya in the south, had never gotten off the ground. A jagged north-south spine of mountains marks the border between Algeria and Tunisia, the only way into Tunisia being through several passes or along the coastal road. Once we landed in Algeria the Germans raced reinforcements into Tunisia to keep the back door open for the Afrika Korps. They stopped us cold. What should have been a walk against light resistance would turn into a bitter fight that would hold up to us an unflattering mirror of all our inadequacies.

The reserve troops training in Casablanca were ordered into the fight. We loaded onto trains for the thousand-mile ride to the front lines.

6

Tunisia

Early on the morning of March 7, 1943, we started our move
to the front. It took five trains, loading up across three days, to
carry our eight hundred men, eighteen M-7s, and all our other
gear. Yet again, a train was taking me to the next step in my life.

The trains were like something out of World War I, the classic
boxcars labeled "Forty and Eight" and small flatcars that could
barely fit an M-7, pulled by wheezy old steam locomotives.

For all of us, it was a time of mingled emotions. On the one
side there was the excitement of a journey across an exotic landscape. As we puffed our way out of French Morocco we crossed
up and over the snow-capped Atlas Mountains. When we hit
the long grades, the train would slow nearly to a crawl. When
we hit a tunnel, we'd all be choking on coal smoke and steam,
and at times the train would stall there for a moment, the engineer struggling to build up a good head of steam. By the time
we emerged into the daylight, everyone would be gasping and
wheezing, all our equipment covered with rust-stained water,
cinders, and oil. Later in the war, in Italy, a train loaded with
refugees stalled in a tunnel, and a thousand people died.

At times we'd pull off onto a siding to let a westbound train
pass or to refuel. At one stop, a small village along the tracks,

the locals took us for the ultimate tourists. The men were allowed off the train to stretch, take a break, and look around. Well, soldiers being soldiers some immediately ran off to the nearest wineshop. The French wine in North Africa was a sour, disgusting drink, but for many a soldier it was still alcohol. The whistle blew, signaling that it was time to load up, some of the men staggering as they headed back.

I carefully looked at the men. Here and there I'd see a bulge in a pocket or under a shirt. I motioned the man over, had him produce the bottle, took out my .45, and with the butt of the gun broke it.

"Ah, come on, sir!" more than one of them groaned.

Sure, it made me look like a martinet, but the last thing I wanted was a trainload of drunken soldiers, especially aboard that train. Half of them would have wound up sprawled alongside the track, pitched off on the rocky ride or pulped under the wheels. The men who were drunk—well, I found some ways to get them sobered up real quick and then feeling a bit miserable afterward with extra details.

We were heading into a combat zone. In fact, we were already within range of German aircraft, and a wheezy French locomotive, hauling artillery, would make a real tempting target for any pilot.

We finally rolled in to our assembly area near Tebessa, Algeria, close to the border with Tunisia on March 17.

It was pouring rain, and a miserable night, as we gathered our men and prepared for our first move. Our orders, to attach our unit to the 1st Armored Division, part of Patton's command, which was preparing to counterstrike after the horrific disaster at the Kasserine Pass.

Kasserine Pass is one of those battles that is pretty well forgotten today, unless you are a student of the war or a veteran of it. In scale, the battle was small when compared to the vast operations we'd be undertaking only a year and a half later, but at the time the American defeat was one hell of a shock.

Kasserine Pass is the main avenue through the mountains bordering Tunisia and Algeria. Rommel struck first by launching a surprise attack up and through the pass. The American troops caught in his path were slaughtered.

Our Grant tanks were death traps, nothing but slow-moving targets for Rommel's 88s and Mark IV tanks. Our men were ill prepared and poorly deployed and showed all the weaknesses of an amateur army gone to war. Tragically, a country at times needs such a harsh lesson in warfare, a wake-up call, if it is to learn and then go on to win.

In this type of warfare everything depends on proper deployment of troops, flexibility of command, quick mobility, and training. We had none of them. Our casualties were in the thousands. Entire units broke and ran. Close to two thousand men were taken prisoner.

The Germans thought the battle was a joke, especially after their two years of combat experience in the deserts and mountains of North Africa. But they took the wrong lesson out of that battle. They came away with contempt for us, believing that this would always be the way we would fight . . . and run. They had little idea of what we were about to become.

I see this battle as offering a profound lesson in warfare. For the losing side, if they do not learn from their loss, will continue to lose. And the winner should never assume that the next match will be as easy as the last one.

We passed through the battlefield a couple of weeks after the action. If ever there was an object lesson for me and my men, this was it. At Kasserine we saw a battlefield after an armored attack, and it was frightful: equipment blown apart, the sides of the road clogged with blown-out trucks, ammunition carriers, shattered field pieces, discarded equipment. But it was the smell that haunted. Even after sixty years a veteran will suddenly recall the smell, a nightmare memory that catches him in its grip. When a tank gets hit, it usually burns, immolating the crew. The smell was the smell of cooked bodies, now rotting.

So this was war. From the newest draftee to the oldest NCO and officer, it was a bitter foretaste of what was to come. It was not an encouraging moment, an encouraging sight. This was not the army civilians saw in the newsreels in 1945, triumphantly marching forward to victory; ours was a new army, unsure of itself, trying to learn how to survive, facing tough professionals having years of experience. Our way of trumping them was to use our innovative thinking and our mass-production capabilities to get ahead.

That drive through the Kasserine Pass was an education in reality, a transition between what we had left behind and the dark land of what we would become.

By March 22 we had hooked in with the 1st Armored Division and were part of an end-run sweep, attempting to get around the flank of the Germans. We had fired a few times, taking on a distant outpost, but it hadn't quite seemed real. The twenty-second was our true day of initiation.

We went into position, and the Germans knew where we were. The first time you hear an 88 coming in, well, it's an "interesting" moment. At times, you just might hear the distant thump of the gun firing, the sound racing across the fields while the shell arcs up if the range is long. It comes down faster than its sound, however, so all you have is the "thump," and then a second later the "wham" of it detonating; then comes that weird screaming sound that you hear in the movies. In the movies it is always several seconds long, telling the audience something is going to blow. In real life you don't get that warning.

If they are firing on you in a direct-line flat trajectory (meaning they are literally aiming the gun straight at you from only a mile or two away), there is no warning. Just the explosion if it hits, or the spine-tingling *rip*, almost like the sound of a very big zipper being rapidly pulled open and shut, as the shell streaks past you.

If their gunners are really good, and aiming at you individually, one of two things happens: either you are dead, or you get the crap scared out of you as you feel the shock wave of that shell streaking past your head.

It wouldn't happen until a year later, in France, when I had one of these direct encounters of the worst kind. We were moving along a road and I got a call that a German battery was on a parallel road about a thousand yards away. I got out of my jeep, crawled up the embankment on the side of the road, half stood up, exposed from the chest up, and carefully started to look for them.

They knew we were there. A damn good battery commander had aimed his 88s straight at me. Three shells hit. My shell struck the berm just about a foot or two below the lip and blew. I'm still not sure how I lived through it. Most likely the blast of shrapnel spread out in a cone, and I was just inside of that cone, hit only by the shock wave. Amazingly, I was still standing. Later, my men got a chuckle out of it. They said I was as white as a sheet for the rest of the day.

When the 88s start landing, it isn't like the movies. They're on top of you before you know it. When that first shell hits, your whole perspective on the war changes.

We took our first incoming that day in an olive orchard near Maknassy. Up till that moment it was an abstract, a mental exercise, a wondering of how we would shape up, whether we could do our job, whether we would have the guts for it, and what the shock of battle would be like.

When that first shell hits, war suddenly becomes very personal. Someone out there, someone who is a total stranger but wearing a different uniform, is trying to kill you. It is a curious feeling, a mixture of disbelief, anger, shock. Hell, you never really wanted to be in this. If only the damn fools running their country had left well enough alone, you could be home with your wife. And now you are out here in the desert, in some strange country, and people are trying to kill you. And you now, to the best of your ability, start to kill back. The Stukas used us for target practice, though it strikes me that the pilots were second rate, with most of the bombs hitting a hundred to two hundred yards away. I had a Thompson machine gun, and when they came in, I'd blaze away. Kind of foolish, but it made me feel good, a bit like a gangster character firing away.

We had our first serious firing mission, and the technique our battalion employed was a first. The countryside was totally non-descript; it was a great open void of rocky plains, hills, a few olive orchards, but no sharply delineated landmarks or structures. We were simply given a coordinate and told to hit it.

In order to properly hit a target when it is just a coordinate, you not only need to know where the target is, but also where you are, right down to the foot, so that you can calculate the proper settings for your guns. Out there, in that great void, we weren't quite sure of either point.

We ordered the fuse setters to set for airburst at a thousand feet. The guns fired a salvo. Seconds later, as in a fireworks display, forward observers saw the puffs ignite. By either great skill or luck, the air bursts were right over the target, and the forward observers called it in, plastering the landscape.

The response was swift, and a regular duel ensued. Then the Luftwaffe appeared. They dropped bombs all around us. Later in the day they caught the battalion commander in his half-track and strafed the hell out of him. The half-track was a wreck, but thank God he got out okay.

The following morning the Luftwaffe came back in. An ME-109 peeled off and dived straight at us. The first time you see that, it definitely sets your hair on edge. The plane comes screaming in at three hundred miles an hour, the ground around you starts to "stitch" from the impact of machine-gun fire and 20mm shells. You feel like a rabbit caught out in the open.

One of the reasons I loved the design of the M-7 was that pulpit holding a .50 caliber machine gun. Every one of our gunners opened up, putting up a blizzard of fire in return. And we nailed him, tearing a wing clean off. The plane flipped into a violent spin and slammed into the earth, exploding, pieces of it and of the doomed pilot plastered across the Tunisian country-side.

The dueling continued in support of Patton's move. The following morning is when we really got hit, after being ordered out of the protection of the olive grove and into the open. The Germans had us zeroed in, and in fairly short order we lost two M-7s, along with most of their crews. A number of men were wounded. We were out there for two hours, then they pulled us back.

There was yet another terrible step in my education, the sight of my own men getting hit. Long before, going all the way back to the first days at West Point, it is drilled into a soldier that the mission is everything. You will lose men, that is a given of warfare, but you must transcend that moment and all that you grew up with in the civilian world. You must take it in, then push it aside, calculating how to continue the mission in spite of the loss.

The reality of that moment, the first time you lose men, is a horrible dividing-off point, a transition from the abstract to the real, and if you do not deal with it swiftly, you will fail or crack up.

Two M-7s were hit. Men were down. Orders came in to get the hell back under cover, and we pulled back.

Men of my battalion, men who had staggered through the staging area at Fort Kilmer, men who had lined the deck and watched the Statue of Liberty recede, men who six months ago had no clue as to where the hell Tunisia was, now bled out on the windblown soil of that forsaken land.

Deal with it, that is what I had to do. I remember a sergeant who had just lost a man coming up to me, yelling, "Where the hell is my replacement sir? I need a replacement now."

I didn't react; I knew what was going on. The man had just lost a buddy. If he allowed that to fully sink in, he'd go down. So he had buried it behind a shield of feigned indifference. Maybe later, maybe that night, maybe not for fifty years, he'd finally deal with it, but not then, not at that moment.

Strange things happen in war, and the following morning I had the first of many of them. People talk about "gut instinct," a voice whispering in your head, the hair prickling up on the back of your neck because someone, hidden, is looking at you, that weird sense that something just isn't quite right.

Our fire-control center, the backbone of the battalion, with all its complex electronic equipment, radios, links to division, was dug into the orchard. We'd taken random hits throughout the morning, but no real damage yet, just what you'd call harassment or probing fire.

Something struck me, a "bad feeling" as we'd call it. I went up to the men and told them to get the hell out, to move everything a quarter mile to the flank.

There were some moans and groans. This movement wasn't simply a matter of standing up, getting into the trucks, and driving off. They had to pack up all the gear, go to the new location, get their shovels out, and dig back in, then set everything up again. After men have dug into a place the first time, they get a bit attached to the ground, after all they've sweated to make their post. Leaving for no good reason seemed like nothing but more useless work. At that moment I think the men thought I'd gone a bit weird.

"Do it now!" was all I said in reply.

So they loaded up, drove a quarter mile, got out, dug in, and set everything up again. Just as they were finishing, all hell broke loose, a full-scale barrage. The Germans must have had a couple of battalions' worth of 88s pouring it in, all of them zeroed in on the ground I had just gotten out of. One of the men, trying to keep count, later claimed that something like two thousand shells came in that morning.

The orchard was absolutely shredded, and the ground where the fire control center was located looked like the surface of the moon.

For the rest of the war, whenever I got that "bad feeling," no one asked why, they just did what I said.

Maybe, in war, that is the difference between living and dying. Maybe, if there is indeed no reason, no logic to the universe, something I do not believe, it is just random chance. Maybe it is some inner voice, a guardian angel, a subtle reading of things you are not even aware of, but it is the difference between life and death. Talk to nearly any vet and he'll have a similar story, a pilot who suddenly decides, for no apparent reason, to change direction but a few degrees, and thirty seconds later a barrage of flak tears the sky where he should have been; a GI, asleep, who suddenly awakes, just knowing something is out there, and it is; a marine about to take a step, and something tells him to look down, and there is the thin trip wire of a booby trap all but concealed in the high grass.

Across the next two weeks we stayed in the same position concealed in olive groves just outside of Maknassy, moving slightly back and forth to try and throw the Germans off on their target practice.

The landscape was similar to New Mexico or Arizona, rocky hills, bare except for a few scraggly trees, open valleys between the hills, and ridgelines that were absolute killing grounds for anyone trying to cross. Olive orchards were one of the few places you could get some concealment, and as a result they were pounded relentlessly.

When that first shell slammed in, everyone dived for cover, unless we were in the middle of a fire mission, and then the gunners and fire control people grimly hung to their work.

I remember one shelling in particular. It's amazing how quickly you come to love a good slit trench, lavishing extra attention on it if you are in the same spot for several days, digging it down a bit farther when you *had* a few extra minutes.

We were getting hit hard. I heard one round come screaming

in. I was flat-out down in the bottom of my trench and heard
the thump of impact. It was close, but no explosion.

I peeked over the side and saw one of my men, who became
a trusted comrade and friend, Sergeant Edwards, scrambling out
of his half of our L-shaped slit trench like it was full of snakes,
and roll into my half. The poor guy was white and stuttering.

After the "storm" was over, I went and took a look. There
lying in his hole was an 88mm shell, a dud. It must have hit the
lip of the trench, or bounced off something, ricocheted, and
fallen in right on top of the sergeant. If it had hit him dead on,
it would have crushed him. I wonder whether he still has nightmares about that one.

In turn, we pounded back, paying particular attention to the
olive orchards on their side and to haystacks. The Krauts took a
liking to hiding their armor inside haystacks, something we
learned to our dismay when advancing into one of their positions. A cloud of exhaust shot out the back of a stack, and a
German Mark IV burst out, guns blazing.

After that, any haystack in sight got the treatment. Ninety-
nine times out of a hundred some poor Tunisian farmer was the
only victim, his hard labor going up in smoke, but a couple of
times a huge secondary explosion and telltale greasy black smoke
told us we had nailed something concealed within.

The air battles were a daily show as well. A year and a half
later, in France, we pretty well had control of the air (but not
always, as I most definitely learned to my dismay at one point).
In North Africa all you could see overhead were iron crosses. A
lot of times the Germans would come roaring in low and fast,
skimming across the valley floor at three hundred miles an hour.
No warning and they're on you. Out there, still green to combat,
fighting in a strange and alien world, the American soldiers suddenly felt very vulnerable. Across the last sixty years American
troops accept as a given that we own the skies. North Africa
might very well have been one of the last battles where we
definitely did not. German medium bombers regularly plastered

rear areas, while Stukas, ME-110s, and the small, agile ME-109s tore along the front, strafing anything in sight.

One day we had a gaggle of 109s decide to give us a full going over, and I finally got some of my first personal shots in. I had popped a few shots from a pistol and a Thompson machine gun at them before, but this time a .50 caliber gun mounted to one of our half-tracks was open and right in front of me when we spotted them coming in.

I scrambled in behind the gun, chambered the first round, took aim, and opened up. Whether I was actually hitting them or not, there was something damn satisfying about manning a .50 cal. It's a tremendous weapon, puts up a hell of a racket. The tracers arc up into the sky, while with each passing second that tiny dot of a target seems to be doubling in size.

I guess I got the pilot's attention because he peeled off and came straight in at me, guns blazing back. If I had been in the M-7 I'd have had a little bit better chance, since the pulpit surrounding the .50 caliber gun is armored, whereas on a half-track the gun is just bolted on top and out there in the open.

Anyone under fire like that knows the moment. You suddenly realize that, to use the technical term, your position is "untenable." In common language, you're about to get your backside blown off if you hang around for another second. I baled out just as that 109 dropped a small bomb. It seemed to be coming straight in.

I slammed down on the opposite side of the half-track, waited those few seconds that always seem like an eternity, and the bomb impacted on the far side of the half-track, the 109 roaring over so close I could have hit it with a rock, and then it was gone.

Shaken? Hell, yes! My backside did feel a bit breezy. Reaching around, I discovered that the back half of my trench coat was dangling from the side of the half-track, torn off when I jumped over the side.

Those moments made you or broke you. There's a learning

curve to survival in a combat zone. That first day or two, you hear something strange, a hum, a vibration, or a whistle, and for a second or two you think, "What the hell is that?" Wham, one goes off and darn near kills you. After a week or so you barely hear the whistle and you're already into your slit trench.

Once you got that survival skill down, your odds were fairly good, though skilled or not, if an incoming shell had your number on it, that was it.

Some men just never got it, others dwelled on it, something that's easy enough to do, and it started eating them up. We come from a culture that sanitizes death, and when someone "passes on," you finally see that person in a funeral home, and everything is in its proper place.

The first real shock of war is not just the brutality of death, it's the random casualness of it. You talk with one of your men, a barrage hits fifteen minutes later, you hear the screams for a medic and you find what is left of that man. Death is not clean; in fact, you are the one who has to do the cleaning. You have to have the body taken care of, and then write the letter. There's no funeral director, no preacher, no doctor to do it for you.

You see, as well, the horrible destruction that you deal out, especially in a running battle across the plains and hills of Africa, columns of greasy smoke and bodies. The nightmares linger.

We had one nasty encounter with a German artillery battalion that still bothers me. Their fire was so good, that one of the first rounds in sent me sprawling, muddy clay covering me from the burst. We were on a totally flat flood plain, and we were definitely at a tactical disadvantage, and yet we beat them. Both of us were on the move, the folds of the land keeping us concealed from each other as we moved along the edge of a lake, and then suddenly they were there, just fifteen hundred yards away, murderously short range out there on an open plain. Our lead battery slammed to a stop and immediately went into firing position. The Germans scrambled as well. It was a race. The one big difference between them and us: Their entire battery was horse drawn, like something out of a different age.

They were damn good, obviously experienced troops, and, amazingly, they actually got one of their guns dismounted, deployed, and slammed off the first volley. That's really about all they got off, because then we opened up and smothered them. It was so close I could stand there with binoculars and watch it all, and I saw what happens when a 105mm shell bursts on top of a team of horses.

Ironic, isn't it? We automatically accept the wholesale slaughter of our fellow man in war, and yet when it comes to horses, men will sicken, even break down into tears.

We slaughtered the German battalion, their horses dying with them. What I had once contemplated while learning to drive a team of artillery horses at Fort Sill had indeed come to pass, except it was the Germans and their horses on the receiving end.

After two weeks near Maknassy we were on the roll again. Movement always lifted my spirits. There's something about the M-7 that implies mobility and speed. It's not a weapon, like a standard towed 105, that you feel should be dug in so you can just sit and wait for a mission. The M-7 is designed to run fast, to maneuver with mobile armored forces, to pull over, deliver the firepower on the point of attack, and minutes later get back on the road again.

In those opening weeks of our combat experience we began to master our own methods of operation, techniques that would be honed, refined, and used till the end of the war.

My battalion commander, Bernard McQuade, and I believed in rapid fire: Hit the target with everything you have and then overwhelm it before the enemy has time to react. Therefore, we always kept the ammunition lockers mounted inside the M-7s full. As fast as rounds were fired off, loaders passed up replenishment from the towed trailers, and the towed trailers were reloaded in turn from the deuce-and-a-half ammunition trucks. We yanked the ammo for an entire battery off one truck, and the moment it was emptied, that truck went racing to the ordnance supply depot in the rear. Unlike the arrangement, in some units, where one truck would support a single gun until it was empty and only then go back to reload. That meant that ten to fifteen trucks might be following a battalion around, each of them with only a half load. If a heavy firing mission hit, that battalion would quickly run short and have to drop its rate of fire.

Another simple trick added to our firepower. We swiped an engine from the ordnance reserve. Standard procedure was that when an M-7 lost an engine, the gun was out of action until ordnance came up with a new engine, pulled the broken or shot-up engine out, and replaced it. Through a little playing around with the papers, we got an extra engine and hauled it around with us. When an engine burnt out, we replaced it on the spot, called up ordnance, they came up, and then we "traded" them the old one for the new. In the meantime our gun was already fixed and back at the job.

The same was true of fuel. Even if we drove only a few miles and stopped, we topped off the fuel in all vehicles, drawing our supply from one of our tanker trucks or a load of jerry cans. The moment a fuel truck was emptied, it went racing back for more gas.

These might not seem like much to a casual observer, but if we ever found ourselves in a fifty-mile race for a position, or suddenly got engaged in a bitter firefight, we wanted every shell, every gun, and every vehicle ready for the moment.

I noticed from the start that our men, six hundred of them green draftees only months before, were developing a certain espirit. We didn't look like much; we lacked the spit and polish of the Brits and Germans. We were, as Shakespeare wrote, "but warriors for the working-day; Our gayness and our gilt are all besmirch'd with rainy marching in the painful field. . . . But, by the mass, our hearts are in the trim."

We were working warriors of a free society. We weren't professionals. Most all of us would rather have been doing something else, but since the Germans had pushed us into this fight, by God we were going to see it through. It was a job, and we quickly learned to do it without fanfare, but do it we did.

One of the proudest moments I had across forty years in the military was the day a high-ranker came to inspect us. He already knew the reputation we were gaining for fast shooting, and for putting down in a few minutes the equivalent of several battalions' worth of fire on the Germans.

His inspection done, he turned and headed back to his jeep, and was overheard to say, "There isn't a man in the lot who looks like a soldier, but by God they sure can shoot."

Those weeks around Maknassy, dodging shells, dueling with Messerschmitts and Stukas, and giving back as good as they gave was the initiation of the 58th and of myself.

After two weeks we pulled out, swinging north on a march of nearly three hundred miles. The noose was closing around Tunis. The Brits were driving up from the south, and our effort now was to roll in alongside them and squeeze in from the west.

Spring followed us. We passed through beautiful valleys carpeted with flowers of every color. If there was no shooting going on, for a few minutes we could rest in a field and enjoy the moment. The only problem was, such a moment inevitably made you think of home, your wife, a world left behind. One day we crossed through an area with a lot of vineyards, and one of my observers came in, a bit wobbly, soaked to the knees. "It's all wine," he announced, having found a vat full of the stuff.

We pushed back into the front, in the vicinity of Beja, then going into the line at Djebel Zeraris, and then from there to Eddekhelia. It's interesting to me even as I write those place names, but to all but a few, either students of the war or the men who fought there, this campaign is all but forgotten today. Yet it was so crucial for all that was to come. It changed us from that ragtag bunch who had landed the previous autumn, through the winter, and now into the spring, in spite of many of the screwups of higher command, into seasoned fighters. There was criticism aplenty to go around after North Africa was finished, but for the ordinary fighting man on the front line there should be none. Many had been civilians just six months earlier and there they were, fighting like seasoned professionals and driving back some of the best the Nazis could throw against us. Already our victory at Normandy and the Bulge was taking shape, there in front of Eddekhelia and Hill 609.

Hill 609 became our last big fire mission of the campaign in support of the assault. It was a bloody head-on assault, one of our biggest actions in North Africa, and it demonstrated, as well, a graduation. The three months since Kasserine had wrought a profound change in all of us. Hill 609 was a murderous fight, our infantry were out in the open charging up a steep slope with almost no cover. Our guns were firing until the paint damn near blistered off, trying to put down a curtain of steel in front of our men who were getting slaughtered.

I will never forget, after that fight, crossing the ground our troops had charged. The hillside was covered with poppies, a symbol so evocative to my generation because of the poem "Flander's Fields." All the way up that slope you could see, here and there, where the flowers were crushed down, and an inverted rifle was stuck into the ground, bayonet first, marking where a G.I. had fallen, his body yet to be retrieved. It was a sight that made the strongest of us weep, and to this day the sight of a poppy blossom takes me back to that time and place, to a battle forgotten by history. The survivors of that assault I would meet again . . . on Omaha Beach.

There was one dark side of that fight that must be recorded as well, the fact that the battle got out of control at the end. As the infantry stormed the heights, the Germans began to surrender, throwing up their hands at the last second and shouting "Kamarad." Some of our men, driven over the edge by the slaughter on that hill, gunned the surrendering Germans down.

As an artilleryman I had plenty of moments of up-close combat, but, of course, nowhere near the intensity of the line infantryman, yet I cannot excuse that breakdown in discipline. Word of it quickly leaked, and it is one of the reasons why one of the officers in command was relieved and sent back to the States.

It is a hard discipline to maintain, yet I've always believed that the American soldier must stand to the highest level of discipline and self-control in battle. It must be our moral position, and pragmatic one as well, because by holding to that discipline it ultimately saves lives. Our opponents, by knowing they will be treated humanely, will be more willing to surrender rather than fight to the last man.

From the German side it was a doomed campaign. They should have cut their losses and run after their defeat at El Alamein and after we landed on the flank. Instead, they poured an additional quarter of a million men into the front, troops that could have been far better used in Russia or in preparing defenses in Sicily or France.

We fell back in with the 1st Infantry Division and supported them on a brutal drive in the hills around Mateur. Besides the infantry the Germans were also funneling in their new Mark VI Tiger tanks, a machine with frightful firepower, but in its earlier model still rather slow and cumbersome. One of my batteries caught a Tiger out in the open and, doing direct fire, at only eight hundred yards, took it out with white phosphorus. If you could burst a "willie-pete" near a German tank, it got sucked into the engine and set it on fire.

The following morning, May 7, we got into a direct, close-in counterbattery duel, the flashes of the German guns clearly visible on the crest above us. Yet again our professionalism was beginning to show through. German shells were impacting throughout the battalion area, but my men kept at it, observers calling in the adjustments, the gunners at times able to see their own bursts because the range was so short. We kept our nerve and wiped the enemy off the crest.

What followed was the last day of the campaign in North Africa. For our battalion it was a field day. The Germans were falling back into Tunis, their backs to the wall. Targets of opportunity studded the plains, and it was a continuous day of firing missions, nailing convoys of trucks, retiring armor and infantry. The scene that spread out before us was apocaplytic, with fires soaring to the heavens, burning throughout the night.

For those of us who were prewar army, it was almost beyond imagining, a profoundly great distance from the maneuvers in Louisiana two years earlier, a demonstration of what America could indeed do if aroused, and then marshaling the guts to get the job done.

Shortly after 11:00 A.M. on the morning of May 9, 1943, the battalion CO received the message "Cease firing in all present positions—Germans have surrendered."

Later that day the enemy started to come out of the hills, yet another moment etched in my memory. They came in with typical German style at that point in the war. Though they had been defeated, you could never tell it by looking at them. They had brushed off their uniforms, formed in columns, NCOs and officers in the lead, and came out of the hills marching and singing.

It was a chilling sight. As they marched past us, more than one taunted us, "We're going to America while you go to Germany to die."

We stood there silent, watching them, and I thought yet again about the contrast between us. Here were the professionals, looking like pros even in defeat. We were ragged, filthy, exhausted, no military polish after two months' hard campaigning, but we were the ones who had won. We had won because of who we were, just as surely as they had lost because of their own arrogance.

Yes, we were going to Germany, and after we were done, that arrogance was finished as well. By the end of the war, our prisoners weren't singing anymore, and they were damn grateful it was us they were crawling to rather than the Russians.

It was May 9, 1943, and on that day I celebrated my twenty-eighth birthday. I was glad to be alive to do it.

7

Sicily

We had been through the crucible of war, our first testing, and found that we could indeed stand the fire.

As I stood before Tunis, on May 9, 1943, I had just turned twenty-eight years old, I was a major in a combat battalion, had seen battle, and on that day saw an enemy vanquished. Such a change in just a year, from a young man, eager and yet untested from a nation aroused, but untested as well to one that had fought and won. The pride of the Africa Korps marched past us, defeated, but also, as yet, unbowed, taunting us with the fact that they were only the beginning of what we would face.

The cease-fire and surrender in Africa was a profound moment, the first real triumph of American arms over the Nazi juggernaut. Personally, it had a certain surreal quality as well. Only the day before we had been in hot pursuit of the Germans, firing hundreds of rounds, the plains and hills around Tunis carpeted with burning wreckage, dead bodies, vast columns of troops from both sides on the move.

Now it was quiet. For the first time in weeks I could stand up, walk around, and not keeping one ear cocked for the whisper of an incoming, an eye heavenward for a 109 or a Stuka screaming in on the wind.

It is, in a way, amazing how swiftly one adapts to combat. You train for it for years, you lay awake nights wondering how you will react, whether you can do your job, whether you can lead, and then the moment is upon you. What comes afterward is a blur, a jumble of memories, a fact any veteran will attest to, that certain moments, perhaps only seconds in length, will stand out starkly clear . . . the tight smile of a friend who has just survived a near miss, a quiet moment at sunset, the fear as you hear one coming in and swear that it is coming at you . . . and then there will be days, even weeks, that are all but impossible to recall.

I do remember, though, thinking that what we had passed through was only a foreshadowing, a brief test of all that was to come. Yes we had won in Africa, but that, even the most egotistical of us knew, was only the sideshow. The real battlefields would be on the mainland of Europe. Hitler was not about to roll over and disappear simply because we had taken Tunis. Germany would not surrender as long as it held nearly all of Europe by the throat. That was ahead of us and we knew that we would be the ones to face it. Those of us who could even think beyond the present campaign knew that even if we got through Germany, there was still Japan. There were years of war, some of us thought perhaps even a decade of it, to come. To be twenty-eight with that before you was not a reason for optimism, and yet we had a growing confidence that we would see this job through to total victory.

Where next? A few soldiers talked about England, saying that we would stage there to invade France later in 1943. A few talked about Greece and a stab into what Churchill called "the soft underbelly." Most anyone, though, with even a taste of military history in their education surmised it would be Sicily.

Across three thousand years of history Sicily had always been the key to control of the Mediterranean Sea. The great war between Sparta and Athens in the fifth century B.C. had spilled into Sicily; next it was Rome and Carthage, then the Byzantines, the

Arabs, the Normans, the Turks, the Spanish, and the French. He who controlled Sicily controlled, or at least could impede, all east-west traffic across the Mediterranean, a plane could hop from there to the North African coast in thirty minutes, and an army from Sicily could threaten all of Italy, or even stage to assault southern France. Here would be our next battle.

Across May and June we went into bivouac, catching up on maintenance on our gear, which had taken a terrible beating in the fast-moving campaign across Africa. Then, on July 7, 1943, we staged to Bizerte.

Given the limited transport, we were ordered to divide the battalion into two elements, the primary assault or combat team, and the support team. We stripped everything down to the essentials, a small headquarters and fire-control detachment, the gunnery crews, ammunition-hauling crew, and a small service element. This cut us to just over three hundred men; the other five hundred went into reserve, sitting out most of the campaign in Sicily.

Strange how we are at times. Natural instinct should be that if given the chance to avoid getting killed, a man would be absolutely jubilant, relieved to have been given an honorable way out of the carnage. And yet more than one man screamed and hollered to go and tried to pull any strings possible to get sent in.

We loaded into an LST in Bizerte Harbor. The LST, "landing ship tank," was another one of those wonderful and yet unglorified tools of war that were essential to victory, but gained none of the praise that would be lavished on her far more elegant and lethal sister ships, such as the battleships and cruisers. It was a big, ungainly thing, really nothing more than a long shipping container with a motor slapped on one end and giant hinged doors up front. It rolled like a tub, had no armor to speak of, and had just a few guns on top, more for the psychological support of the crew and men riding it out below decks than for any real attempt at self-defense. And yet it was a miracle of production and American ingenuity.

It could haul darn near anything, from dozens of tanks, to ambulances, to crates of ammunition (which must have been one hell of a nerve-racking experience for the crew), and it could even haul smaller landing craft, the far more famous Higgins boats.

Being flat-bottomed the LST could literally come right up onto the beach, open its clamshell doors and start unloading, then turn around and steam all the way back to the States for another load. It wasn't a first-wave assault ship, it was simply too big for that, though on D-day more than one did come in under intense fire and wound up getting destroyed. It could even be partially flooded, the lower deck inside submerging, so that the Higgins boats could start up and go charging straight out the open hatch.

Though I sing its praise, I never would have wanted to spend the war on one. The quarters were tight; it was guaranteed to make even the most seasoned sailor sick to his stomach as it rolled, and if ever it were hit, well, you were dead.

We loaded onto LST 351 (they didn't even rate names, just numbers). I was a bit uneasy over the fact that we didn't have our precious M-7s with us. Someone higher up the chain of command had decided that our weapons would be temporarily transferred to the 3d Infantry Division and its organic artillery battalions. If you get attached to a weapon in war, you get attached to it big-time. That is "my gun," "my plane," or "my M-7," and woe to anyone who touches it, or, worse yet, messes it up. I had little trust in anyone other than my own men and myself taking care of our pieces.

Just before we steamed away from Bizerte, a rather embarrassing incident occurred. Ike decided to show up to wave us off. The way he did it showed a definite lack of public relations savvy. He pulled up to the dock in a shiny new car, and the driver was a stunningly attractive British female. That alone was enough to set my men off. Ike stepped out, dressed in a neatly pressed uniform, grinned, and waved.

Frankly, it smacked a bit of "So long, guys, but I'm staying back here." My men certainly had a few other comments and thoughts to add to that one, given the driver. Within minutes every GI in the flotilla was hooting and swearing at Ike.

Wilting under the blows, he beat a hasty retreat.

Sure, it was embarrassing to be an officer who had to get the men settled down after that fiasco, but as I look back on it, it shows as well a bit of the uniqueness of what we were as Americans. The men had no fear of sounding off at the supreme commander in the theater (as long as they were safely in a crowd on a ship about to go into combat). In a lot of other armies every last man would have been hauled off and shot or sent to a labor battalion. Ike took his roasting at face value, got the hell out of there, and learned a lesson. Never again did I see him make that mistake. When he visited men in the field after that, he wore a common uniform, and the swell-looking girl was left behind.

The 58th was not present at the main landing near Gela, which was part farce and part tragic fiasco. The Brits landed on the right flank, and then, typically, Montgomery promptly did nothing, though the road straight up the coast to Syracuse and Messina was wide open for the next few days. The few Italian troops guarding the beach promptly took off or surrendered. The situation in the air, however, was different. Stukas and ME-110s hit the invasion fleet, not causing any serious losses but jarring everyone's nerves. Later that night an airborne regiment came in overhead, and the entire fleet panicked, opening up on the lumbering C-47s. Hundreds of men were lost, entire sticks of paratroopers jumping early when their pilots in all the confusion hit the green light, and the heavily laden men came down in the ocean and disappeared.

Our own landing, at Licata, was uneventful. The crossing had not been a bad one. We came straight in to the beach, the clamshell doors opened up, and out we stepped into the bright summer light of Sicily.

For the men in my outfit who were sons of Italian immigrants, it was a bit of a homecoming. The stereotype you see in so many war movies of units having at least one GI who knew the local lingo, and might very well have come from the town, was true. Culturally, it was far different from North Africa, which had been a depressingly rundown mix of corrupt French colonialism and destitute native populations. I'll have to admit the young Sicilian girls were darn pretty, and in general the local population greeted us warmly. Sicilians have never really seen themselves as Italians, and have always resented the dominance of the mainlanders, especially those from Rome and northern Italy. Mussolini had made a major effort to try to crack down on the locals and some of their more "colorful" attitudes toward law and order. Therefore, we were not alien invaders, we were liberators.

On the following day our M-7s were brought up. To our amazement they had not been messed with and in fact had never even been used in action. I guess no one over in the 3d knew what to do with them.

That, I found, would be common throughout the war. Our battalion was a hybrid. We were viewed by the traditional artillerymen as being armor and thus not part of their team. A 105mm gun, mounted on a tank chassis and designed to set off in hot pursuit and get right into the front-line action, was somehow beyond the pace they were trained to at Fort Sill, where artillery came in behind the lines, set up their cumbersome communications, and would sometimes take an hour or more to prepare for a mission that we might have to respond to in seconds if we were to survive.

We became a unit attached to support the 3d Infantry Division as it began its arduous trek across the spine of Sicily. The marriage was, at best, one of convenience, with little love shared between their high command and us.

We engaged in a number of firing missions, and occasionally two or three shells would come winging back in against us, but, in general, after we pumped out a salvo or two against a target, we'd see the Italian infantry throw up its hands and come running into our position, damn grateful to be able to surrender to us. It was a nice way to fight a war. We grew a bit complacent over our supposed enemies, and as a result it damn near killed me.

I can't remember the name of the town now, some small village, typical of Sicily, with old stone houses atop a hill (nearly all the villages were atop hills or mountains, remember this was ground fought over for thousands of years). I was at the head of the battalion, racing ahead in a jeep. We tore into the village and suddenly we were confronting a well-dug-in pillpox with every indication that there were troops inside. By this stage of the campaign that was no problem in my mind. So what if they were carrying guns? They were reasonable opponents, they knew we had them, so I assumed they were just waiting to surrender.

I got out of the jeep and walked up, expecting their officer to come running out, salute, and offer his pistol.

He came out, and he had his pistol—aimed straight at my head—and he was yelling for his men. It was a very long few seconds. Like I said before, there are moments that stand out while others are forgotten, and this was one of them: that man charging out, his pistol raised, hammer back, the bore aimed right between my eyes.

This was no cowboy movie with a showdown on Main Street. This was real. I will admit it; I froze. I started to fumble for my own Colt .45, but I was way too slow on the draw. A shot rang out, incredibly loud, frightening, and the Italian officer was down.

My battalion CO, who had been riding in the jeep with me, had dropped him.

Needless to say, I was pretty shook up, and I learned never to assume anything ever again.

There was a moment of silence, one jeepload of GIs, a pillbox full of Italians armed to the teeth, their officer shot and sprawled on the pavement. And, thank God, that was the end of it. Rifles dropped, hands went over heads, and the moment was over.

It was one of those incidents you joke about later. The story, of course, instantly swept through the battalion, but it was something that stayed with me. It haunted my nightmares long afterward.

We continued our advance through central Sicily. The drivers took one hell of a beating. The engine was red hot. If the driver missed a turn in the road by even a few inches, he went down into a ravine. We lost one M-7 that way, most of the crew getting killed when the vehicle went over the edge and fell fifty feet. The roads were Sicilian mountain roads, narrow, with switchbacks and our M-7s edged along, with only inches to spare, above vertical drops of hundreds of feet. Resistance was light, but the thought of our column getting caught in the open by just a couple of ME-110s was a constant worry.

Finally, near the town of Corleone (yes, the same town featured in the *Godfather* movies) we experienced the ultimate frustration. We ran out of gas.

There we sat for a day, furious until we got resupplied. With that resupply we were finally given a mission. Maybe because the 3d Infantry didn't know what to do with us, the division commander cut us loose with orders to race for the north side of the island, seal off the coastal road out of Palermo, and link up with the 45th Infantry Division, advancing on our right. We were to hold a cordon nearly fifty miles wide until the rest of the division came up.

It was one of the finest moments for my battalion, a true charge of the light brigade. Unsupported, without infantry or tanks, we took off on our own, charging for more than fifty miles into enemy territory. Some of us wondered if the higher-ups with the 3d Infantry were hoping we'd just disappear forever, but we didn't care. We stormed through village after village, far ahead of the rest of the army. Now, when I think about it, the move seems insane. A determined company of enemy, armed with just a few antitank guns and some mines to block the road first, could have shredded us.

When we did hit resistance, we simply lowered our guns, blasted away, and poured in close fire support from the .50 caliber guns mounted on each M-7. Hundreds of Italians literally poured out to surrender.

Just outside of Ventimiglia, near Palermo, a retreating enemy unit blew the bridge. American ingenuity came through. Our men dismounted, eyeballed the ruins, started piling up the rubble into a makeshift causeway, cut a ramp on either end to get on and off the road, and in short order we were on the charge again.

By the end of the day we were on the coast, as ordered, dragging along eighteen hundred prisoners. The following morning we broadened our perimeter, moving up and down the coastal road, accepting the surrender of an entire battalion of Italian artillery and a coast-defense command unit. In a little more than a day we had over three thousand prisoners. I believe this was a record that was unique in the war, an artillery battalion at the van of a charge, penetrating more than fifty miles, seizing a coastal defense from the rear, and dragging in thousands of prisoners. In fact, we had nearly ten prisoners for every man in the unit.

When the 3d finally caught up with us, I'm convinced they didn't quite know what to say, since we had definitely stolen the show.

A couple of days later we were transferred, assigned to support the 45th Infantry with the II Corps, Patton's first command. With Palermo taken, the drive was on to race along the north coast and cut off the German retreat from Messina.

The rest of our battalion finally came up, the men left behind more than a little jealous of our tales of conquest.

We were moved back off the coast and in general were out of action for several days. The enemy was changing. We were running into Germans again, some of them from the elite Hermann Goering Division. Bridges were getting blown, counterbattery fire was picking up, and the going was slower.

We were briefly pushed forward, but the terrain was almost impossible for our M-7s to deploy, steep rocky hills with deep narrow valleys. At one point the Germans were trying to lay shells into us, but we were in good defilade, ground that could not be directly hit, and the shells either impacted on the crest above or plunged into the sea behind us. Unfortunately, one shell did burst directly over A Battery, killing one of my men, our first combat fatality in the campaign.

After our headlong charge the slow pace was grueling. Two weeks passed and we were still just inching along, stalled by the Germans near Mount Etna. Our advance was reduced to crawling a few miles a day, the Germans blowing every bridge on the road as they pulled back. That road was literally hung on the side of the cliffs, sometimes a thousand feet or more above the ocean.

Now started the famous "rush" by Patton to break the deadlock and get into Messina. Some claim he wanted to beat Monty, who was slowly crawling up the opposite coast. I don't buy it. He simply wanted to get the damn campaign over with, for at the rate we were going, we'd finally reach Messina sometime in 1945.

Two batteries, A and B, were now detailed off. Limited naval support had finally moved in along the north coast, and Patton opted for an end run, a quick amphibious jab, putting a battalion ashore behind the German lines supported by two batteries of M-7s. A and B got the job. It went off to perfection. Our two batteries landed near Sant'Agata, poured the fire in while the infantry secured the road, and the deadlock was broken, a couple of thousand Germans getting bagged as prisoners. Next day the rest of the battalion moved up and rejoined the triumphant batteries that had made the landing.

And then things unraveled, both for me and the battalion.

Ever since the race to the coast I had been feeling under the weather, a low-grade fever at first, something I tried to shrug off as simply a bad cold. Then the cold shakes and the sweats started.

My fever spiked to over 104 degrees and I collapsed. I was down with malaria, compounded by yellow jaundice.

Just as orders came in for the battalion to embark on another amphibious end run, I was loaded into an ambulance and hauled away.

I guess the hand of God intervened. I was supposed to lead the next amphibious operation for my two batteries, and this time the Germans were prepared. They had Mark IV and Tiger tanks concealed and waiting. The second assault went in near Brolo. Within minutes, all but two of the M-7s in the attack were destroyed, the last two making it off the beach and up onto the coastal road, attempting to engage the tanks head-on at nearly point-blank range before they, too, were blown apart.

The battalion executive, Maj. Stuart Lamkin, who had replaced me as commander of the attack, was found dead, slumped over the side of an M-7, hands still on the machine gun. He had died trying to cover his men as they fought to get off the beach and up the hill.

More than forty men of the battalion were dead, wounded, or captured. Some of them, once darkness fell, ran back down to the sea, got in the water, and then swam west, to try and escape. Others fell in with the infantry and fought it out, either dying or hanging on until the relief force finally broke through to the pocket.

One of my favorite comrades with the 58th was a young man who had grown up in Palestine and at age thirteen had fought with the underground, and who had been drafted within weeks after his family immigrated to America. For him there was no thought of surrender to the Nazis. He survived the landing, joined up with the infantry, and fought it out. Two months later General Patton would personally pin a Silver Star Medal on his chest.

Another comrade, a Navaho Indian, was caught up with part of a unit that surrendered. He wasn't about to take that lying down. When the compound where he was being held in Messina was bombed, he made a break for it. He finally got back through to our lines and was furious with, as he put it, "our damn officer who turned me in to the Germans."

These two friends, like hundreds of thousands of other comrades, show the uniqueness of our Army, one a Native American, the other a Jewish refugee, both under the American flag and fighting with courage and resilence.

In the movie *Patton* it is this amphibious attack that triggers Patton's rage as he pushes his men up the coast to try to relieve the beleaguered survivors, who are pinned down and fighting for their lives. Patton has been wrongly portrayed as someone who lusted for blood. No, he understood war, that it is through aggression that one ultimately saves blood, by overwhelming and intimidating an opponent into either retreating or surrendering. Men were trapped, fighting for their lives, and he was going to get them out. No war was ever won by someone trying to be "reasonable."

I would witness this firsthand in one of the most famous incidents of the war.

I was in the next tent when Patton slapped the soldier.

I don't recall much leading up to that moment. I was half out of my head with the fever and chills. All I know was that I finally wound up in a field hospital, surrounded by sick and wounded GIs.

We'd been told that Patton was coming to visit, and we were excited. He was respected by nearly every man in his command. We heard the jeeps pull up and the commotion as the hospital staff scrambled.

We heard him in the next tent, talking with the men. His voice wasn't like George C. Scott's; actually, it was kind of high and squeaky. Some people laughed when they first heard his voice, since it didn't fit all the stories about him, but God save you if he heard you laughing.

Suddenly all hell broke loose. A nurse came running into our tent, all upset, and cried that Patton had just slapped a soldier and yelled at him to rejoin his unit and act like a man. One of the guys in my tent asked what it was all about, and the nurse told us.

Every last man in that tent who could muster the strength, myself included, cheered as the Old Man left.

I guess to a lot of people today that might sound barbaric, our cheering Patton for slapping the hell out of a poor guy who was supposedly shell-shocked. I think only someone who had been in combat over there could understand our response.

This was the middle of 1943, when it was still quite possible that we could lose the war. We were fighting for our lives, and when there was time to think about it, we realized as well that we were fighting for our nation's survival. That's hard for people to understand today, but at that moment there was the distinct chance Germany would win and that America and the rest of the free world would be crushed.

The German soldier was without a doubt one of the toughest in the world, and the fundamental question was, Did American soldiers have the guts to stand up to them? Could nice, clean-cut American boys go toe to toe with a professional army that had been kicking the ass of everyone they'd come up against for nearly four years? A lot of American kids were going to get killed before the war was over. The question was whether they would be killed running away or going forward, making the Germans pay in blood until we finally won. That's what the war was going to come down to, trading blood for blood, and the side that lost its nerve first would lose the war.

So far, the prospects didn't look too good. At Kasserine Pass our men had run like sheep and were slaughtered. We won in North Africa mainly because the Germans had foolishly poured troops into a fight that was already lost, and in the final weeks they were totally cut off from supplies.

After North Africa was won, the British stepped forward and were making a lot of noise to the effect that they were the ones who had really won while we just provided backup. In a way you couldn't blame them; after all, they'd been fighting in Africa for three years, and we were the Johnnie-come-latelies of that fight. So our self-confidence wasn't quite up there yet.

In Sicily we were facing the elite Hermann Goering Division, and it was coming down to a test of nerves. A hell of a lot of our guys were not doing their jobs. A significant number of men were wandering around behind the lines, dodging MPs, and, when caught, claiming they were either lost or their nerves had "cracked." Every guy who wasn't at the front, either for good reason or not, meant one less man doing a job, which meant that the ones still there had to carry the extra burden.

I do have sympathy for soldiers who truly crack under the strain of prolonged combat; ultimately, every soldier will crack if pressed hard enough and long enough. A year later, just before the Bulge, two years of war caught up with me, and for four long, intense days the stress bedeviled me, until finally I caught my wind and got back into the fight. Better men than I, not so fortunate, never got that wind back.

I think if that soldier Patton slapped had been in it for a while, a vet who had seen one too many battles and was sitting there with a "thousand-yard stare," Patton would have prayed with him and shown sympathy and respect, but at that moment, in Sicily, there wasn't time for sympathy, and we'd only been in action for a month. Men were dying only a few miles away, and a lot more were going to die. Patton knew that. That slap was aimed not just at that one kid, but at every man in the army; in fact, it was aimed at the entire nation. I'm convinced Patton knew what he was doing; he hadn't flown off the handle the way it is portrayed in the movie. It was a calculated move meant to show everyone that there was only one of two outcomes in this war: either we ran away and died or we fought and won. Every man had to pitch in and do his job to the max.

As he walked out of that tent, I'm convinced he did so with a clear head and a clear conscience. He knew the message would spread through the entire army, show backbone, and get the job done. I know, because I was there as it happened. In spite of my fever I knew how I felt about it, and I knew how every other man in that tent felt. We cheered Patton as he left.

There wasn't a frontline soldier who had the slightest sympathy for the kid Patton slapped. The people who went after Patton were five thousand miles away, safe in the States, and Patton was right, they knew about as much about war as they did about fornicating, though that wasn't the word he used.

A couple of months later, when all the crap started, we couldn't believe it and thought the people back home had gone crazy. Here they were slamming our best general over a lousy slap. None of them had ever walked across a battlefield after a fight, looking for a buddy and finding him blown in half or seen parts of bodies scattered all over a field that the Germans had just nailed with their artillery and tanks. They were weeping over one slapped soldier, but we heard precious little about the guys who stuck to their jobs, got killed doing them, and afterward were tossed into a grave if what was left of them could be found.

Sure, we lost men with Patton, but the Germans lost a hell of a lot more, and that was the bottom line. Patton was the one American general the Germans were really afraid of; I know, I talked to more than one prisoner who said they were scared half to death when they knew it was Patton they were facing.

So they forced Patton to go to every unit in the army and apologize for his "terrible crime." When he came to my unit, the men wouldn't let him speak; they cheered him the moment he got out of his car and shouted their support. He was in tears when he left us, and so were we.

He was removed anyhow, something we couldn't believe. As his replacement we got Mark Clark. (It was my profound misfortune to be one of his aides after the war.)

A year passed and the word went through the army like lightning, "He's back!" The first man who shouted that did not need to say "Patton," or even "George," simply "he." We knew who he was. The day we heard that, we knew there was going to be a lot of tough action ahead, but it was action that would lead us to the end of the war.

If we had listened to the critics, the ones who wrung their hands about one poor boy getting slapped, while men were dying in agony by the tens of thousands, we'd still be over there, all of us dead, and the Nazis in charge of what was left. Unfortunately, it seems at times that such critics are the ones in charge of things today.

By the time I got back to my unit, the fight in Sicily was over. Thanks to a lot of foot-dragging by commanders other than Patton, the bulk of the German army had escaped Sicily and that meant we'd see them again, in Italy.

Here is yet another forgotten tragedy of the war, the result of the campaign in Sicily and what happened afterward in Italy. If Patton had been listened to and properly supported, a hundred thousand Germans might have been taken on the island, leaving the rest of Italy all but naked.

Next was the failure to exploit even the partial victory. The landings across the Strait of Messina and at Salerno would not take place until weeks later. Even then, when the army did go in, the road all the way up was wide open. Mussolini's government collapsed, and the Italian government surrendered, bailing out of the war.

For a precious few days, even then, all was wide open. A few of the more aggressive types screamed to ram an amphibious landing right in front of Rome, and if need be, to drop every airborne trooper we had in an all-or-nothing bid.

We dragged our feet and did nothing. The Germans who had escaped Sicily dug in, and then through the Brenner Pass an entire German reserve army swarmed into Italy and took over.

It was brutal. The Italian people had been lukewarm in their support of the war to start with, and now the Germans turned on them with ferocity. Thousands of Italian soldiers were murdered, the country was occupied, and as we finally dragged ourselves up the bottom of the boot of Italy we stalled just north of Naples, in front of a mountain called Monte Cassino.

The war in Italy would drag on for another year and a half, hundreds of thousands would die, and a beautiful country would be devastated.

Meanwhile, back in Sicily, George Patton was forced to go from unit to unit, humbly begging forgiveness for having dared to slap a coward who had let his buddies down.

The 58th, after the mauling it had received at Brolo, had been pulled off the line to refit and thus missed the final action around Messina. It was ordered into reserve, to prepare to go into Italy. Then we waited.

September dragged into October, and still no action. Finally, in early November we received our orders—to turn in our beloved M-7s, the surviving vehicles among the first to come off the assembly line. We were to turn them over to our new and favorite allies, the French.

We did as ordered. Long afterward, those of us with the old 58th learned that our M-7s, now with the 5th French Armored Division, were the first allied vehicles into Paris. If a machine could celebrate, I bet they had a wonderful time.

I found out, as well, that I was leaving the 58th. I had been promoted to take command of the sister battalion of the 58th, the 62d.

A couple of days later we loaded up, boarded ship at Palermo, and steamed west, not to Italy, but to England.

8

England

It was a time of rapid change on all fronts. Though the Sicilian campaign had failed to achieve all that it might have gained, nevertheless, we had learned. The mistakes experienced on the beaches would be studied, analyzed, and used in the planning for what was to come. Though we had failed to gain what might have been a tremendous advantage in Italy, with a rapid follow-up after Mussolini's abdication, still we had taken one of the Axis powers out of the war. We were a far different army than the ragtag bunch that had landed in Casablanca but nine months before.

Our valiant Eighth Air Force was starting its first deep-penetration raids into the heart of Germany, facing horrendous loses but still pressing the fight. At home the flood of production was truly kicking in, and the training programs were finally turning out the next wave of units for what was to come.

I look back now and still consider the campaigns in North Africa and Sicily to be a forgotten phase of the war. Little is written of them, public attention is focused on the climax, the invasion of France, the drive into Germany, and in the Pacific the bloodbath at Iwo Jima and the fight for Okinawa. The ragged, ill-equipped, dog-tired veterans of Guadalcanal, New

Guinea, Trebassa, Tunis, and Palermo will tell you different. Those battles were our primary school, our first bitter taste of battle. Those battles taught us what we were doing wrong; they were the terrible harvest of all the years of neglect, of burying our heads in the sand. And they gave us something else, the sense that we could indeed do it, that a reluctant nation, once aroused, could stand the fire.

I believe that it was in those months that the profound question of the twentieth century might very well have been settled: Could the people of a free republic, the inheritors of all that western civilization stood for, stand against totalitarianism?

For the first half of the twentieth century it was said by many that the liberal traditions that had emerged in western Europe and the New World had reached their climax, failed, and that the "new" state that could merge the labor of its subjects into a single unified will was the wave of the future. This state, combined with, as Churchill said, "the lights of a perverted science," was the future, and nothing, especially a polyglot of citizens who wasted most of their time bickering, or pursuing their own ends, could stand against it.

In North Africa and Sicily, at Tarawa and Bougainville, the reluctant soldiers, who wanted nothing more than to go home, had stood against the supposed supermen and defeated them. I think that the taunts of the Afrika Korps soldiers on the day they surrendered expressed their doubts and fears about their cause. Yes, they were going to the safety of America, a unique fact right there. They knew they would be treated well in America and, in fact, lived in relative luxury as our "guests." We were going to their country and, if need be, we would flatten it. They had started the war; we would finish it.

It was a profound time of personal change as well. Like all young officers who in two short years leapt from second lieutenant to major or lieutenant colonel, I had my own inner fears: Could I do my job? Would I freeze under fire? Would I make a terrible mistake that might cost lives? Could I do all that I had been trained to do?

I now knew that I could. I had grown more in those nine months than at any other time in my life. I had helped transform a confused band of draftees into a fighting force that could leap seventy miles in a day, take thousands of prisoners, go toe to toe with the best, and in its final terrible action, die fighting.

I loved the 58th. I still do. It was my first taste of leading men in battle, and I will never forget it. After coming back from the hospital, I was heartbroken to see the crossed-out names in the roster and yet proud of all that they had done.

As we waited to go into Italy, I knew we were ready, and I was eager to go in with them. And then came the transfer order, that I was to take command of the 62d.

For me, as for any soldier given his first independent command, it was an astonishing and humbling moment. The realization that someone higher up had said, "Give it to Bennett," was a bit of a shock. It meant that someone up there figured I was the man who could take the responsibility and get the job done. There is a heady moment, a sense of freedom, that now you can truly run things the way you want them to run. My CO with the 58th was one hell of a good officer, one of the best, and yet, ultimately, I had to answer to him, to get his permission for each and every act. As the commander of an independent battalion of mechanized armored artillery, I was now the head man, at least on the tactical level, and I could fully implement all that I had learned.

If there was a touch of sadness, it was that I was leaving the 58th. The men whom I had first seen straggling into our camp at Fort A. P. Hill had become comrades and friends. I had shared slit trenches with them while 88s screamed in, including those strange tight grins when a round hits close, and you look into another man's eyes and are awed that you are both still alive. I had seen the look in soldiers' eyes as we swept out of the mountains and down to the coast of Sicily, that triumph as thousands of dazed prisoners marched before us. I was leaving them, and part of me hated to go.

We had been sitting it out near Palermo, waiting for the word to load into the next LST and head for Italy when word came through of my transfer. So I packed my gear, said my good-byes, and drove the short distance over to the bivouac of the 62d. The reception was polite but hardly enthusiastic. The battalion had fought through North Africa and Sicily under the command of Lt. Col. Raymond Conder.

Colonel Conder was a remarkably good officer, well respected by the men of his command, and his departure to move up the chain of command was accepted by his men as the natural order of things, but they weren't too happy about it. Conder was a veteran of World War I, a father figure, traditional and by the book, but well reasoned and fair, and who the hell was this young guy from West Point who was replacing him?

My transfer was official as of November 11, 1943, and on the same day I was informed that both battalions, the 58th and 62d, were standing down from Italy. We were heading to England.

The anticipation of going into battle within a matter of days was gone, replaced with the realization that we were heading to the big one, the eventual invasion of France, for already it was clear that Italy was devolving into a secondary theater of the war.

We prepared to ship out from Palermo, which had turned into a bit of a wild and woolly place, so much so that one of my first orders was to detail off a "riot squad" to back up the MPs. The city was packed with thousands of GIs, most of them veterans of two campaigns, waiting for orders either to go into Italy and the increasingly nasty fighting near Naples, or to stage back to England, and they were getting somewhat out of hand.

We staged into a holding area just outside Palermo, and there, on November 15, General Patton came to decorate some of the men of my battalion, to thank us for the job done under his command, and to go through the embarrassing ritual of apologizing for having slapped a coward. When he came to that part, the men of the 62d broke into cheers of support and Patton was in tears. It was a heartwarming and heartbreaking moment. We had fought under this man, knew his mettle, we were leaving his command and assumed his career was finished. Little did we know . . .

As we prepared to ship out, the 58th and 62d stripped down. All of our combat gear was being left behind, eventually to be turned over to the French 5th Armored. The only thing we'd take along were personal side arms and our B-bags.

Two days later we loaded aboard the British transport ship *Aorangi*. After LSTs it was like boarding a luxury liner. The *Aorangi* was an old P&O liner on the Vancouver to the Orient run, a true prewar steamer of nearly twenty thousand tons. In many ways the Brits truly knew how to run a ship, in wartime or peace. Though converted to the mass shipping of men to battle, the ship still retained some of its old classical touches, with brass work, clean dining areas, and even a few 4-F types who wandered around with polish and rags working on the trim.

In one sense the *Aorangi* did offend American sensibilities in that the class consciousness was everywhere. Officers had suites that most of us never could have afforded in peacetime. Below decks the men were divided off as well into separate quarters for sergeants and finally steerage for the privates. At least the long shuffling lines for meals were gone, replaced by smaller messes in which everyone could eat his fill. After nine months in the field, this was heaven. The ship was big enough, as well, so that even the queasiest stomachs could hang on, unless we ran into a major blow.

As the new CO this should have been a time when I wandered every inch of that ship, dropping in on the messes, learning names, letting the men get to know me, working to establish my position, but it never happened. Though I had been out of the hospital for well over a month, I never really got my footing back and was still shaky, though I tried not to admit it. A couple of days after we weighed anchor and left Sicily behind, I awoke with chills and a fever, and when I looked in the mirror I thought I was staring at a canary. I had come down yet again with yellow jaundice, a common side effect of a bout with malaria. Jaundice is a disease of the liver, and if you've ever had it, or something like hepatitis, you will know what I mean about wishing you were dead. It's amazing just how disgusting your body can get when the liver goes bad.

I went from my room to sick bay, and there I spent almost the entire voyage. The few times I did get out to try to do my job, I must have been less than inspiring to my new command. I always had a wiry frame, and still do. With a liver ailment, though, you shed weight if for no other reason than sweating and shaking. I must have looked like a skeletal yellow ghost; I was as weak as a half-drowned kitten. This was not the type of man that seasoned troops would want to follow into battle. It was frustrating because the men of the 58th knew who I was, they were even on the same ship, but I could well imagine that the men of the 62d were wondering just who the hell I was.

In peacetime the voyage from Sicily to Britain would have taken only four or five days, but the coast of Spain and France was still a hunting ground for U-boats. While we had been battling in North Africa and preparing for Sicily, the great battle of the North Atlantic had reached a climax. New sonar and microwave radar, combined with light jeep carriers and hunter-killer groups, had fought out a deadly campaign with Admiral Doenitz's subs and won, pretty well sweeping the vital lifeline between America and Britain clear of the U-boat menace. It was another unsung campaign of those first two years of the war. If the U-boats had not been defeated, making it safe to transship millions of GIs and their equipment to England, the Normandy invasion never would have gone off in 1944.

So rather than swing up the coast of Spain, once we cleared Gibraltar after anchoring there for several days, where it was assumed that spying eyes in Spanish territory would observe our convoy, we dashed straight out into the Atlantic and just kept on going. We darn near crossed the entire Atlantic, pushing far out into waters rarely traveled in peacetime, and then swung up to the northwest. Once into position there we fell into the "cleared channel" for passage to England, covered by long-range aircraft and heavy fighting ships. After the sun of Sicily the wintry Atlantic was a shock for everyone.

On December 9, 1943, we steamed into Glasgow. What a sight that was, the last great surge of the famed Scottish shipping industry, turning out the tools of war, rousing from the Depression and soon afterward to fall silent again. Every inch of dockside and yards was swarming with activity as the famed Glasgow workers turned out ships of war. Anchored there as well was the great *Queen Mary*, its bright prewar colors now covered over in battle gray.

The Brits had everything well organized. As soon as we docked, the battalion disembarked, led by their canary-colored CO. Greeted with hot coffee and donuts, we were quickly led to the rail station where a train was waiting. As soon as the last man was on board, we were under way. It was a model of efficiency, designed to get millions of men out of the harbor area as quickly as possible and dispersed into the countryside. It impressed the hell out of us.

For nearly all of us this was our first glimpse of fabled England. For me it held a special meaning since this was the land of my parents. It was, as well, a country that had been under siege since 1940. Though Scotland was far outside the area of heavy bombing, everyone could see the impact of four years of struggle, the austerity and tight rations. We GIs, though fresh from a distant battlefront, were nevertheless well fed and well clothed, and our pockets were filled with pay.

Our train took us down to the Midlands, where, on the following morning, we got off at Bloxham and from there transferred to a vast country estate, Wyckham Park. Wyckham was a true English country estate. A vast park surrounded the manor house. Before the war over seventy people worked there, as butlers, servants, groundskeepers, and grooms for the horses. Taken over by the government at the start of hostilities, the estate had been stripped of all the luxuries, and an ugly spread of Nissen huts had sprung up around the manor house. So many of those estates, holdovers of a distant age, which to Americans seemed both appealing and a bit repellent to our egalitarian sensibilities, became home to hundreds of thousands of boys from Brooklyn, Mobile, Duluth, and Santa Fe. For those of us out of a combat zone, it was heaven, except for the lousy climate, which throughout that winter of 1943–44 was unrelenting rain, mists, and chill. In both the Nissen huts and the manor house, it was freezing.

Billeted in the town was a unit fresh from the States, and our first encounters with them were amusing, and a little tense, until the "pecking order" was straightened out. The new GIs had brand-new uniforms adorned with ETO and good conduct medals, while my men were still outfitted with uniforms worn and battered from Sicily and, as was typical of combat vets, they tended not to wear any "spaghetti," especially those good conduct medals. At first encounter the boys from the States had a good laugh, believing our raggedy outfit was some sorry bunch that had just shipped in as new draftees. That matter was quickly settled, and after that, respect was shown.

The nearby town of Banbury, the Banbury Cross of the nursery rhyme, was soon overrun with Americans. In so many ways we were the harbingers of things to come. Banbury was typical of so many small English towns and cities of that time, still firmly entrenched in the nineteenth century, barely conceding to the speed and pace of the twentieth century. We changed all of that forever.

The quiet, sedate pubs, of which Banbury had close to ninety, a place for a quiet pint, a game of darts, and talk of horses, farming, and the doings of the local nobles and squires, were transformed into the hangouts of fast-talking, fast-spending, jitterbugging GIs. It was a wonderful, curious mix. I know that in some ways we must have been resented, if only because every able-bodied Englishmen was off at the front, manning the planes of Bomber Command, or languishing in a POW camp, taken in 1940, and our young men had come flooding in to replace them. The streets were packed with jeeps and deuce-and-a-halfs, the music of Glenn Miller and Benny Goodman echoed, and school-boys got hooked on gum and, when they could sneak them, Lucky Strikes.

For the older folks, like all men and women of middle age whose sons were away at war, they looked at us and saw a re-flection of their own loved ones. Pretty soon a lot of GIs were "adopted," some forming a circle of warmth and love that would endure for the rest of their lives, whether it would end on a beach in Normandy or go on for long years afterward. Men would be invited to Sunday dinner, go to church. Romances bloomed, and many a case of rations helped to feed families living on the edge. We were allies, of the same blood, and in the same fight. It was without a doubt one of the best and strongest alliances in history.

Throughout that cold winter we were a battalion of artillery without guns, so I kept the men busy as best I could, the old routine of drill, classes of instruction, especially on radio gear, and inspections, and, in general, I tried to keep the men in shape. It was a time of waiting.

Christmas was tough. The previous year I was in Casablanca, immersed in getting ready for my first fight. This year I was in England, and there is something about that land that, at Christ-mastime, connects you to home. I had not seen Bets since leaving A. P. Hill, and it was enough to drive me crazy at times. All we had to hang on to was the memory of how much we loved each other. I eagerly awaited her letters and I tore them open the minute they were in my hands.

Every one of us knew that this winter was a final moment of breathing, of safety, and that ahead was the invasion. England was filling up with troops, the joke being that if one more man or tank landed, the island would tip over and sink. We all knew we were there for only one reason, and thus there was always a shadow of dread over the future, a realization that whatever we had faced before was but an indication of what was to come.

Around February 10, 1944, I had that first glimpse of the reality.

We had gone through a number of shuffles. We were attached or assigned to first one command and then another. That was the lot of an independent battalion, to be slotted in where it was needed, then shifted somewhere else. I was finally informed that we were now designated to V Corps. The 1st Infantry Division, veterans of North Africa and Sicily, were in this corps, and it didn't take a genius to figure that they would be in the initial assault, wherever that might be.

I was called up to 1st Division headquarters for a briefing, led into a highly secure area, and the maps were laid out before me. Normandy, a beach code-named Omaha, a sector code-named Fox Green, on the left flank of the attack.

If, today, someone walked up to you, and said but one word, "Omaha," chances are you'd think of one of two things. The city, of course, but then "that day," D day. Even the term *D day* was nothing but a code word. Today it is part of our lexicon, a significant event, but then it was nothing but a word without any emotional meaning attached, the same as Omaha, the same as Fox Green.

Up to that moment, that briefing, all that was to come was abstract. Yes, I knew an invasion was coming, but when, where, how, was a mystery. It could be Normandy, but then again it could be Brittany, Belgium. Some even said we'd go into Norway first. As for my battalion, we might not even see the invasion, the same as in Italy, where we staged and then waited for weeks, finally to be transferred somewhere else.

Fate was now drawing me in, and I was taking that first step toward a beach on the coast of France and all that it implied. The briefing officer shared only what I needed to know. The 1st Infantry was in the first wave, here, on this beach. We'd go in at low tide. The advantage: The obstacles designed to rip the guts out of a landing craft would be exposed and above the waterline. The disadvantage: We then had to get across several hundred yards of open beach. Then, once across that beach, we had to go up an escarpment a hundred and fifty feet high, studded with German dugouts, bombproofs, pillboxes, and reinforced concrete fortresses.

I was told that the area would be plastered. Damn near every bomber in England would have hit the landing area; tens of thousands of paratroopers would have already landed; and the firepower of dozens of cruisers, destroyers, and battleships would pound the Germans into dust.

Sure.

Highly censured word was out about what had happened to the marines at Tarawa when they hit a fortified beachfront that was supposed to have been bombed back into the Stone Age.

My mission was to bring in my battalion of M-7s. On the run in to the beach we were to engage, laying down fire support. That was a novel idea, a 105mm gun mounted on a tank chassis, sitting in an open bobbing and rolling landing craft, an LCT (landing craft tank), an oversized version of the smaller Higgins boats. I was to figure out how to accurately fire my guns during this run in, then have the LCTs lay off the beach, continuing to fire until we came in two hours after the first wave hit, the beach and the heights above secured.

It was all laid out, a brilliant master plan. Across the entire front of Omaha Beach two divisions would secure the position within a couple of hours, gain the heights, then drive inland, eventually to seize St. Lo, while on the left the Brits would take Caen. We would take casualties, but the beach was manned by third-rate German troops and draftees snatched from the Ukraine.

I walked out of there with a knot in my gut.

Anyone involved in the planning of an operation can be placed in one of two groups. The first, and God save us from them, conceive a plan. They are, at times, brilliant men. They sit down, figure out the overall grand strategic design: Do we invade in Normandy or Belgium? If Normandy, why there? Once that is settled, they focus on the details. How broad a front? How many ships do we need? What kind of resistance can we expect?

Information is gathered. Pilots risk their lives in unarmed planes to get photos, resistance fighters are to find out who is in command of a certain sector, commandos sneak in at night to snatch samples of sand and gravel to compute out the load-bearing capability of the ground a tank will drive over.

Engineers, scientists, and even quacks design equipment. Statisticians figure out how many hospital beds and premade crosses will be needed.

Troops are trained, maps are drawn, orders are broken down from division level to battalion, to company, to platoon, and to squad, each man numbered to a certain landing craft, a certain ship, and timed to the second as to where he will land and which trail he will secure on which beach.

And when the first shot is fired, the whole thing goes to hell.

That is where you pray the second type of planner comes in. The first kind gets so caught up in it all, they come to believe the plan is a reality. Yes, we need that kind of planning. Without it we have nothing but chaos, but to believe that it will all work as conceived is seductive. Hell, the planner is doing his best, but over time, too many come to think it will actually go off correctly, for never in history has something been so carefully thought out.

That's where the second kind has to step in. These planners assume that at some point the entire thing will SNAFU. The weather goes bad without warning, the Krauts for reasons unknown shift units at the last second, faulty batteries get issued for a crucial radio, the radio operator simply disappears in the first ten seconds, ships get lost, bombers get lost, some men panic, good men die (such as my old CO, Colonel McQuade, with the 58th, who was killed within seconds after stepping off his landing craft).

Maybe I'm a bit egotistical, but I'd like to think that through most of my career I was the second kind of planner. Yes, the paperwork looks great, the lines on maps are neatly drawn, the timetable is to the second, but it never happens that way, whether you are Caesar, Lee at Gettysburg, the raid to try to free American POWs in North Vietnam, (of which I was one of the planners), Desert Storm, or action now against terrorist states. Assume the plan will screw up, for it most certainly will. Victory then comes from guts and the ability of men on the ground to think and make the right decision while hell is coming down all around them.

I was driven back to my battalion area, went to my room, sat down and started to think, "Now what the hell do I do to pull this off?"

Within a few days our replacement combat equipment arrived, nearly all of it brand-new from the States: M-7s, fire-control equipment, camouflage, trucks, everything. That was signal enough to my men that things were gearing up.

With the gear came orders that our winter of relative peace in Banbury was over. We were shipping out to a training area at Piddlehinton (another one of those lovely and slightly comical English place-names).

As we prepared for this move, I had to work up a plan for the mission. I had yet to see an LCT, and locked in my head was a beach named Omaha, in Normandy, a secret known only to those of battalion-command level and above in the first wave.

I became so paranoid that I finally told my XO and duty personnel who might be around when I grabbed some sleep, "If I start to talk while asleep, wake me the hell up."

I knew where we were going. My men were in the dark, and maybe that was for the best.

9

Getting Ready

I left that briefing with orders to proceed to Slapton Sands, on the coast of England near Portsmouth. Slapton was the testing ground for our invasion force. The beach and bluffs were rather similar to those in Normandy, and there the training was to take place for D day.

One of my gun crews, and the chiefs of each piece in my battalion, met me there. Our job was to figure out how to fire an M-7 from the open deck of an LCT in support of the infantry landing.

The plan was for four M-7s to be loaded on each LCT and accompany the first wave, laying down suppressive fire as we went in, until we stopped a thousand yards offshore. There the LCTs were to continue to fire until the initial landing area was secured, and then our landing craft would come in and lay my M-7s on the beach.

That, at least, was the plan.

The first question, which no one had yet to figure out, was how to fire a 105mm gun, mounted on a tank chassis, which was lashed to the deck of an open landing craft, and to do so without killing yourself or hitting another landing craft or killing your own men on the beach. Quite simply, it's relatively easy to shoot an M-7 on the ground, once you've mastered the technique; it's an entirely different game when at sea.

On the way down to Slapton I cooked up a scheme that I thought might do the job. I had to account for several factors. First was the up-and-down pitch of the boat, and the rocking back and forth. The LCT is fairly big, a rather cumbersome landing craft, and it rolls like a cork. It doesn't slice through waves like a destroyer, it goes up the face of a wave, then over, and then wallows back down. In a matter of seconds the elevation of your gun might shift thirty degrees or more, and the traverse would shift just as wildly.

At Slapton we met up with our LCT training crew, a British unit commanded by a young lieutenant. We rolled our M-7 on board and lashed it down; otherwise, if the gun shifted due to the rocking of the boat, it'd go right through the side and we'd all be dead in the Channel, since this was still February.

It was fairly calm for the Channel that day, and we headed out to sea. Dead amidships, up on the top of the loading ramp on the landing craft, I had one of my men tie a firing stake, which is really nothing more than a stick to use as an aiming point, just like the front sight on a rifle.

Next I posted a man in the middle of the ship, armed with a huge cooking pot and a potato masher, not the German grenade, but the real thing, a big wooden tool used for mashing potatoes. He was the timer. Standing next to him was a man with a stopwatch.

Finally, I had the battery commander up on the small catwalk across the stern of the ship, standing directly amidships, literally above the weld line that ran up the middle of the boat from bow to stern.

This was my high-tech answer for fire support on D day. The battery commander, standing amidships, eyeballed the firing stick as it bobbed up and down and weaved back and forth. In that split second when the stick was vertical and lined up on the target, he'd scream, "Fire!"

Meanwhile, the man with the stopwatch would be counting off the seconds, and every thirty seconds he'd yell for the man with the cooking pot to whack it with the potato masher. We were supposed to go in at six knots, so every thirty seconds equaled roughly a hundred yards. The banging of the pot was the signal for the gunlayers to drop range by one hundred yards.

Finally, a forward observer, up at the bow of the ship, tried to see the fall of our shells and would call out adjustments if we were short or long.

That was it. No gyro stabilizations, no sophisticated sighting equipment, just men eyeballing the target and one banging on a pot. Thus my plan for the invasion of Fortress Europa.

All right, I was realist enough to know that unless we were on a flat-calm sea, we couldn't have hit the broad side of Berlin, but that wasn't the main idea. The thought was that all hell would be breaking loose, thousands of guns firing, and somewhere, somehow, someone was bound to hit something. I knew as well that, for the guys going in on those first waves, it was damn important to hear one hell of a lot of steel flying over their heads, and, for the Germans, to see a display of firepower unlike anything ever witnessed before.

So we made our way out into the Channel a few miles offshore, pointed out to sea, rigged everything up, and loaded a shell into our M-7. The powder charge in a 105mm gun is variable. Before loading the shell the casing is packed with prepackaged powder bags, going from "charge one" up to "charge seven." Charge one will barely put the shell out of the barrel and is for close-in work; charge seven will lay a shell out to eleven thousand yards. We opened with a charge one and fired several rounds. In general, the shell impacted ahead of the craft where we wanted it to.

I took us up to charge two, three, and four, our LCT motoring along, our British crew intrigued by what we were doing and eager to help in any way they could.

Finally we went up to charge five. That, I realized, was a bit of a showstopper. The recoil was tremendous. On the ground, when you start moving up to charge five and above, and you are standing near the gun, the shock wave goes right through you, the entire piece lurching back. When we fired that charge five, the recoil seemed to bring the LCT to a standstill.

The LCT was designed almost as a throwaway ship, nothing more than some steel plates welded together, a ramp forward, a diesel engine, and tiny crew quarters aft. No one had thought about reinforcing it for use as a gunnery platform. My British lieutenant expressed some dismay over the pounding his ship was taking, and I agreed. It was clear, too, that my original thought of having all four guns aboard fire in salvo was out. Except at short range, we'd have to fire in sequence, otherwise the recoil would sink the ship.

It was cold out there, so I told the men to relax for a few minutes, to go warm up. I went to the stern of the ship and into the tiny galley to have a cup of tea with my host.

WHAM!

The entire LCT surged backward, nearly knocking me off my feet. The lieutenant and I scrambled out, and there were my men, looking a bit sheepish, gunsmoke whipping astern with the wind.

"What the hell are you doing?" I roared.

"Well, sir," someone replied with a bit of a grin, "we wanted to see what a charge seven would do."

And then the Brit lieutenant started to shout.

"You've split my boat in half!"

Sure enough, the recoil had popped nearly every weld on the boat. Water was spraying in, and we were eight miles offshore.

My men just stood there like a bunch of kids who had lit off a firecracker next to the school and now the entire building was burning down. Our boat was sinking, and we were out in the Channel with a water temperature of maybe forty degrees waiting for us if we went into the drink.

The lieutenant whipped that boat around, gunned the engine,

and started racing for shore. The minuscule pump on board was overwhelmed, and everyone, using helmets, pots, and pans, bailed like crazy. For a couple of minutes I figured we'd really bought it, that the damn boat would simply split right down the middle into two halves and we'd go down like a rock. What made it worse, the faster we went, the more slamming and vibration tore into the boat.

We wallowed along, water sloshing back and forth on the deck ankle-deep as we reached the inlet. Our poor British lieutenant, with an unrelenting homing instinct, wanted to try to get back to his base, but it was obvious we were going down. I persuaded him to race the boat straight in to shore.

He turned out of the channel and roared straight toward the beach, hitting it hard, water sloshing back and forth on the deck, the boat wallowing. We hit land, and for a moment everyone just stood there.

"Let's get the hell out of here," I muttered, and before the lieutenant fully realized what we were doing, we unchained our M-7, lowered the ramp, and all my men scrambled onto our M-7. They gunned the motor and started off the boat.

"Colonel, sir, what am I supposed to do now?" the lad in command of the broken LCT cried. "What have you done to my boat?"

"Thank you for your cooperation, Lieutenant," was all I could say, trying to hide a grin. I patted him on the shoulder, hopped on board the M-7, and told the driver to get us the hell out of there.

As I've said before, the alliance with the British was one of the finest in history.

I waited to hear a report, a call from someone up the chain of command who would chew me out, but there was never a whisper. I hope that boy didn't get hung for having his first command washed up and wrecked on the beach, within sight of his headquarters, and I hope he made it through the real show four months later. Most of the LCTs went down.

Actually, it was a good moment. Up till then, my relationship with my command had not been the best. We had got off to a rocky start. The previous commander was well respected, and more than one man thought that the new CO should have come from their own ranks rather than from outside. Then I got sick. I was still staggering when we docked in England, and we just didn't seem to click. That experience on the LCT started to forge a bond between me and the 62d. Once we were back at our base word of what had happened spread around, growing in the telling, as all such tales do.

With our full load of combat gear in, and our transfer down to Piddlehinton, we felt like a military unit again, one getting ready for battle. Though I could not tell a single soul about our actual mission, the mere fact that we had taken that ride on the LCT and were fully outfitted with brand-new equipment fresh off the assembly line was signal enough to everyone that we were in the big show. When the realization hits a combat unit that they are going into battle, and that it will be a big one, everyone buckles down. I felt at last that I was really in command of the battalion and not just stepping into someone else's shoes.

The buildup was evident all around us all the time. Units were redeploying to the south of England, security was getting tighter, training schedules went into high gear. Just a week after our first experience aboard the LCT, we were detailed off for Fox Exercise.

I knew it was the first of what would be several training exercises, but my men didn't. That was part of the whole idea. You announce that this is just a drill, and everyone relaxes a bit and the pressure is off. The drill was necessary if for no other reason than to rehearse the most complex military operation in history, but it was also to get the men conditioned psychologically as well.

All the vehicles of the battalion were waterproofed, full combat loads of ammunition were put on board the guns and towed trailers, equipment was convoyed and moved down to Weymouth and nearby Portland harbors and loaded up. The first time a battalion goes through this, there can be utter chaos. You are merging a ground-fighting force into the requirements and needs of the navy, coordinating as well with British forces and facilities. These runs were to work out the kinks.

One thing I noticed immediately was just how much equipment our battalion was expected to take to the invasion. It was simply too much, and something was going to have to be done about it.

Once loaded up, the ships were "locked down," the men forbidden to get off. Those aboard the LCTs lived right on the deck, since the crew area astern was designed for only a dozen men and was not even as big as an apartment bedroom.

I had already made the decision that on the day of the invasion I was not going in with the LCTs. I knew my place was not to be out there bobbing around in the Channel, where at best I could control only four guns. I had decided to go in with the second echelon of the first wave, bringing in with me a headquarters unit and radio gear. Once on the beach I could help direct the fire and then establish the rally point for the entire battalion to form up on. We were supposed to come in at H + 110 minutes.

After a couple of days of miserable cramped conditions the fleet weighed anchor and headed out to sea. More than one of my men was convinced that this was already the real thing. We steamed through the night, though actually we were sailing in a great arcing circle to simulate the sprint across the Channel, and at H hour we were off Slapton Sands . . . and all hell broke loose.

Every ship opened up, including my LCTs, plastering several miles of English coast. This had been a populated area before the war, of farms, villages, and coastal cottages. The entire community had been evacuated and relocated, yet another tragic uprooting caused by the war.

The bombardment ripped the beachfront to shreds, and our landing craft charged in. At least, this time, it went according to plan. One big factor, of course, was that no one was shooting back at us.

My batteries slowly came in, every gun of the battalion firing, though at low charges, of course, and not in salvos, while the smaller Higgins boats and LCVPs stormed toward the beach. We saw a number of LCTs loaded with rockets that were fired off in great tearing salvos, volleys of hundreds of rockets arcing up and then smothering the beach and the hills beyond.

There were more ships in this one exercise than in the entire Sicily invasion, a stunning realization of what we and the British were producing in anticipation of the "day of days."

Some of us there knew, as well, that this rehearsal was but a simulation of a beachhead, one of five that would be spread along fifty miles or more of Normandy coast.

Exactly as planned, we came in on schedule, though with this first rehearsal the off-loading of the M-7s and the dozens of trucks needed to haul our ammunition and equipment was more difficult than anticipated.

The training gained here, at least in terms of loading up an invasion force and getting it to the beach, was beneficial, but beyond that it was essentially play-acting. Once the first man hit the beach, all live firing stopped, a necessary precaution, perhaps, for reasons of safety, but not realistic at all in terms of what would really be going on.

In general, though, Fox Exercise was a success and heartening. At least we all didn't drown or start shooting at one another. But only a fool would think that this was a demonstration of how combat would really be. No one was shooting back, all fire support ended at the beach, there were only a few simulated obstacles, there were no wrecks, no bodies, no burning equipment, and everyone was careful when it came to where the real ammunition was raining down.

On a later exercise there was a taste of the real thing, but it sent such a scare through the highest levels of command that not a word of it was leaked until long after the war was over. An

LST loaded with an entire battalion of engineers simply disappeared. A German E-boat, a small surface raider, an upscaled version of our PT boats, wandered into the exercise area in the darkness, ran straight into an LST, and opened fire. Within minutes the ship sank, taking hundreds of men to their deaths.

The ship was gone, just gone, and no one knew where. Finally, some bodies were spotted, and it was surmised that a German ship had taken it out, but no one knew how, or whether there were survivors or prisoners. Afterward it was realized that some maps were missing; someone had apparently taken classified charts on board against orders. And for several weeks it was feared that the security of the entire invasion had been compromised. What happened was so secret that the bivouac of the lost battalion was sealed off, and notification to families was withheld until after the invasion. Then they were simply informed that their loved ones had been lost on June 6. Not until after the campaign was over were they told the truth.

Since I was in the know regarding the invasion, and had highly classified information in my possession, security for myself was tight. No map could be checked out; any and all paperwork that might reveal a detail had to be kept locked up and never taken aboard a ship. It was clear as well that if ever there was a screwup, my being taken prisoner was not an option.

This was not a game; all of us who had been briefed, so far, were fully aware of all that it implied. One ill-spoken word, one idle boast or act of stupidity, could result in the deaths of a hundred thousand men and change the course of the war.

It is hard today to fully express the "gravitas" of that time, how men who today would still be defined as boys carried themselves, bearing knowledge that could save or kill hundreds of thousands, and did so with maturity and dedication, even unto death.

As my men trained, I attended briefings, studying and reviewing the latest intelligence on Omaha Beach. Hundreds of men were risking their lives—pilots, resistance fighters, commando

teams—to get down every detail of the beach and the ground
clear back to St. Lo. Each obstacle was marked and numbered.
I was expected to have the entire beachfront memorized so that
no matter where the 58th landed I would be oriented. Direct
ascent up the bluffs dominating the beach would be out of the
question for my equipment, so the defiles—ravines that cut
through the bluffs and in a more peaceful time provided access
roads to the beach—were the key points to seize. Of course,
they would be the most heavily defended.

I became familiar with the men of the 16th Infantry Regiment, 1st Infantry Division, the troops I would be directly supporting on Fox Green, along with the elements going in on Easy
Red, the beach on my right flank. We had to figure out how to
work as a coordinated team. They needed my firepower; I
needed their close-in infantry support. The plan assumed that
the first wave of infantry would take heavy casualties but would
clear the beach area within minutes. I would come in as the
second echelon of that first wave, landing thirty minutes into
the assault, part of a group of twenty-two landing craft carrying
approximately one thousand men across a front of four hundred
yards in those first two echelons.

Once on the beach, I would immediately establish radio contact with the LCTs of my battalion, which would be positioned
a thousand yards off shore, and guide them in, the entire battalion ashore at H + 2 hours. The headquarters unit going in with
me would hit the beach aboard a LCVP (landing craft, vehicle
and personnel), a slightly larger version of the Higgins boat and
capable of carrying fifty-five men or several jeeps and trucks. I
planned to have a team of fifteen men with me from my battalion, radio operators, the battalion XO, who would take over
for me if I got hit, the battalion recon officer, and several fire-
control officers who would go up the bluffs, supposedly secured
by the first wave of infantry, and from there call in the first fire
missions. Then, as soon as possible, we'd proceed up the ravine
in front of our position, gain the heights, and begin to pour fire

in as the 16th went forward, moving with them to reduce strong points and provide direct fire support.

The follow-up support elements of the battalion, the trucks loaded with additional ammunition, and all the rest of the equipment of the battalion would land later in the day and join up with us inland. Coming in then, as well, would be two crated-up Piper Cub spotter planes, assigned to the battalion. Once off-loaded, they'd be assembled on the beach, take off, and provide aerial spotting as well.

That was how it was supposed to be.

Throughout March we continued to train, taking part in firing exercises, drilling in procedures, and in general toughening up with road marches. An honest artilleryman will admit that he can get fairly soft when compared to an infantryman. The infantry, who were always eager to point this out, had to lug nearly every ounce of fighting gear, ammunition, and rations. If there was any luxury item, they hauled it on their backs or dropped it by the roadside. Gunners, in contrast, stowed their personal equipment aboard the M-7s, and the rest of their battalion hauled everything else aboard the quarter-tons and deuce-and-a-halfs.

The farthest any of us walked was from one truck to another, so it was damn easy to get out of shape, at least your legs. In contrast, any gun crew member will tell you what it's like to load five hundred shells, each weighing nearly fifty pounds, while under fire. The gunners had backs and shoulders of iron, even if the rest of them might sag a little. Therefore I thought it important to get the men out marching on the roads whenever I could to keep them in shape, myself included. On the beach, in those first hours, we might all be doing one hell of a lot of running.

An item of great personal satisfaction came through on March 27, my promotion to the rank of lieutenant colonel. A commander of a battalion was suppose to hold that rank anyhow, but still it was something that really hit me. I had been out of the

Point less than four years, and most graduates would have spent
twenty years or more before even beginning to hope for such a
position. In a way it was hard to conceptualize that, but nine
years earlier, I had been a kid swinging a sledge on a New York
Central work gang, and now I was in command of a battalion
of men about to take part in the greatest invasion in history.

While my gunners trained, I participated in a number of map
exercises to evaluate our plan held by the 1st Infantry Division
and V Corps. I had only a general idea of what the other beaches,
Sword, Gold, Juno, all of which were British and Canadian, and
Utah, looked like. But Omaha was beginning to look like a
killer.

In France, Rommel had first concentrated his defensive efforts
on fortifying what German high command believed was the primary target, the Pas de Calais region, but Normandy was getting
a lot of attention in early 1944. Each intelligence update revealed
more barriers, beach obstacles, and fortifications. The heights
above the beach, which in places rose over a hundred and fifty
feet straight up, offered one hell of a killing ground against troops
going in at low tide. Yet again the optimists were projecting that
the first wave, though it would take a beating, would still secure
the bluffs within the hour. The pessimists, or should I say realists,
saw the potential for a debacle. If that first wave got pinned
down, every wave behind it would pile up at the water's edge
and get shredded.

I knew that using the M-7s as floating artillery aboard the
LCTs would only have minimal impact. Those guns needed to
get ashore as quickly as possible, but if the bluffs were still occupied by German defenders, they'd be fish in a barrel. If we
did come in under those conditions, our survival might be calculated as a matter of minutes, at most. My hope was that the
bluffs would be cleared, but the realist in me figured that my
guns would be in the fight only a few minutes, but so long as
they lived, I hoped I could direct their fire to maximum effect.

Part of the plan included floating a wave of Sherman tanks

ashore. They were to be dumped off in deep water and then motored ashore under their own power. An inflatable skirt surrounded each tank, and snorkels were attached to the air intake and engine exhaust. Thank God, no one thought of doing that to my M-7s.

In the middle of April we started to prep up again, this time for Exercise Fabius One. It was a full rehearsal for the lead assault waves. My battalion was divided off according to the ship each unit would load on to, every piece of equipment was waterproofed, and we shipped down to Dorchester. This was as close as possible to the real thing. Yet again my men were led to believe that it was indeed the real thing. More than one wrote his farewell letters.

The marshaling area was fully locked down, carpeted with camouflage, and heavily secured. Something that unnerved us was that the Luftwaffe had found our position, or at least it semed that way, when we were hit by a bombing raid on April 24. It made many of us wonder whether they were on to us or had simply wandered in by accident.

On May 1 we moved to Portland, loaded up, and again spent a couple of very uncomfortable days on board the LCTs and LSTs. I decided to stay with the LCTs for this exercise so that I could directly observe my men in action rather than be on board the ship I would actually take in the invasion. We finally sailed on the night of May 3, did the simulated run yet again, and went in on Slapton Sands on the morning of May 4.

It was even more spectacular than the Fox Exercise, an indicator of just how much the buildup had surged in the last few months, and a foreshadowing as well that we were getting close to the real thing. If I had any personal problem with the exercises it was that we again ended the exercise once we hit the beach. My battalion formed up without firing a shot once the first troops hit the beach, proceeded a short distance inland, and then that was it. Nor did we practice a "worst-case scenario," for example, suddenly declaring that the first wave was "dead" and that the follow-up waves were now going to have to figure out what the hell to do next.

Across all my years in the military I always saw this as a problem. We get married to a plan, and then we come to believe the marriage is real and not just a "best case" rehearsal. I knew that the potential variables for all that could go wrong were almost limitless: The invasion is spotted before leaving port and hits heavy resistance from E- and U-boats, the command is hit, crucial LSTs are hit, or—a possibility we didn't seriously consider—the high rate of loss of landing craft in the first two waves hinders the bringing in of the follow-up waves. Exercise Fabius One went off, but it didn't prepare anyone, fully, for all that might go wrong.

Leaving Slapton, we loaded up, returned to the shelter of Piddlehinton, and immediately set about reviewing our checklists yet again, rewaterproofing all equipment, and waiting. And I saw a huge problem.

The army, and the tens of millions of civilians working back home, were doing everything possible to make sure we went in with everything we needed. The problem was that in their largesse there was simply too damn much. I was focused on but three things, the guns, the ammunition, and the minimum of equipment needed to keep my men alive. I decided that everything else was going to be stripped out. We were already overloaded, and my obsession was that when we went in, we go as a fighting unit and not one burdened down with equipment that might be nice, but wouldn't make a difference if things got tough.

The battalion essentially could be seen as comprising three waves. The first would be the actual fighting vehicles, the precious M-7s, and the command element. We would go in aboard the LCTs, and my headquarters unit would go in with the 16th Infantry aboard one of their LCVPs. The second wave, with the rest of the equipment, was spread out aboard several LSTs, mingled in with various support elements. I wanted that second wave to be ready for action and not waddling ashore incapable of directly adding to the fight on the first day. I had a gut feeling that this operation, in spite of all our optimistic planning, would be anything but a cakewalk. Finally, a third wave of a hundred and twenty men would cross the channel after the invasion, bringing up auxiliary equipment and supplies.

I called my staff and officers together and passed the word. Each man in the battalion was to sort what was absolutely needed from what he could live without, from the equipment issued to the entire battalion right down to the personal gear in his pockets.

For example, four deuce-and-a-half trucks were loaded with camouflage. Great stuff, we most certainly needed it in North Africa where the Luftwaffe had air superiority, but I didn't see it as first-day equipment. The Army Air Force was planning on having thousands of aircraft over the beach. Those deuce-and-a-halfs should carry an extra five hundred or so rounds of ammunition instead of those hundreds of yards of material.

So we started the "Great Divide." It went from camo to winter equipment to the absolutely ridiculous gear only a paper pusher back in the Pentagon could have thought of. On a personal level, if you take off but ten pounds of gear per man, and multiply that by five hundred men, that's two and a half tons of personal equipment, enough to load an entire landing craft. Add in everything else, the camo, tents, heaters for tents, cooking gear (we would be eating C rations cold), and by the time we were done, I swear the pile of discarded equipment must have covered half an acre of ground and cost millions of dollars, and that is in 1940s' money.

We were stripped down. I piled back in, many times on the sly, extra FM radios for communications, ammunition, backups for fire control equipment, small-arms ammo, extra medical supplies for the battalion surgeon—the things I felt were essential to keeping us alive in the first twenty-four hours.

It was the latter part of spring, and even the greenest private

knew that if any campaign was to be opened in 1944, the invasion would have to go in no later than midsummer.

The schedule was grueling, and the knowledge in my head
was a constant source of worry. I looked at the men entrusted
to my command, wondering how I would lead them. I was
obsessed with trying to make sure that every detail was thought
out and planned for. What happens if I get wounded, or killed?
Who will take over? Can he do the job? Which battery commander is my strongest? Which one needs some watching? How
many men might I lose? And as I looked into the eyes of each
of those men, was I doing everything possible for them?

It is hard to recall a clear picture of those final days of preparation, for all that came afterward would overwhelm the memory. Of course, the mere fact that I am writing this, sixty years
later, means I was one who survived, and yet so many that I
knew did not. What did they think in those final days?

We all knew that we were part of the greatest military buildup
in the history of the United States. Though we were locked up
in a secure area, that was obvious. Every village and town in the
south of England had been transformed into an American city,
packed with GIs from every branch of service. The sky overhead
was darkened at times not just by dozens of planes, but by planes
in the hundreds, vast formations of C-47s towing gliders for
maneuvers, bombers heading over to the continent, fighters on
patrol, the air thundering and humming with their passage.
When units deployed to Portland for maneuvers, the harbors
were packed with destroyers, cruisers, transports, LSTs, LCIs,
LCTs, ferries, barges, old passenger liners, almost anything that
could float and carry men into battle.

It was a stunning transformation from all that we were but
three short years earlier, the most telling example in history of
what a modern republic could achieve once aroused to action. I
remembered what we were only eighteen months earlier, shipping out of New York, bound for Casablanca, green draftees

staring wide-eyed at the Statue of Liberty, over 80 percent of the men in uniform little more than a week.

The gut-turning thought that could keep me awake at night was wondering just how bad it was going to be. What had happened to the 58th when cut off at Brolo, Sicily, was never far from my nightmares. Trapped on the beach, with Kraut armor on the bluffs, every M-7 was blown apart.

Of the hundreds of thousands going in, very few had any real combat experience. On paper the 1st Infantry was a hardened outfit, but in reality many of the men were replacements, sent over to reconstitute the unit after North Africa and Sicily, while many of their veterans were transferred to green units in an attempt to beef them up with seasoned men. Other first-wave units were entirely green. Even within my own battalion a lot of the men were new, for the army constantly siphoned off experienced personnel to "leaven" new units just coming in. Very few of the airborne troops, in spite of their pride and swagger, had seen action, and those who had, carried with them the memory of the debacle over Sicily, when the 82d had nearly been annihilated by so-called friendly fire.

Ultimately, it boiled down to a question that had haunted me in my first days at the Point, when we came to that first startling realization that America would eventually be at war: Could we face war as a nation when war came? In spite of our pride in our achievements in North Africa and Sicily, they had been sideshows, and we knew it, but they were good training exercises. France would be an altogether different story. The nightly German propaganda broadcasts, which we all listened to at one time or another, constantly hammered on that theme: They might have lost on distant fronts, but never would they give up France without a fight. Battle-hardened units, including the much-feared SS, were being transferred to France after years of action in the cauldron of Russia. Men who thought nothing of annihilating tens of thousands of men in the Red Army in a single day would be waiting to greet us.

We might put on a bold front when talking among ourselves, but down deep any man who was a realist, in England, in that distant May of 1944, held little hope that he would ever see home again.

I thought often of Bets, wondering how she was, longing to hear her voice, longing to just hold her for a moment. I wondered as well how she would bear up if I should not return. Of course, like any man of that time, I never alluded much to my concerns for myself in my letters; that was considered to be bad form, and I still think it is. At such times the best a man can do is to be the man he has to be. It's strange how men and women will fall into those roles in a time like that spring of '44. Our letters were filled with the chatty news of home, for that is something we all longed for. How are friends and parents? What is the spring like? And mingled in would be the little code words that revealed just how much we longed for each other. If she had any fears, it was felt to be bad form for her to openly express them other than by a simple "Be careful and take care of yourself."

I could not tell Bets anything other than that I was in England. Any kind of detail, especially about the impending invasion, was strictly off limits. So I filled my letters, in turn, with what little chatty news I thought might be of interest and in some way tried to allay her fears.

Every letter I received was a cherished moment. Knowing that the envelope I held had been in her hands, that the letters of each word had been traced out by her hand, provided comfort. I saw men at mail call, filled with rapt expectation, eagerly snatching up each precious missive, and later I saw more than one in quiet tears, for the touch of home had opened with it all the aching, the fear, and the loneliness.

Yes, there is a romance to war, and that might seem shocking at first glance, but I must hasten to add that the romance is in the memory of war. It is afterward, in that wondrous moment when you first catch sight of each other again in a smoke-filled station, or a dock at dawn, and you are both alive, still young, and safe, that the romance arises, when the fighting is over and you are alive. Then in the long gentle years afterward you talk about it, you remember, you share the good times with your children who sit before you wide-eyed or bemused or bored, for they will never fully understand. Then it might seem romantic, and in fact is. As it is when you see your comrades of old at a reunion, for it is they who, across the years, are the only ones who truly understand.

For all those with me in that spring of 1944, clutching their letters, staring at the ceiling of the tent or barracks at night listening to the cold rain, it was not romantic, not yet. That would only come in distant years.

For those who would never get off that beach, and for those who would carry in their hearts the memory of the telegram telling them of that beach, there is nothing I can say even now to capture what those final days were like. How can one who survived fully explain to those who were not there what the final days of precious life must have been like for comrades lost, the final days of dreaming that everything will yet be all right, only to have those dreams wash away and disappear forever?

The final days were indeed upon us.

At midnight, on May 25, 1944, our base at Piddlehinton was sealed off. That morning I was told that it was time to brief my officers on what I had kept concealed from them for months. The telling was, in a way, cathartic. I was at last able to share the truth with my comrades, and yet, as the maps were spread out and I went over the details of the plan, I could see it in their eyes now, the realization of what we were getting into, of what was expected of the men of the 62d.

We went over it again and again with each man, and each in turn was cross-briefed on the responsibilities of his superior officer in case that man went down. If there was a part of my plan I was really anxious about, it was that we as a battalion were apportioned to ten different ships. My intent was that, by going in with the second echelon of the first wave, I could immediately establish a rallying point for the rest of the battalion, but suppose I was killed? My XO was briefed on every detail, but suppose our landing craft was blown apart before we even got out, and every man of that first wave died? I wanted to make sure that my battalion could still function, that each battery, aboard a different LCT, was fully capable of fighting independently until they were somehow formed up by whoever replaced us.

It's strange how, at such a moment, we are so cavalier when talking about our own deaths and the deaths of others. "If I die, you know what to do" sounds so simple. I would ask, "If he gets killed, you know what to do?" and I would point at one man, and then another. How different it is from peacetime. When someone is laid off in an office, waves of shock run through an entire company, but few grasp the fundamental point: The guy is still alive. That evening he will go home to his wife. He will not be rolling in the icy surf.

The following morning all the enlisted men were gathered and briefed in turn. Given their experience of the exercises at Slapton, they had figured out that we were among the first waves and would go right into the belly of the fight. I could see the sober looks when the charts were revealed, place-names given, details gone over, and then gone over again. I wanted each man, from private to my second in command, to know it all by heart, to be ready to take over, ready to fight, if need be as an individual with a gun in hand if everything else went to hell. Privates knew the jobs of sergeants, sergeants of captains, and captains my job.

Across forty years of military experience I have never known another such moment, such concentration on what had to be done. We were not in this because we sought war, but now that we were in a war, we were going to see it through to the end. Words fail me. Only those who were there, locked in those depots in that final week before the invasion, fully know what it was like and carry that memory with pride.

With the sealing of our base we knew the invasion was at hand, no more false games of exercises. Last-minute paperwork was taken care of, and with that the final letters, the ones that could reveal nothing but somehow, between the lines, said everything, and those that might be sent later, if your body was found, the note tucked into a pocket.

Starting on May 28 we began to move out, shipping to the departure areas of the ships we were to be loaded aboard.

Every civilian in the south of England must have realized at this moment that the invasion was on, and it is truly one of the great miracles of the war that such an operation was mounted without a single leak. It was never to be forgotten how the people of England responded during those last days. They stood in the streets and greeted us. Few cheered, for in reality there was nothing to cheer about, but their looks, the tears in their eyes, the calls of "Good luck, Yanks," spoke their concern. All of it I will never forget. This was the land of my parents, of my blood, and it will forever be my second homeland as well. If I were destined to die for any other nation, England, with all its gentleness, beauty, history, and green rolling hills, was that land. It was and forever shall be worth that sacrifice that so many made.

On June 1 the main battle force of the battalion was fully loaded aboard ships in Portland Harbor. It seemed that the entire harbor was paved over with floating steel, and I knew that this was but one of dozens of points of embarkation. The air cover was constant, for if a single Nazi reconaissance plane had gotten through, the secret would have been out. Out to sea a cordon of ships constantly patrolled.

The next three days were torturous. The original plan was for our departure on the afternoon of the fourth in order to hit the beach at dawn on the fifth, but the weather closed in, a blow strong enough that the weak-stomached, even in harbor, were leaning over the rails.

I made my final rounds, trying to get to each ship, to go over briefings one last time. Photos of the beachfront were distributed, showing each man the perspective from the water's edge, our approach routes, our primary sector at Fox Green, and distinguishing landmarks.

The fleet actually started to sortie on the afternoon of June 4. Our convoy formed up and cleared the harbor. It was a nightmare, with huge seas rolling in. I was aboard a heavy transport, and it was bad enough there. I could only pity the men on the flat-bottomed LSTs and LCTs. After several hours the order came in to stand down and put back in to harbor. The invasion had been postponed. Such a moment triggers a mad mix of emotions. You have an extra day, but the anticipation is relentless, any hope of sleep banished. During that night the rain lashed down, and I wondered if it would ever end.

I was now aboard my assigned ship, the *Empire Anvil,* which was primarily carrying the men of the 16th Infantry of the 1st Division. I had fourteen men of my battalion with me, my XO, my recon officer, several forward observers, and a signals unit.

We were hunkered down together, smoking incessantly, and just waiting.

It was in this final twenty-four hours that all officers were called in for a final briefing, and it was one to put an extra knot in your stomach. Omaha Beach had been reinforced by a full division of German infantry who had just deployed in to the area. That meant several things, all of them bad. Had the Krauts figured out that we were on our way and were now racing to deploy? Even if that was not the case and random fate had rolled against us, it meant that those bluffs would be occupied by more than third-rate garrison troops. This unit was a standard mainline division of German Infantry, and they would be waiting for us. No one talked about calling off the invasion. That was out of the question. We absorbed the information and looked at one another and nodded. The game had gotten tougher, but that didn't change what we planned to do.

Finally, at midmorning, on the fifth, the word came down. Ike had given a go. The weather was supposed to lift for a day or two, enough to get us in; otherwise, we'd have to wait until June 19 for the next window, when the combination of tides would be right. History would later show that a delay would have been a total disaster, for a major storm struck that day without warning.

Until the last day of my life I will never forget that moment when we set out. Across the harbor hundreds of diesel engines that powered the landing craft rumbled to life; the funnels of the larger transports and fighting ships were smoking; the vibration, the hum of it all, filled our world. It was all-encompassing, and it breathed with it the power of America and Britain, who after years of struggle and preparation were embarking on what truly was a great crusade. Mingled in were the flags of a half dozen other nations, Canada, Norway, Poland, Holland, and France.

If ever there was a moment when I personally felt that I was indeed part of something that transcended my own life, it was there, at that moment. Though I had only a passing knowledge of Shakespeare's immortal words from *Henry V,* they did indeed apply to all of us that day, this was *our* St. Crispin's Day.

The fleet sailed, ship after ship swinging out into the Channel, clearing the breakwaters, rising up into the storming seas, waves breaking off the bows, the air heavy with diesel fumes and salt. Columns formed, destroyers in the lead of each, flying their distinctive banners. Any ship of size towed barrage balloons meant to ward off low-level air attack, but the wind laid them over, in many cases right in the water. For the smaller ships they were a clear hazard, so that more than one captain simply had the cables cut and the balloons disappeared into the clouds.

In the mists I could see the vast columns, and beyond the mists, beyond my sight, I imagined an armada was gathering, seven thousand ships pouring out of every port and inlet.

England fell behind, our place of refuge, preparation, training, and waiting. The place that we were defending disappeared astern. But looking back, I saw an entire nation coming with us, ships as far as I could see, braving the waves, storming ever south and eastward. Overhead, hundreds of planes cut back and forth, flying low, keeping below German radar, ready to pounce on any intruder.

And so darkness settled over us, a single small light, forward and astern, marking each ship in the column. Belowdecks the infantry was geared up, each man burdened with anywhere from sixty to well over a hundred pounds of equipment—rifles, grenades, mortar rounds, extra ammo for machine guns, rations, knife, first-aid kit, poncho, and sleeping bag, maybe a few packs of cigarettes tucked into pockets. They were so heavily laden they could barely move. As for the poor guys carrying flamethrowers, BARs, mortars, or bangalore torpedoes, I still don't know how they did it.

It was one of those times I did thank God I was an officer, gladly trading that burden for the distinctive white stripe painted on the back of my helmet that German snipers loved to get in their crosshairs. I would go in with a .45, ammunition, some K rations, a few packs of smokes, and not much else.

Someone, in his infinite wisdom, decided that the appropriate meal to send us off with would be macaroni and cheese. To this day I can't look at it, or smell it, without being there again, and to this day, I can't stand the taste of it.

The meal was slopped into our plates, and before we were even done, men began to vomit it back up, either from nerves or from the steadily rolling seas.

The passage took ten hours, with the armada anchoring ten miles off the coast under cover of darkness, which at that time of year didn't come until around ten. Shortly after midnight the engines dropped off and then there was the frightfully loud rattling of the chains as the anchors dropped. That is yet another amazing thing to me about that moment—how thousands of ships, struggling through the rolling seas, under all but complete blackout, could each find its slot and do so without one major collision. The vast majority of the men conning those ships were kids who, but several years back, were in high school or standing on lines looking for work. My hat will always be off to the navy and coast guard for the job they did that night in bringing us in safely.

Then the command echoed belowdecks: All troops of the first wave prepare for departure.

The time had come. It was just after midnight, June 6, 1944.

10

June 6, 1944

There is much mythology about D day, but then that is true of all great battles. Memory fades, erasing the darker recollections for all those who "outlive this day and return safe home." In that forgetting is born much of the mythology, embellished through the years by those who come afterward and try, sometimes nobly and sometimes feebly, to write of what they did not see.

Certain events in the history of any people become part of a society's culture and sacred memory. I know D day has achieved that status, aided by books, some good and others not so good, and by movies.

I think it is fair for me to mention the efforts of Stephen Ambrose here, for it is his writings more than any in recent years that have become synonymous with the story of D day. I applaud his efforts, if for no other reason than the fact that he has raised the consciousness of all Americans as to what happened that day, though I will, as a participant, disagree with many of his general observations, especially the claim that the battle was mostly fought without benefit of leadership by officers. I think it is fair to say that I have earned the right to object, and to speak as well for so many of my comrades who never had a chance to lead on that beach because they died within seconds of landing.

As I have contemplated the writing of this chapter I know it is the one that many readers will turn to first and will examine most closely, for we Americans perceive D day to be the pivotal moment of the war. Perhaps that is true, and yet it is a shame that so many other days of that war are overshadowed or forgotten. Few speak of Kasserine, of New Georgia and the Slot, of Cape Esperanto, Malta or Kursk, of Leningrad and the skies over Regensburg, Peleliu and Attu, of Monte Cassino and Okinawa. I wonder, at times, about the tens of millions who fought on so many forgotten fronts, of the millions still alive in old age, who when they hear so many speak of the horror and triumph of D day, ask, "And what of where I was, where I fought and bled?"

Perhaps what I shall try to explain now will at least in some way reflect upon them as well, for the shock and horror of combat, whether it was on Fox Green of Omaha Beach, in the frozen woods of Russia, or beneath the tropical sun of the South Pacific is the universal. My tale is theirs as well. I hope that in some small way this is a humble salute to those comrades I have never met who fought on other fields and seas and under other skies.

To those who have never known battle, I must add this. Though one might see a movie, such as Steven Spielberg's noble salute, *Saving Private Ryan*, one must never forget that it is a movie, and it can never truthfully and fully convey the overwhelming reality. Though I have never met Spielberg, I suspect he would agree with this.

Many speak highly of the realism of the first twelve minutes of *Saving Private Ryan*. Yes, they are riveting, but a distortion of so many things. First, is time itself. From the moment the ramp drops until the heights are gained in the movie, twelve minutes elapse. In reality, four hours passed. Imagine sitting through four unrelenting hours of such a film.

Notice as well that I say "sitting." On the beach sitting still was death. While watching the film, consider that you are a part of it, and do so after first standing in a landing craft for six long, icy, wet hours. Imagine that you are shaking from the cold and from fear.

The other thing is what I would call density—density of men, of equipment, of time and experience. The movie compacted hundreds of men into a fairly small space. Fox Green was suppose to be hit by one thousand men in the first hour across a front of four hundred yards. That is roughly one man for each foot and a half of beach, which was three hundred yards wide at mean low tide. But if you do the math, figuring the square yards of front, you will see just how lonely it seemed at times out there, though later in the day, as more and more troops piled in, it did get "dense," at least in the physical sense.

Of the experience, it is all but impossible to convey anything. Psychologists who study men under extreme stress can explain it in technical terms far better than this old soldier can. The world is strangely distorted: time shifts, seconds might seem like hours and be frozen like a razor-sharp image in your brain, and hours might disappear forever, never to be recalled, though at times, in the darkness of dreams, they momentarily reemerge to shadow the day to come.

So I shall try now to tell all as I remember it. Or, more truthfully, to tell most of all. In the reality of battle there are men, the most ordinary of men, who transcend and achieve greatness. Some are singled out because so many witnessed what they did, and, ironically, so many are forgotten because no one saw what they did, or those who did, died seconds later. And yes, there are some who failed. Across the years memory of them softens and they are best forgotten.

With the fourteen men of my command I joined the hundreds of others on the deck of the *Empire Anvil*. All was blacked out except for occasional flashes of hooded lamps. Our landing craft, LCVPs and the slightly smaller Higgins boats, edged up alongside of us in the darkness, and heavy woven mats were rolled over the sides of our ship. It was, as often seen in movies, men going over the side, climbing down the mats into the landing craft.

It was, I should add, shortly after midnight. The night was dark, the wind gusty, the seas running ten to fifteen feet. Going down the mats was the equivalent of scaling down the side of a building four stories high. If I had taken the time to think about it, I would have been terrified. In truth, at that moment, I was so focused on what had to be done that I didn't give serious thought to just how risky the whole proposition was.

Here is an interesting side thought, how the mind can react to what should be terrifying in the extreme. I blanked out any thought of what might happen on the beach in seven hours, and of how a single misstep on my part, or of the man above me on the loading nets, could kill me. I was obsessed with getting into the landing craft, getting my men in, and getting ready.

I went down the net, the bulk of the ship at least blocking some of the waves, the landing craft bobbing up and down, timed my jump, and let go just as the craft was at the peak of a wave, falling only a few feet. A man alongside me came down hard, breaking his leg. More than one man, I was told later, simply missed the boat completely, and with eighty or more pounds of gear went straight down and disappeared. It's a horrible death, to fall like that and keep going down for hundreds of feet until you drown in pitch darkness.

Once aboard I did pull rank. I pushed my men forward to the bow. We were sharing the landing craft with forty soldiers of the 3d Battalion, 16th Infantry, 1st Division, and I didn't want my men tangled up with them. Frankly, I had a gut feeling about what would happen. It is strange how different views develop about such things. Some argued that the best place to be was the first man forward; when the ramp dropped, you'd get off and the men behind you would catch it. Others said it was best to be in the back; the first men would get nailed, and then you could get off when the enemy turned its fire somewhere else or had to reload. I'm glad I chose the former.

Once we were loaded, the LCT pulled away. As we cleared the bow of the *Empire Anvil*, the roller-coaster ride started. There, ten miles offshore, the seas were a nightmare. More than one Higgins boat swamped in the darkness, all men disappearing. Waves crashed over the bows. As we circled about, waiting for the rest of the landing craft to form our assault wave, the ocean seemed to come in from every direction. We were packed in like sardines in a can, the infantry burdened down, men leaning on each other for support and vomiting on each other as well.

How hundreds of young coxswains handling the landing craft even knew where the hell to go, let alone get us in to the beach, amazes me still. A lot has been written about the confusion, the fact that some troops landed hundreds of yards, even miles from their assigned sectors. I cannot be too critical on this. No rehearsal can adequately prepare one for the reality of navigating off a strange coast in choppy seas that were barely suited to such operations and doing so while dodging thousands of other ships in the pitch-black night. Add in the smoke, the noise, a cross-current that was far stronger than anticipated, and it's a miracle we landed in France at all. And once the shooting did start, we in the landing craft, for a few merciful seconds, were protected, even if it was simply a couple of sheets of laminated plywood, while the nineteen-year-old coxswain piloting the boat was exposed from the chest up, bearing the awful responsibility for our lives, the brutal obstacles, the incoming rounds clearly visible and unnerving as he tried to con his way in between the barriers and Teller mines. If he survived that, he was then supposed to back off, head out, pick up another wave, and then do it all again.

As in all such things it was hurry up and wait. We bobbed around in the Channel for hours, slowly circling about, waiting for the formations to organize. Then, just around dawn, we started to move up to our jump-off line, roughly four thousand yards out from the beach. I could not see the rest of my battalion; in fact, my entire world had shrunk to the back of the man alongside me, a rather upset radio operator. Somehow, most likely just before going over the side of the *Empire*, he had picked up his radio. Only after we were aboard the landing craft did he discover that he had some other unit's radio. Someone, aboard another landing craft, had my Model 510, set to communicate with the rest of my battalion, and we now had a different model set to infantry communications. To say I wasn't pleased would be to understate my feelings, and I was kicking myself for not bringing along a couple of backup radios. Before we'd even hit the beach, my plan had unraveled, and I would have to find some other way to contact the rest of my battalion. The point would prove to be moot anyhow, since the radio went into the drink in the first seconds after landing.

So far, the entire affair was anything but dramatic. We had loitered for hours in the dark, and everyone was sick. There was no God's-eye view of the drama, the sweep, the scale of this vast undertaking. For all of us going in, it was just a few feet of the universe around us, cramped, smelly, wet, miserable.

As dawn broke off to our left, all of that changed. We passed through the five-mile line, out where the bombardment support had formed up, the battlewagons *Texas* and *Arkansas*, heavy cruisers, light cruisers, and those valiant destroyers that would run in with us.

Suddenly and without warning all hell broke loose. I think any GI who was in those first waves into Omaha will remember the moment when the *Texas* and *Arkansas* opened up. It most likely scared the crap out of them!

My landing craft was passing directly in front of the *Texas* when it lit off. The shock wave from those big fourteen-inchers literally flattened the waves, the blast rocking our boat. I think we all let out a yell, because the blast felt like we'd been hit. It truly did sound like a freight train roaring down a mountain pass when those great shells tore overhead, winging in toward the beach. After that first salvo someone would try to keep an eye on the *Texas,* to shout a warning when the next salvo cut loose.

We never saw the fleet of several hundred bombers, sent in

to crater the beach and thus give us some shelter when we landed, flying across the beach just before the naval bombardment opened up. And I will testify, as have so many others, that they missed the beach by a mile or more. I don't give a damn what the air force's after-action reports say. There wasn't a single bomb crater on that beach when we landed, other than the impacts from the naval bombardment and the incoming German 88s and 105s.

My landing craft went into its holding position at four thousand yards, waiting for the first wave to start the run in, going with them the poor ill-fated crews of the allegedly floatable Sherman tanks. In the heavy seas their inflatable curtains collapsed. Some tanks simply rolled off the end of their landing craft and went down. The horror was that when the Shermans sank, they didn't go straight down; they tended to roll over first, blocking the top escape hatch. Almost all of those men died. Only four vehicles even made it to the beach, and those were shot up within minutes.

Without a radio I was cut off from the rest of my command. I was kicking myself for not bringing along a couple of extra backups. We were circling at four thousand yards, all hell was opening up, and my ship was bobbing about like a cork. I pulled myself up to see over the side of the landing craft, to try and get oriented and see if I could at least get a visual on my LCTs. It was hopeless, but at the same moment awe-inspiring. The first wave was now running in toward the beach, eleven Higgins boats for the Fox Green sector. To the right, toward Easy Red, I could catch glimpses of the first wave running in toward that beach but sensed that any concept of organization and order was already breaking down. The bombardment fleet was really pouring it in, the sharp crack of five-inchers, the heavier eight-inchers on the cruisers, and those deep thunderclap, volcanic roars of the big fourteen-inch guns.

I wish all the naysayers about what Americans can accomplish, both contemporary to that time and today, could somehow have been there to witness that moment. I was watching the righteous wrath of my nation unleashed in all its fury, and though at that moment it was impossible for me to feel any pity for the Nazis, I could at least sense it later, when passions cooled. It must have looked like the gates of hell had just been opened as a power, undreamed of in their darkest fantasies, was now stepping forward and demanding retribution for all their crimes and sins.

The first wave stormed forward regardless of loss. We were timed to come in thirty minutes after the first wave and the obstacle demolition teams hit. Our wave of ten Higgins boats and my LCVP waited. Our naval guide boat came racing in to lead the way. The coxswain gunned the engine and pointed us straight in toward the smoke-shrouded beach.

As we crested the waves, I was able to catch momentary glimpses of the beach, and nothing seemed to be in the right place. After four months of study I had the sector we were supposed to hit memorized—the bluffs, the ravine we were to ascend, distant church steeples. None of it was in place. I was up at the bow of the boat, and at that moment there was no way in hell I could push my way all the way to the stern to "negotiate" with our lone coast guardsman about trying to find our proper slot on the beach. I knew the kid was doing the best job he could, and our guide ship was most likely just as lost as we were and intent now on just getting us in somewhere, anywhere. Our landing craft were spaced roughly one every fifty yards, the navy guide boat racing ahead, though it would turn aside at the last moment.

Random small-arm, mortar, and artillery fire started to pock the water as we got down to a mile. The amphibious Shermans, which were already supposed to be up on the beach, providing direct fire support, were nowhere to be seen, and I already assumed they were dead. There was a continual roar as outgoing and incoming crisscrossed overhead. Geysers of water kicked up, and puffs of smoke appeared on the bluffs ahead. And those damn bluffs looked impregnable. It was one thing to study them in photos and map exercises, but the maneuvers at Slapton had not prepared me for the sight of them now, towering as high as a fifteen-story building, flashes of light winking along their crest from fortified positions.

Of the first wave I could see little. The landing craft in it were supposed to drop their men off, back away from the beach, then roar out to pick up another wave. All I could see was floating wreckage and pillars of smoke. It looked as if the entire first wave had been wiped out, along with the demolition teams that were to come in ten minutes behind them on a couple of Higgins boats.

The first wave was timed to hit at exactly mean low tide. On that section of the beach the tide fluctuated twenty-two feet, rising close to four feet every hour. Obstacles that were to be fully exposed and taken out by that first wave, in order to clear the way for subsequent landing craft, including the heavier LCIs and eventually the huge LSTs, were still in place, the ones placed farthest out already half submerged again. Chances were, if we went all the way in, the bottom would be ripped out of our boat and then blown apart.

The plan was shot completely to hell in the first thirty minutes.

It was getting hot, damn hot, incoming foaming the water. I ducked back down, looking at my wide-eyed men. Everyone could hear it now, the impacts, water splashing.

A heavy pinging rippled across the front of our boat, machine-gun rounds impacting on the armored bow ramp.

"When that ramp drops," I screamed, "break left or right! Don't go straight out. Get the hell away from the boat!"

There were a final few seconds for prayers, a deep breath.

"Get ready!" It was the coxswain shouting a warning.

I'm not sure now, but I think I turned back, looking at the infantry behind me, and shouted for them to break left and right or go over the sides. I'm not sure because those seconds were both the longest and the shortest of my life.

I could feel our boat hit something, engine surging, nearly knocking me over, more surging, the rear of the boat rising up, falling as a wave broke against its stern, the bow digging into the soil of France.

The ramp dropped.

Even as it rattled down, I scrambled upward, dodging around the cable winching out and leapt, hitting the water, going under, feet hitting bottom, pushing back up, gulping for air.

The memories are a kaleidoscope now, the sound of incoming, bullets zipping past, the cold of the water, that horrid feeling of trying to run when one is chest-deep in water, except it is not a nightmare, it is real, and someone is trying to kill you.

I know I cleared the side of the ramp and scrambled through the surf to get away from that boat. I think I looked back, or maybe the memory is what someone else told me later. The infantry that had been behind me in the boat had panicked under fire and piled into the back as machine-gun fire tore into them, tracers flicking past, sparks flashing, rounds hitting bodies. In their last seconds no one was going forward. I think I was screaming for them to move, to go over the sides, but they didn't. In an unrelenting stream of fire those poor souls did not stand a chance. They were slaughtered to a man.

Mortar rounds were dropping in the water around me. I surged forward, staggering, falling, getting up, and pushing forward and away from that doomed boat, for when the slaughter was done there, the gunners would pick off whoever was left around it.

Years later a comrade, one of my men from the 62d, said that he was floundering in the surf, looking for cover, and suddenly saw me standing in front of him.

"Goddamn it, come on," he said I screamed at him. "You're holding up the war!"

Strange, I don't remember that, but I must grin now at what I said, since it sounds so Hollywood. I guess in a time of stress like that, you fall back on the familiar.

I was up on the beach, out of the water and looked back again at my boat. Everyone aboard was dead, a mortar round hitting it, the boat exploding, burning, wallowing in the surf and going down.

There wasn't a damn thing I could do now, and I turned away. Before me was hell on earth.

The first wave had all but been annihilated. A scattering of men was visible here and there, crouched down behind barriers, the dead littering the edge of the surf, which was creeping ever higher, a heroic few racing out to drag wounded comrades to higher ground.

It was not, as I said before, a scene crowded with men. It was frightfully lonely, a few men here, others there. Up on the bluffs, three hundred yards away, I could see at least a half dozen strong points, tracers zipping down from them, kicking up that damn sand, which seemed to engulf and trap you so that you took four steps just to slither one step forward.

It was obvious to me that any semblance of order and coordination of plan was dead at the water's edge. Of the twenty-two landing craft comprising the first two waves, twenty-one had been destroyed, either on the run in or within seconds of discharging their men. I did not know it then, but Fox Green was cut off; high command, believing we were all dead, had abandoned the sector.

I was recently asked by a historian how I functioned at that moment. What enabled me to take the responsibility I was supposed to take as the senior officer on that beach?'

That is one of the toughest questions I could ever try to answer. A lot of it, I guess, was training. The four years America had invested in me at West Point was now a debt to be paid off there, in the next few minutes. I think a lot of it, to use the psychologists' term, was conditioning. Across eight years I had been conditioned for the next few minutes.

If I thought about my personal safety, I was doomed. Any rational man, at that moment, would find the nearest place to hide and curl up. But war is a continuing act of irrationality, a transcending of all our instincts to preserve our own lives. Comradeship was a damn big part of it, too. Everywhere I looked men were dead, dying, wounded, screaming. My own men were loosely gathered around me, eyes fixed on me, silently asking, "What the hell do we do now, sir?"

I had to act, to do something, anything, and everything within me screamed that I had to do it quickly. I felt, at that moment, that we were all dead men anyhow, and the training, and the pride in what I was supposed to be, told me that if I was going to die, I might as well do something, anything, in those few remaining minutes that just might make a difference.

I think, as well, that lingering somewhere in the back of my mind was the Cadet Prayer. That might seem quaint to many today, but the old saying about there being no atheists in foxholes is true. That prayer, across the years, had conditioned me for what was ahead, to go up that sloping three hundred yards of beach, a killing ground as deadly as any faced by soldiers in American history.

It is a bit embarrassing to write this now, for in a way it is a violation of "the code." Veterans who were there know what I mean. We don't like to talk about what we did. For we survived. Far too many of our comrades who did what had to be done died doing it. In our hearts we wish not to speak of ourselves, but rather of them, if we wish to speak at all. And yet, perhaps this telling is a reflection on others, rather than on myself, for what I did was meaningless if others had not been there with me, many of them dying because of the orders I would give.

Standing up, I started forward.

It is that simple. Someone has to stand up. Once that is done, from that moment, it becomes almost easy. He has crossed a line. He no longer thinks of himself, or what he is doing. He no longer thinks of the possible pain, of his wife, his kids, for to do that would paralyze him. He thinks of the mission. He thinks of the men he must lead and prays that in leading them more will live than will die through his actions, versus his inaction.

I stood up. Down the beach I spotted a couple of antiaircraft guns. How they ever got on the beach was beyond me, but there they were, beautiful quad .50 caliber guns mounted on a light vehicle. I told my XO to head down to them and get them to start laying in suppressive fire along the top of the bluffs.

I told the rest of my command to follow me up the beach.

It was a long, laborious zigzag run as we moved from obstacle to obstacle. About half of my men were hit. Amazingly, though, none were killed. At some point I took a round or shell fragment through the wrist. A remarkable wound. It didn't touch a bone, a major vein, or an artery, just went clean through. I didn't even feel it at first.

Elements of at least four companies of the 16th Infantry were scattered on the beach without any real semblance of organization. As I went up the beach, I found the captain of one company, who must, across all these years, remain nameless. He was in a blind panic, frantically digging a hole, refusing to move. I left him behind.

At last I found Captain Richmond of company I, 3d battalion of the 16th, and a true hero. His battalion commander and battalion XO had opted to come in on a later wave, so Richmond was the senior infantry officer on that beach, and he was alive and functioning. We hunkered down together, all hell roaring about us, and hurriedly worked out a plan. Several of my officers I detailed off to him as infantry commanders, slotting them in to take over whatever men they could round up.

Fire support was out. I was without a radio. My battalion had no idea where the hell I was, nor I they. A look back out to sea showed utter chaos. Landing craft were burning, support ships cutting back and forth, geysers of water erupting, banks of smoke eddying, obscuring the view. I couldn't see any follow-up wave coming in, and I think it was then that I realized we were cut off and most likely abandoned. So my men and I became infantry.

The plan Richmond and I came up with was damn simple and straightforward. We had to get those men up off the beach. Once under the bluffs, we'd have some defilade, ground out of reach of their 88s and mortars, and we could then close on the German bunkers dug in along the bluffs.

Easier said than done. There were still at least two hundred yards of open ground ahead. Most of the other officers with the 3d of the 16th were dead, so I put my people in and sent them out to get the men moving. This is the key point of my objection to the statement that the battle on that beach was not a fight led by officers. I am not speaking of myself now, but of the lieutenants and captains who had a life expectancy of a few minutes.

I started to push forward myself. A sharp, clear memory is of coming across an entire squad of infantry, all but one of them dead, most likely caught by a machine gun and riddled. I went up to the one man still alive and knelt down and said something about how he'd be all right.

"No, sir," he sighed, "all my buddies are dead. It's okay about me. I just want to go with them."

There was nothing I could do. A few minutes later I crawled back to him, and he was dead.

The next two hours are a blur, as we tried to get across that two hundred yards of open ground. Many have seen one of the few extant fragments of film of that fight, of four or five men getting up out of the surf, heavily laden, and trying to stagger forward. Within seconds two of them go down. I was near where that happened later in the day, and the same machine gunner almost got me. It was like that. Four or five men getting up, dashing half a dozen yards, a man or two drops, the rest go to ground. They take a deep breath, and then sprint forward again. And they are burdened with upward of a hundred pounds of equipment, they are soaking wet and cold, and trying to get up a sloping beach of wet loose sand.

I was obsessed with getting the men to start fighting back.

Most of the guns were jammed with sand and grit in spite of the plastic wrappings (and condoms) on the muzzles. If you want to do a truly maddening task, field-strip a Garand under fire.

You could see the Germans up there, for the trench connecting the strong points was only about waist deep. They'd pop up, fire, duck back down, then pop up again a few seconds later to the left or right and fire again.

I started getting men to lay down suppressive fire to start throwing off the aim of the Krauts.

The bluffs were so damn close and yet the final sprint to them felt like an eternity. By ones and twos men gained the momentary protection of the base of the bluffs, a trail of casualties behind them clear back to the waterline, where the wreckage of the landing boats rolled and bobbed, debris and bodies littering the high-water line as the surf crept up behind us.

I think at this point we were down to fewer than five hundred living men on the entire sector, and they were spread across several hundred yards.

Wire entanglements, mines, and deadly fields of cross fire were still ahead of us on the face of that bluff.

There's a note in the battalion log that shortly after nine I did make radio contact with my units still offshore. I'm not sure now how the hell I did that. We did have a navy liaison unit on the beach, and perhaps it was through them that I managed to relay a message that the landing zone was still too hot for the M-7s to come in. Though I desperately wanted their firepower, I knew they'd get hammered before they were even off the landing craft.

Captain Richmond and I started to grab men to push up the bluffs, but now we got into a true short-range killing zone. All the Krauts had to do was lob grenades down at us, and every approach was covered by interlocking fields of fire, barbed wire, and mines.

I'm not sure where it came from, but out in the surf there was a beached Sherman, stalled and half submerged. The gun was still operational, though, and by waving and pointing I got their attention. The guys in that tank had guts. We pointed out targets to them and they just poured it in, and they in turn became a target for every German gunner on the heights. The tank kept on firing until it was finally swamped by the rising tide.

And then came the miracle. Even now, as I recall it, the memory brings tears to my eyes. A United States Navy destroyer came to our rescue. The men of Fox Green will forever be indebted to their comrades aboard that ship, for it was obvious that they came in, not just to fight, but also to draw fire away from us, to give us a needed breather so we could get up that slope.

The destroyer came slicing in out of the smoke, so close that I swore it was going to beach itself not two hundred yards away. At that range it suddenly looked huge, like a battleship going in harm's way and every damn gun on that ship opened up, from five-inchers, to 20mm and 40mm antiaircraft, to machine guns, and I suspect more than one man had a rifle or pistol out.

They just blasted that crest and the bunkers at near point-blank range. Rounds were literally shrieking in only a few feet over our heads, tearing across the cliff face, rubble raining down. My God, how we cheered them. We had not been forgotten. Some sailors out there were risking their lives to give us a fighting chance.

That beautiful ship came almost to a stop, the water around it foaming as the Krauts, unable to resist the target, foolishly lifted their fire from us and poured it out to sea.

That was our signal to go. Richmond and I started to urge the men forward, to get the hell up that bluff while we had the chance, charging upward with the naval shells striking above us.

The destroyer slowly, ever so slowly worked its way down the length of Fox Green, firing away with everything it had. It reached the edge of the front, turned sharply about, closed back in, and opened up again.

Across forty years of service I've had a lot of rivalry with the United States Navy, but always in my heart I've felt that debt of gratitude for that ship whose name I do not know. I would not be alive now if it had not been for them. I would gladly embrace every man on that boat if ever I had the chance to meet them.

There, if such a thing can be said about war, is the beauty of what can indeed happen even in the depths of hell. Comrades you will never know, perhaps passing them by on the street years later without realizing it, come forward and risk their lives to save yours. You could tell those sailors wanted into the fight, and were willing to lose their ship if it meant saving us. And they did save us.

They tore the crap out of that crest, and under their protective fire we rushed the high ground, taking casualties, but pushing forward to the bitter, close-in killing range, wiping out the Kraut bunkers with nothing more than rifle fire, a few light machine guns, and grenades.

And suddenly we were on the crest, the few Germans still alive up there giving back, abandoning their position, running into the fields and woods.

We had our toehold on the coast of France, all of a couple of hundred yards of it as high tide pushed in, but we were there, a battered few. Why we were alive and so many others dead, well, that is the mystery of God's will. For me there is no other answer. The round that clipped through my wrist might very well have been through my heart, or head, as it was for so many others.

Captain Richmond had command of the top of the bluffs, his men digging in to secure the position.

I feel I should add a strong point of clarification here. When accounts of a battle are written, historians often say that General Smith took this position or Captain Jones seized that hill. In reality, of course, that is absurd. It was and always will be the men of their unit who did the fighting, bleeding, and dying in order to take and hold those places. It is they who took and held the bluffs above Fox Green against near impossible odds. On that point I do agree with Stephen Ambrose. The individual fighting men on Fox Green were superb, and they were the ones who truly did it. It was a place where uncommon valor was common. We fought that battle as a team in the best tradition of the United States Army and Navy and Coast Guard.

It had been roughly four hours since I had called for the men around me to break left or right once the ramp dropped. My battalion was still, to the best of my knowledge, out at sea. It was time for me to step back into the job I was originally intended to do.

I wished Richmond good luck, left my observers there, and, taking a sergeant with me, hiked down the length of Omaha Beach to see if any of my M-7s had come in. I needed to start organizing my command.

It was the longest hike I've taken in my life, a walking tour that I will admit gave me a chance to observe nearly the entire beachfront from one end to the other during the climax of the battle.

I hooked up with my XO, Major Bowman, and he took on the task of reconnoitering the ravines that led up to Colleville-sur-Mer and St. Laurent. I grabbed Sergeant O'Brian, and we started down the beach together, moving along the bottom edge of the bluff, for in a lot of places the Germans still held the high ground.

It was a walk through a surreal, battle-scarred landscape. In some places our forces had gained the bluffs, pushing the Germans back so that you could actually stand up and walk for a few feet, keeping an eye out for mines, of course. In some places there was an unreal silence, no one in sight, neither American nor German, the entire beach empty. In other places we had to crawl on our guts, as machine-gun fire still raked the beach.

If ever there was a testament to the cost and waste of war it was there. Thousands of men in some places carpeted the beach, bodies rolling in the surf, the shocked wounded sprawled under the protection of the bluffs, medics frantically working to save lives. In the four or five hours since I had landed, hundreds of craft had come in, a good many of them wrecked. Higgins boats, LCVPs, LCIs (which carried roughly a company of men), LCTs, and even some LSTs had by this point come in and been torn apart. Everywhere there was shattered plywood, boats torn in half, boats with their bottoms ripped out by the obstacles, shattered hulks, some burning, others just water-logged and rolling in the surf, abandoned.

Millions of dollars of equipment was scattered everywhere, rifles, machine guns, mortars, ammunition, and so, too, frighteningly, were the men who had carried them.

More landing craft were frantically struggling to come in. Any sense of orderly progression, of assault troops, followed by demolition teams, followed by troops to exploit the breakthrough, followed by support personnel—all that was gone. In places it was like a rush-hour traffic jam, boats jockeying for position, bumping against each other, trying to squeeze into a place between the wreckage. With the tide having peaked and now starting to recede, the underwater obstacles yet to be cleared were still a deadly menace. Landing craft would brush against a Teller mine and everything would blow apart. Landing craft trying to back out, a difficult job even on a calm sea in a friendly port, would ram into an obstacle and get instantly gutted.

Just offshore the sea was carpeted with wreckage and rescue craft weaving back and forth, pulling survivors out of the water, while destroyers, heedless of their own danger, came within spitting distance to lend their support. I understand that several grounded that day, and I hope the captain of every ship that grounded got a promotion and medal, for it showed they had the guts to get in there to help us out.

Eighty-eights were still coming in, in some places with deadly accuracy, in others with random fire, since their observers were gone, but if they hit anywhere on the beach or a quarter mile out to sea, they were bound to hit something. I remember seeing several 88 shells bracket a landing craft, then hit it dead on, blowing it apart.

I could only spare an occasional glance to the sea, and when I did, I was intent on trying to spot my LCTs with the M-7s on board. I found out later that they did attempt to come in, as planned, starting at H + 90 minutes, but the intense fire held them back, the ship commanders deciding to turn about and go back out to the jump-off line. I think this was wise. A huge LCT coming in on that beach in the first two hours would have been blanketed with shells, and every gun of my battery, so desperately needed later, would have been lost.

I pushed on. I remember coming up on that spot immortalized in that brief film clip of several GIs getting hit. I had to sprint across the same spot, the sand kicking up around my sergeant and me.

We finally slid in under a large black piece of wreckage and hunkered down. Bullets kept zipping by to either side of us. I was catching my breath when O'Brian looked up, and his eyes grew wide.

"Hey, Colonel, we're hiding under a rubber boat!"

Sure enough, we were curled up under an inflated raft. We both stood up and got the hell out of there!

Some Kraut must have had the spot under observation because we had barely made twenty or thirty yards when a well-placed mortar round whacked in, bits of rubber boat fluttering back down.

I was still looking for my lost command, not sure where, or whether, they might have landed.

Around 3 P.M. the first element of my battalion, other than those that came in with the first waves of the 16th Infantry, finally made it through the chaos and confusion, bringing in three M-7s, one of which immediately hit a mine and was destroyed. On the same landing craft a jeep was totaled and a half-track damaged. My first guns were ashore and set up literally at the water's edge. In all that confusion I didn't know they were there yet, and they worked desperately to establish radio contact with the forward observers, still with the 16th, who were now acting as infantry officers.

A second LCT pushed in, this one on Easy Red, the beach adjoining Fox Green with the rest of B Battery's guns. They had made five previous attempts to get in, and, when they finally did, it was on one of the hottest sectors. One of the M-7s took a direct hit, killing or wounding most of the crew.

I finally found some of my men crouched down behind one of the guns.

What happened next was one of those strange, wonderful moments, so typical of the American GI.

One of my men spotted me and called over to me, shouting, "Hey, Colonel, how about a cup of coffee?"

I slid in by his side. He had a little gas stove rigged up and was boiling a cup of water as if he hadn't a care in the world, while just a few feet to either side incoming fire was screaming past us.

He got the water to a boil and mixed in some instant coffee. I suddenly realized I hadn't had anything to eat or drink since that ghastly meal of macaroni and cheese nearly sixteen hours earlier. I placed my order for coffee, got up, and sprinted off to keep looking for my men. I finally wandered back to get my cup of java, and the sergeant was laughing.

While he was brewing the coffee, a head had popped up from a nearby crater to see what was going on.

"Hey, Sarge," the onlooker shouted, "look at those goddamn sons of bitches. They're making coffee!"

Another head popped up and took a look.

"I'll be goddamned."

And then, a few seconds later, he stood up, looking down at his men.

"Come on, you bastards," he shouted. "Let's go!"

With that a squad of men emerged from the hole and stormed forward, disappearing into the fight.

They stood out for me, at that moment, as a sterling example of what we were. My sergeant and I, having a cup of coffee out there, stirred something within them, and, in turn, their gallantry stirred me as well.

I finished the coffee, invigorated. The cigarettes I had stuffed into my pockets were all soaked clean through, but someone had a dry butt. Later, when I had a chance, I put the wet cigarettes out to dry, and I smoked every one of them. I didn't think till later that they'd have made a hell of a souvenir of that day.

Gradually, I started to get my command together. By around six or so I had a hundred men with me, and half a dozen M-7s. Part of A Battery had finally come in. In their first attempt at landing, two M-7s got off, then the half-track loaded with ammo floundered and jammed on the ramp. Then the ramp took a near direct hit from an 88 and the LCT's lieutenant decided to get the hell back and pulled off the beach, an understandable move since the wreckage of the half-track blocked the way forward.

I now had a composite group of six guns on the beach. Their usefulness at this moment, however, was limited. We still weren't clearly linked to our forward observers, and along most of the front we were not even sure where our lines ended and the Germans' began.

I wanted to get the men up and off the beach as quickly as possible. In several places our troops had pushed over a mile inland and needed our support on what is called "the forward edge of battle."

We finally managed to queue up and get through the ravine at St. Laurent. These ravines were the choke points that first day. Everywhere else the bluffs were damn near vertical, and, needless to say, the ravines were heavily defended death traps, carpeted with wire, booby traps, and mines, a lane having to be cleared through them first, and the wreckage of destroyed equipment pushed aside.

The smell was something you can never forget. Everywhere

equipment was burning, gasoline, diesel, rubber, hot metal, cordite, and when you were near the wounded and the dead there was that terrible scent of raw flesh and blood.

Just before dusk we gained the top of the heights with our first composite battery of six guns, a few half-tracks loaded with ammo, and a couple of jeeps. I posted details along the entire length of the beach to spot the rest of the battalion as it came in and give them our rally point.

Again, my memory is not sure on this, but I think it was as we went up the ravine, though it might have been the next day, that I saw my old tactical officer from the Point, Omar Bradley. I was in a jeep, going past where he stood, watching us. I stood up and snapped off a salute.

General Bradley started to return the salute then broke into a grin and shouted, "Hey, how are you?"

He was called the GI's general, and for me, if ever he demonstrated that touch, it was there. He remembered me, a shavetail cadet, now filthy and feeling a hundred years older, and still he remembered me. It is amazing how such a touch, at such a moment, can do so much to restore the human spirit.

I finally made contact with Division Artillery for the 1st at around 8 P.M. and was ordered forward to a position five hundred yards to the northeast of St. Laurent. The infantry had pushed forward about two miles from the beach, and we were to be ready to provide support.

I went forward, did a quick recon, and brought up my six guns and had them deploy, but received no orders to fire.

Everywhere, that evening, was the front line. Snipers worked our position over, incoming was arcing overhead, slamming the beach. Just before dark a lone ME-109 came roaring in. I swear he wasn't more than half a dozen feet off the ground, skimming the beach—and he didn't fire a shot. Either he was totally insane, completely fearless, or a touch of both. It was a remarkable display of bravado, as if he were flipping off the entire landing force. I was almost glad he got out of there alive.

As darkness closed in, I took stock of all that had happened. I had six guns ashore (out of eighteen) and three definitely were lost, along with a lot of other equipment. Of the men around me I knew we had taken heavy loses. I had about a hundred of my battalion with me. I had no idea then of the fate of the rest, and could only pray they were still alive out there. The view out to sea was almost beyond the ability of men to comprehend. Thousands of ships stood off the beach; landing craft were jockeying to find a slot to get in; rescue boats were still at work; destroyers, cruisers, and battleships were relentlessly pouring fire in over our heads, over troop and supply ships, LSTs, and Rhino ferries waiting to off-load.

It was, indeed, our St. Crispin's Day, as it was for our British, Canadian, and French allies down the coast and far inland in the drop zones.

As the darkness came down, pyres lighted the beach, ships, trucks, tanks, and men, the smoke and fire of their military offering drifting up into the sky.

Later I would be told that I would receive the Distinguished Service Cross for my actions that day, along with a Purple Heart. The only reason I mention that now . . . that medal rests with the memory of all those who were with me, Captain Richmond, the kid of a coxswain who died with our landing craft, the men of the 3d of the 16th Regiment, the captain and crew of the destroyer, the sergeant who calmly made a cup of coffee, and that boy who softly told me not to be concerned, for all his comrades were dead and he was ready to go with them.

That is where the medal rests.

I sat down, and to myself, as I did every night, I recited the Cadet Prayer.

My Day of Days had come to an end. It was June 7, 1944, and I was still alive.

11

Normandy

After securing my unit on the bluffs just above Omaha Beach I managed to grab two hours' sleep, the first real rest I had had in a couple of days. Some of the men in my unit might have thought it strange, but I had actually packed along pajamas rolled up inside my sleeping bag, which had safely made it ashore. I changed into the pajamas, settled down, and was out like a light. I think somehow I was trying to make a statement as well, that the little civilities can be maintained even in the middle of a nightmare . . . or maybe it was just an eccentricity, but at the time I didn't ponder on it.

We were in a slight defilade that offered just enough cover from the stream of incoming that arced over us all night. The beach was still within easy range of the Kraut artillery, and they made the most of it, the only drawback for them was that nearly every observation point had been wiped out, so they were firing blind, but with that kind of density on the beach, they were bound to hit something, and usually did.

There was also the continual racket of outgoing mail, the fourteen-inchers of the battleships, eight-inchers of the cruisers, and smaller calibers of the destroyers sounding like a freight train roaring by. It was unnerving, even for the vets in my unit, let alone the new men. I actually managed to sleep through it, though, and woke up around 4:30.

Some German machine-gun fire was skimming just over our heads, and one of my battery commanders finally got ticked off, rolled up a hundred yards to the low crest, and blew the enemy position away, then came rolling back with a grin on his face.

Strange as it sounds, one thing we had to be careful of was engaging every target in sight. There were certainly enough of them that morning. We had only a limited amount of ammunition on hand and had to conserve it, especially if the Germans launched a major counterpunch, which we fully assumed would materialize.

Around six in the morning I headed back down to the beach with two missions, to find the rest of my battalion and to report in to 1st Division headquarters in order to coordinate our mission. That beach on the morning of the second day was an overpowering sight. It was still under artillery fire, but the vicious struggle up the bluffs had been won. All of the support was now pouring in, a flood of supplies. The sight of it filled me with awe and pride.

Gone was the poverty of equipment and uncertainty of the prewar years. What was spread before me was the vibrant strength of an America and Great Britain resolved to win no matter what the cost. The ocean seemed to be paved with steel. Huge LSTs were now coming straight up to the beach, disgorging tanks, trucks, bulldozers, jeeps, and thousands upon thousands of men. Farther out, the transports had come closer in, waiting to off-load supplies and yet more troops, while the support ships of the navy continued to pour the fire in. High overhead our air fleets kept watch, ready to pounce on any sign of resistance from the Luftwaffe.

The wreckage of our hard-fought battle was evident everywhere, blasted vehicles bulldozed off into piles of blackened steel, abandoned weapons, helmets, busted-up plywood from the hundreds of landing craft, blood-soaked bandages, all of it pushed up by the rising tide to form a grim line of flotsam.

Sections of the beach were marked off as temporary burial sites, and the men assigned to that grisly task, the Graves Registration units, were hard at work. Bodies, covered with ponchos, were lined up, waiting for a hasty interment. Only later, long after the battle had moved on, would the memorial park be laid out on the bluffs above. Until then, most of the fallen rested near where they fell, their grave marked by a simple stake with a dog tag nailed to it.

Casualty clearing areas were set up, mostly out in the open, hard up against the side of the bluffs in order to protect the men from incoming fire. Hundreds of medics and surgeons who had come in on the first day were at work, struggling to stabilize the critically injured. As soon as a supply ship was off-loaded, stretcher-bearers would start running the men down to the ship. That must have been damn unnerving for the injured, to be badly hurt and have to endure those final moments in a cavernous LST, or open LCT, listening to the steady crump of 88s and 105s, helpless, knowing that if the ship got hit there wasn't a damn thing you could do to save yourself.

The one thing you did notice in all this was the supreme effort we were taking to do everything possible to help the wounded, ours and the Germans. In the clearing areas you saw more than one former enemy lying side by side with a GI, for our policy always was to give all the wounded the same treatment and to evacuate them as quickly as possible to hospitals in England.

Our medical treatment was the best in the world, and it was and is a lasting credit to our cause. The latest technologies were in service, the new miracle drug penicillin was at last in sufficient supply, tens of thousands of units of whole blood and plasma had been stockpiled, and every GI had an emergency pack with morphine on hand to treat shock. (And God save the man who abused that, but then again, it was a different age, because at the time the thought never crossed our minds.) Compare that to what we saw the typical German having to endure or, worse yet,

the civilians, or, worst of all, the way the Russians handled their
millions of injured, which was little better than the treatment
American soldiers received in the Civil War.

There were spots where the beach was still hot, or not yet
cleared of mines, so it was cautious going. Moving about a mile
to the west I found most of the rest of my battalion and led
them up the escarpment to the vicinity of Cabourg, southeast of
Colleville-sur-Mer and into position to support the 3d battalion
of the 16th Infantry. The mission of the 16th was to expand the
beachhead eastward and link up with the British. I then moved
the men I had rounded up on D day up to the coastal road to
hook them up with the rest of the battalion. I came close to
buying it during this move. The road had been cleared earlier,
but some Germans had pushed back in. I was in the lead in my
jeep when suddenly we ran smack into the Krauts. This was a
narrow coastal road in Normandy, flanked by hedgerows yet, in
seconds, my driver pulled a one-eighty. How the hell he did it
was beyond me. I sometimes think that like superman he must
have jumped out, picked that jeep up, and turned it around then
got back into his G.I. uniform, jumped back in, and drove off.
However he did it, we were facing the other way, with the pedal
to the metal, bullets zipping around our ears. The sight of the
rest of my men and M-7s close behind, and eager for a fight,
cleared the road, and we finally hooked up, reuniting my entire
battalion.

One final pickup that day was my battalion's air corps. Armored artillery battalions had two spotter planes assigned to provide forward observation. Every one of those pilots was a hero,
and also half insane. In many cases it was simply a matter of a
call going out for a couple of volunteers. They'd be given a few
hours of dual instruction and solo flight, and then they were on
their own, with an observer on board. Their planes were nothing
more than the basic 1940 Piper Cub, a beautiful little airplane
without an ounce of armor or any weapon, though a few of the
more venturesome pilots would sometimes tote along a few hand

grenades and a Thompson machine gun. At best the Piper could do maybe eighty miles an hour. It was a sitting duck, unless the pilot literally flew nap of the earth. Its one defense if pounced on by an ME-109 was to dodge around trees. During the war more than one Piper pilot tried to claim that he had downed a German fighter as the enemy pilot literally flew right into a telephone pole or the side of a hill while in pursuit.

Our two planes came in loaded in shipping crates. Here was another irony of war, for the shipping crate was more valuable than the plane. It was the size of a small trailer, and, intact, made a great temporary house or headquarters. Both of the planes, however, were damaged as they were off-loaded. As was typical of the army of that era, this didn't daunt my air unit in the slightest. The two pilots and two mechanics sorted all the pieces out, took a wing from one, part of the fuselage from the other, and cobbled together a plane that would fly.

In a couple of days, amidst all that chaos, I had my air force aloft, dodging in and out around the hedgerows looking for targets. The other pilot thumbed a ride back to England aboard an empty ship, went straight to the nearest air field, found a Piper Cub, possibly signed for it or, more likely, simply flew away with one loaded with enough gas to make it back to the front. Throughout most of the war the Army Air Force insisted that these men were not real pilots and therefore were not qualified to wear wings on their uniforms. My pilots racked up thousands of hours of air time and could have outflown any Mustang or ME-262 pilot in Europe.

When I reported in to division headquarters, my concern for how my battalion would be handled started to be realized. From my experience in North Africa and Sicily I had become convinced that mobile armored artillery had to be employed rapidly and in mass. Keep the battalion together, assign a mission, pile in the fire sharp and heavy, then move on to the next mission. Granted, in Normandy we were confined to a narrow beachhead, barely a mile wide in many places, but there was room for maneuver, if need be right up on to the front line for direct fire support where it was needed.

Division saw things differently. It wanted to divide the battalion, assigning one battery to each of the three regiments for direct support and then employ them essentially like standard towed weaponry, which meant slow and ponderous action. What followed was the first engagement in a running battle I'd have with nearly every unit we were attached to up to the Ardennes.

The Germans had figured this tactic out long ago. They designated certain units as fire brigades, well equipped, and sent them in to a point of crisis or to exploit a breakthrough. Once the mission was finished, the unit would be detailed to another sector, corps, or even an entirely different army. That was how I felt armored artillery should be employed, and it took a long time to find someone who agreed.

For the first few days a division would get its way, with fire missions divided off to different sectors, lacking concentration. Then they would allow us to re-form on battalion level in support of the lead advancing regiment, but still they saw us as identical to standard towed artillery.

I finally reported back to my battalion at just about midnight and managed to get a few more hours of sleep.

Given the nature of the battle raging around us, the next few days, at least for my battalion, were remarkably quiet, and therefore it was rather frustrating for all of us. We were back together as a battalion and actually supporting regiments to the fore. We had several fire missions, with thanks coming back from the infantry we were supporting (because we were right up there with them), but in general we were putting out only a few hundred rounds when I knew I had under my command a unit that could pump out a thousand or more in a half hour if need be.

The rest of my support personnel began to catch up, though it would be a couple of weeks before the last of my battalion finally reported in from England.

We were up close to the front, which was advancing at a snail's

pace, when I had a bit of a row with the division artillery commander. I had pushed my unit to within spitting distance of the
Germans, literally, and he came forward to check up on us.
Where I was, he informed me, went against doctrine; we were
supposed to be a couple of miles to the rear. The rear, I pointed
out, was getting a regular pounding from German counterbattery
fire. I managed to keep us where I felt we should be, but he left
me shaking his head. I never saw him again.

The terrain here was getting difficult in the extreme. Our situation revealed a decided lack of understanding and prior training on the part of the high command.

For nearly a year, commanders had focused all their attention
on the invasion, on D day, on seizing those beaches and getting
up onto the bluffs. After that, well, it seems as if the plan was
simply to "wing it." There was a complete fantasy-dream that
the Brits would seize Caen, on the left flank, by the end of the
first day, and we'd take St. Lo on the right. They were the two
main towns along the coast, and from then we could drive into
the open country beyond.

The barrier was the hedgerows of Normandy. For a thousand
years Norman farmers had laboriously cleared their land of
stones, piling them up around the perimeter of the fields. Dragging stones is hard work, so the tendency was to simply move
them a few yards and stack them up, so the average field was
maybe only thirty to sixty yards across.

Over the centuries shrubs and trees grew around the perimeter,
their roots building up on each other, so that by 1944 each small
field was enclosed in a fortress wall of trees sprouting from moat-
like walls eight to ten feet wide and almost as high. The narrow
farm lanes enlacing the fields seemed almost to run like tunnels
under the canopies, beautiful to behold, but a death trap for any
offensive operations.

The tendency was for units to focus frontally, each regiment
driving straight ahead, with no effort made to take into account
those penetrations made to flank a position. As a result, a few

defenders, armed with MG-42s, a panzerfaust, and a couple dozen grenades, dug in literally under the roots of the trees, could stop a column cold.

Trying to take a field frontally was an act of suicide. No one dared to step out into the open on those fields. If a unit tried to cut around, it found itself in another tunnel-like lane and would be cut apart by interlocking fire.

Wide maneuvers were the answer.

German forward observers had every crossroad, building, and pasture marked and coordinated, and within seconds they could call down a deadly rain of 88s right on cue. It was a damnable nightmare ground for any offensive. We should have pushed forward far more aggressively in the first two to three days, the way the 18th Infantry did, maneuvering at regimental level to the flanks whenever a breakthrough was achieved, catching the Germans before they could regroup and reinforce, cutting off and eliminating any strong points. We did not, and thus we were stalemated for the next month.

In addition, the invasion plan called for our seizing the harbor at Cherbourg intact, with our supplies then arriving through that facility. We took the city after a couple of weeks, but the Germans made such a wreck of the harbor that it wasn't fully functional until after the war was over.

It seems like no one figured out how the hell we were supposed to take these fortresslike fields, to do so quickly, and push on, keeping the Germans off balance.

As quickly as we were flooding troops in on the beaches, the Germans were finally beginning to move up their reserves, and though we had gained a toehold on the continent, the momentum of the advance stalled (except for the 18th Infantry at the center).

The Brits, to our left, made a valiant show, but frankly, with Montgomery in command, they were even slower than we were. Their big armored offensive, Operation Goodwood, was repeatedly delayed and then turned into a total fiasco, one of the worst armored defeats of the war for the Western allies, with over four hundred tanks lost in a day. At best a mile of ground was taken.

On June 11 we were shifted across the front, eight miles, to a position near Balleroy. Next morning we pushed up to ground that we would occupy for nearly a month. To our south was Caumont, a beautiful village, at least before we arrived. The town sat on a rise of ground, a classic Norman town, and we ripped it to shreds.

There were targets everywhere, buildings to blow down, concentrations of troops, and at one point a heavy fire mission to keep the Germans pinned down while a failed assault was pulled back with its wounded.

During the night a lot of German aircraft flew over, and a warning went out to expect an airborne assault. It never materialized, but we definitely got shaken up when a load of butterfly bomblets rained down right into the headquarters area. (These were the World War II equivalent of the dreaded cluster bombs used in Vietnam, but fortunately they were not as effective.) No one was hurt. We all started to crawl out of our foxholes when suddenly the empty container for the bomblets fluttered down and crashed right in our midst. It scared the hell out of everyone. One of those incidents that make your heart stop, but then you have to laugh afterward.

The following morning Caumont was taken by direct assault after my battalion pounded it into rubble. Division artillery was too far back.

I pitied the civilians caught in the middle of this. This was supposed to be the liberation, and all it was bringing was ruin and death. It was heartbreaking to see the French come into our lines, clutching what few possessions they had managed to salvage. Most of the civilians in the area were German-friendly; those who had been pro-Allies having been relocated long before.

A few days after this the Germans launched a heavy counterattack and overran one of my forward observers. Second Lieutenant Hopkins (the grandson of a Civil War hero), manning the position, finally called for us to pour fire down straight on top of him. It was a heroic act. The Germans were driven back and Hopkin's survived, wounded in the knee by a shell fragment.

On the nineteenth the weather closed in. We were quite a few miles away from the beach now, and thus didn't see the direct effect, other than the fact that we were cold, wet, and miserable. On the beach it was chaos. The storm hit without warning, tearing apart the temporary harbors that had cost tens of millions to assemble. For several days the entire beachhead was cut off. Fortunately, enough supplies had been stockpiled to see us through. None of us knew it at the time, but the nineteenth had been the alternate date for the invasion if Ike had decided to postpone from the sixth. If we had gone in on June 19, the invasion would have ended in complete disaster.

Our daily fire missions continued unabated. We had one, on June 20, that, in spite of the weather, continued with such fury that the paint literally peeled off the barrels of the guns, and several men were burned.

The advance, however, was at a standstill.

Finally, on the first day of July, we were relieved of our assignment with the 1st Division and transferred to the 2d Armored Division. I greeted this with mixed feelings. At last we were getting into action with a mobile unit, but once again we were relegated to a role with too many constraints. Our assignment put us under the control of the 406th Field Artillery Group, with another unit like mine, the 78th Armored Field Artillery Battalion, having priority of mission. That meant that fire control went through the 78th, and we simply took orders from them.

It might seem a trivial point now, but at that moment who we answered to and why was damn important. I wanted my unit employed to maximum advantage. It was frustrating as all hell to see our army stalled in this vicious slugging match, fighting thirty yards at a time as we crawled from hedgerow to hedgerow, taking thousands of casualties. Some of our equipment gave us a clear advantage, and in my biased opinion the M-7 was one of those advantages. It was the same as the pilots flying the new Mustangs. They fully understood their primary mission was to guard the bombers, but at the same time they were begging to be cut loose, to be allowed to get down on the deck and tear into the Luftwaffe in free-ranging missions.

I'll not go into the particulars, but some of the commanders of units like mine understood this fully. They knew that our best mission was to be up close, on the front line, pouring in a terrifying bombardment at the point of contact, in direct support of troops and armor pushing through. Too many, however, still saw themselves as traditional support, with carefully laid fire missions: Get the range with the usual three or four shots, then fire for effect, all of this taking precious minutes that allowed the enemy to get the hell out of the way of our incoming mail.

We shifted over to the front of the 2d and waited. There was, however, an incredible diversion. The 8th Air Force and the British Bomber Command started to lend their tremendous weight to direct tactical support. Groups of B-17s and B-24s began to appear directly over the front, dumping their loads into the German lines, while swarms of Thunderbolts, Lightnings, and Mustangs weaved back and forth. The German antiaircraft fire was intense, and we sweated it out for our brave comrades in the air as they flew through blizzards of bursting flak, more than one plane getting hit.

At such a moment we all seemed to freeze, knowing that up there buddies of ours were dying, their drama played out not in some hole or tangle of forest, but high above, tens of thousands of us watching. You'd hear men shout, groaning, urging the pilot to get the hell out, to swing over our lines, but more than once the plane would just simply fold up and go down in flames.

The Brits put on one hell of a demonstration when their fleet of Lancasters, the heaviest bombers in the European war, just darkened the sky, the ground rolling beneath our feet as thousands of tons of high explosives cratered the German positions. Yet again, at a moment like that, I'd wonder just why the Germans didn't realize the inevitable and give up, when the sea was blanketed with thousands of ships and the sky overhead was already our domain and from it we could rain down destruction.

Over the next several days we did several fire missions for the 2d Armor, but also for the Brits, their Northumbrian Division going in on our left. There was a sense of satisfaction in that, a bit of a salute to the land of my origin. Their thanks were greatly appreciated.

Finally, on July 8, we were pulled yet again, this time to shift fifteen miles to support the American 2d Infantry Division. A big push was about to go in, preparatory to a direct assault on St. Lo.

The fire mission was a classic, that means, in terms of World War I thinking. I went to headquarters and was briefed on the mission. The largest concentration of artillery yet employed in the war was to be unleashed on Hill 193, a key position overlooking St. Lo. The firing plan must have been a pile of paperwork six inches thick. Each battery was given its targets and timing was synchronized. It was to be a classic creeping barrage, dropping down in pretimed fire, at times less than a hundred yards ahead of the steadily advancing troops.

In a positive sense it was heady stuff, a long way from the days in North Africa, where a concentration of only two or three battalions was considered a major deal; but the negative, it struck me, was that it was ponderous, harking back to the days of fixed trenches and fortresses.

The assault was set to go in at dawn on July 11, 1944. Throughout the tenth we prepared; huge stockpiles of shells were brought up, each round carefully checked for the correct powder loads and then carefully positioned. Our worst fear was that, when we were doing rapid fire with a charge three, a load of charge two would somehow get mixed in. Those rounds would thereby drop into our own lines.

Practice rounds were sent out to register all guns, and all along the front we got ready. Of course, the Germans had it figured out; they'd have had to be blind and deaf not to know that something was afoot. Ours were the tactics of World War I, and our opponents were masters at reading the signs.

Once it got dark on the night of July 10 their probing and harassing attacks began; the night sky was crisscrossed with fire. No one could sleep, and I would have thought that the generals higher up on our side could read the signs as well.

That was yet another thing that was increasingly bothering me. In North Africa it was not unusual to see Patton right up on the front line. Throughout that entire campaign in Normandy, just once did I see a star up in the thick of it. That's just my own observation. Maybe it did happen somewhere else, but I would have certainly loved to see a general at one in the morning of July 11 and so have been able to tell him what things were beginning to look like to me.

The plan was for our forward line of troops to abandon their position during the night and pull back four hundred yards, to ensure a safe zone when the barrage opened up. The infantry followed orders . . . and then the Germans swept forward and jumped into our abandoned lines. It was a smart move at just the right time, and yet again a clear sign they knew what was coming.

The barrage opened at dawn, a stunning sight as hundreds of guns opened up. A virtual blizzard of shells, everything from light mortars to heavy 155s rained down on the German lines . . . except there were no Germans there to receive the present.

Finally, our infantry got up in classic World War I style—the only thing missing was officers waving swagger sticks (something the Brits I was told still did)—and started forward, straight into a wall of German fire coming from our abandoned positions.

I'm proud to say my battalion poured it on with precision and dedication. Though we didn't have any flexibility—our firing mission was locked in by headquarters—we worked with passion, putting out close to five thousand rounds. That comes out to roughly three hundred rounds per gun, each crew laying, loading, and firing three hundred shells averaging forty pounds each.

The concussion blasts were constant, a continual roar of fire not only from our guns, but from all the other batteries, while ahead the sky and land was a cauldron of fire. I think all of us were praying for our comrades going into that inferno.

It was one of the most painful days of the campaign since June 6. We finally took Hill 193, a blasted moonscape, by the end of the day, and the fields were littered with thousands of casualties in an advance that took but twelve hundred yards of ground.

I remember that evening looking out across the wreckage of the battlefield, contemplating all the planning, the cost in steel and blood, all of that to move the front twelve hundred yards . . . and it was still eight hundred miles or more to Berlin. At that moment I felt that even if I did survive all this, I'd be a very old man by the time I got home to Bets.

It was one of the low points of the war for me.

We were taking a steady stream of losses as well. Nowhere near as many as a typical line infantry battalion, but it was starting to add up. The day before the St. Lo offensive one of my men was killed when he picked up a souvenir, I don't remember what, most likely a German pistol or helmet, which was their typical trick. It was booby-trapped and killed him instantly. Between booby traps, mines, shelling, and sniper fire, the numbers came to this: After six months or so the odds were against you, especially if you were a forward observer.

The FO had to truly be in the thick of it, right up there with an infantry platoon on the firing line or circling overhead in one of the Pipers. Amazingly, only one of our Piper crews was lost to enemy fire during the war, but the observers on the ground were another story. We had a couple of Sherman tanks assigned to our battalion, to be used to move observers up into hot zones, but the tanks also drew a hell of a lot of fire.

After the St. Lo attack it was back again to the 2d Armored, and I lost a man (killed) and most of one gun crew (wounded) to a near direct hit from a German 88, which came down right in the middle of A Battery.

On July 15 good news came in. We were being reassigned to VII Corps along with the 2d Armored. The assignment was a tipoff to me that something was brewing. The plan was code-named Operation Cobra and we were going to be committed to the main breakthrough punch.

We shifted over to west of St. Lo along with our comrades of the 2d and got ready. Equipment was checked, updates were even given on inoculations, and ammunition stockpiled. This one was going to be different than the disaster at Hill 193, and I was told that the largest air bombardment of the war would open the drive.

There seemed to be better security on this one, with little German response in the days prior to the kickoff, either that or they were beginning to be stretched to the limit after six weeks of unrelenting fighting. Here was one of our greatest advantages in this fight, our control of the sea and air. Fresh troops, new units, ammunition, rations—all of it was moving in just twenty miles behind us by sea while a continual ferry of priority supplies was coming in by air transport. For the Germans, every man, bullet, shell, and ration had to crawl all the way from Germany, usually moving at night, and suffer constant attacks by our air force. They were starting to play out like an exhausted team going into the fourth quarter while we had a bench full of men waiting to get in.

At the same time word filtered out that Patton was back. I was itching to get back under his command, but my assignment kept me with VII Corps, which was a good unit to be with if you couldn't get into Patton's newly forming Third Army.

Cobra, a massive breakout plan, was to open with a huge air bombardment. That was good thinking, at least on paper, since an air fleet could marshal hundreds of miles away and strike the

Germans without warning, unlike the massive buildup for a major artillery barrage. Infantry would push in first, then the 2d and 3d Armored, with us going in as well, would punch through the hole and drive to the southwest, the beginning of a massive end run and right hook around the German lines. If it worked, it would get us out of the damnable hedgerow country as well.

Weather delayed the strike at least twice, but at last, on the morning of July 25, the air attack commenced. It was beyond anything I had ever imagined possible. Across three hours nearly every combat-capable plane in western Europe came in, starting with medium B-25s and B-26s, followed by the lumbering B-17s and B-24s, while a thousand or more fighters circled around the edge of the action, pouncing on any target of opportunity. The ground rolled from the concussion, smacking through the soles of our feet, pillars of smoke and dirt rising thousands of feet into the air.

It was nearly five years to the day since I had stood at Fort Monmouth, New Jersey, a senior cadet, watching the pathetic show of thirty B-17s attempting to act as targets in a simulated raid on New York City (five years that seemed a million years ago). The sky was carpeted with planes, the thunder of their engines a roar mingled in with the continual pulsing of thousands of tons of high explosives blasting through orchards, hedgerows, villages, and forests, instantly turning square miles of land into smoking twisted ruins. At that moment I actually felt pity for the poor bastards trapped under that hurricane, and, worse yet, the tragic civilians huddled in their basements, waiting for the inevitable.

And then the nightmare began to move toward us.

The plan was for the bombers to come in directly over our lines on a north-to-south run with marker panels showing our forward positions, which were, in fact, pulled back just prior to the start of the strike.

For reasons unknown to us and never clearly explained, the strike came in parallel to our lines, and once the bombs began to hit, the smoke, of course, obscured everything. The pattern started to creep toward us as successive waves came in, drifting north of the German lines and closer to our own.

I stood there, mesmerized by the power, something absolutely beyond any prior experience, perhaps not equaled again until I witnessed the detonation of an atomic weapon four years after the war.

From two miles away it was overwhelming, and then it drifted to a mile, the concussions one continual roar, and then a half mile. It seemed as if we were witnessing the end of the world.

Then, all along our lines, we knew it was going to hit us. If you looked up, through the boiling smoke, you could catch glimpses of the bombs plummeting down, angling closer and closer.

Just forward of me the infantry got up and ran like hell. All along our front, men were scrambling. My guns were dug in, ready to support with a follow-up strike, but there was no way in hell I could maneuver them out in time. All I could do was yell for my men to take cover, a rather stupid order when you think of it, even someone who was deaf, dumb, and blind could still tell that a nightmare was marching toward us.

And then, just a couple of hundred yards short of my position it stopped, though just to my right, bombs fell directly into our main lines, killing and wounding hundreds, including a top-ranking general who had come all the way from Washington to observe the attack.

Two infantry divisions went in as soon as the last planes cleared the primary attack area, while farther back hundreds of fighters and light bombers continued to rip into the German rear and logistical supports. Several square miles of land were a blasted moonscape almost impossible to traverse. Resistance was all but nonexistent; the few Germans who were encountered were out of their heads with shock.

Next day we anxiously waited to go in. The hole so far was little more than a needle prick that we were trying to force an entire corps through, but then, on the morning of the twenty-seventh, the great armored offensive began. The 2d and 3d Armored jumped into the attack.

After advancing only a short distance, we came into the "blasted zone." It was frightful to behold. German tanks and armored vehicles were tossed about and torn to shreds as if a blood-crazed giant had stomped through the land. Fragments of bodies, soldier and civilian, cows and horses, were scattered about, sometimes dangling from the tops of blasted, denuded trees. The intact bodies were sickening, already bloating in the July heat. It was obvious that these men had died in terror. Anyone who thinks there's glory in war should spend a day in such a landscape and look at what is left of an enemy who died under a rain of fire and steel. With that before you, all you want is for the madness to end.

Any semblance of a road was completely gone. An order came down from headquarters that the tanks were to have the priority, meaning that I was to stand aside and most likely get left behind.

I would be damned if that was going to happen. I rousted out a bulldozer and told the operator to cut us a path through the wreckage, and we'd follow. There was no resistance, no fear of booby traps or mines and the driver set to work, my tracked vehicles falling in behind. We cut our way along, weaving around blown-out buildings and forests that were still smoking, across hedgerowed fields, fording streams. It was a mad dash to keep up. Ironically, the one supposedly open road was so damaged and overloaded with vehicles that we actually forged ahead. For me it was becoming a race. I smelled a breakthrough, a way out of the damnable hedgerow country. For all of us, from the young lieutenant colonel of the 62d right down to the newest private, our blood was up, and our sense of pride as well. We were on the move, doing the job we had been trained for. Open country, a place to maneuver and fight the way we wanted to, was directly ahead, and we were going to get there no matter what.

At one point I received a call from division asking what the hell I was doing and how did I get ahead of them. "I'm advancing as ordered, sir, and staying clear of your road" was my reply. And the 62d pushed forward.

The breakout from Normandy had begun.

12

---◦---

Breakout and the Race Across France

There comes a moment in life, in a career, that stands forth above all others. It is that moment when years, perhaps a decade or more, of preparation and training at last come to fruition, when all that you have studied, contemplated, and devoted your life to comes at last into play.

The breakout from Normandy was such a moment for me.

For two years, in America, across North Africa, in Sicily, and in those long months of anticipation in England, I had been preparing for this moment. I had seen long bitter months of action, had seen my two battalions (the 58th and the 62d) employed in battle, sometimes wisely, sometimes with great waste, and long had I wished for this moment, to see theory turned to practice, to use the weapon placed in my hands in the manner that it should be employed.

We were designed for movement, for agility, for speed in a new age of war, and now before us was the chance to prove that. A soldier is like any professional when it comes to pride in his skills and in a desire to see those skills and training used to the utmost. We did not glory in it the way those critics who have never known battle might stereotype us. All of us wanted the killing to end, all of us were sickened by the waste and destruction, but all of us wanted to see our weapons used as they were intended to be used, and thus bring the struggle to a swifter end.

As we broke out of the ring that the Germans had held around Normandy, we moved into broad open landscapes of rolling hills and fertile plains, the terrain ideally suited to mobile warfare.

What none of us would ever forget as well was the sheer power of this army. We, a nation that the dictatorships had proclaimed to be weak, were able to show the hollowness of their lies. The power of America literally shook the earth.

As we crested low hills and looked back, as far as we could see the roads, the fields, were choked with our machines, our men, swarming forward like a relentless tide, a power unmatched in history. The horizon was dark with the dust, the smoke, and exhaust fumes of our tanks, trucks, and jeeps. Overhead the sky was darkened as fleets of aircraft, the heavy B–17s and B–24s, the light and agile B–25s and B–26s, the silvery Mustangs and olive-drab P–47s and P–38s swept by, some to pound the fleeing enemy a few miles away, others going deep into Germany. For the average German soldier, it must have been terrifying. You could see it in the eyes of the survivors who straggled in, the exhausted and wounded whom we passed by the side of the road.

So much for the superman and the thousand-year Reich.

They had started it, and we would finish it.

We broke clean through, cutting almost down to Brittany before shifting our charge from the southwest to due east, aiming straight for Germany, drawing a great circle around the German lines, end-running behind them, hoping to close the noose and bag the lot.

For reasons beyond us, the pocket was never fully closed in what became known as the battle of the Falaise pocket. A significant number of Germans escaped, but those who did were, at that moment, a defeated army on the run. They left behind the wrecked equipment of nearly forty divisions.

The routine I had long envisioned for this rapid charge, covering sometimes up to a hundred miles a day, was now brought into play.

Our ace was mobility and speed of deployment; our specialty was taking out strong points blocking the advance, nailing their artillery before they could hit us, catching targets of opportunity before they could get away.

The marching order I set up was a simple routine, a sort of logic I thought should be easy to grasp and self-evident, though only a few units ever adopted it. As we advanced across France, and especially after crossing the Seine, I refined the plan that we would use till the end of the war.

One of my batteries was always to be in firing position, guns deployed in a diamond pattern to the side of the road, weapons trained toward the primary axis of advance. At first light my battalion air force was up, scouting the intended line of advance for the day, looking both for targets and significant landmarks that could be used for pinpointing. At the point of advance would be my forward observers accompanying a light cavalry recon unit, sometimes in the battalion's Sherman tanks, if the situation was very hot, or in jeeps. Behind them would come the lead battery and I'd usually be rolling with them. Following would be the other batteries along with all the other vehicles, supply trucks, wrecking gear for hauling back a damaged weapon, gasoline, ammunition, rations, the battalion fire-control center, and even the quarter-ton truck dedicated to my air force, which had two panels painted on the roof to mark it so that a pilot could set down alongside it when it needed to refuel.

This procession could take up a couple of miles of road when deployed in battle formation, keeping the required distance between vehicles. Once the battalion batteries had passed the lead battery, which had been deployed into firing position, it would quickly pack up and fall into the rear of the line of march. It was trained to move in a couple of minutes and was expected to do so. Meanwhile, the new lead battery would swing off the road and go into the diamond formation and be ready to deliver a firing mission when needed. The routine would be repeated again after the other three batteries had passed, and so on and so on throughout the day—and if need be throughout the night as well. When we were moving swiftly, the lead battery might be in position for only fifteen or twenty minutes before it was swung back into the line of march.

I wanted firepower available *instantly*. Two minutes, three minutes, after contact was too late, and more often than not, a delay meant someone was dead. If a German unit dared to show itself, if they dared to try and block us, I wanted hell called down upon them in a matter of seconds and poured into them with an unrelenting fury. I wanted to scare the crap out of them in the first seconds of contact, to have them looking up in terror, wondering how the hell did they get zeroed in so damn quick and where was it coming from. If the enemy didn't take the hint, in short order, it wouldn't be a single battery but my entire battalion pouring it in.

If we had contact, the battery in position would open up, providing rapid covering fire. If we were on a road without an overhead canopy, I'd sometimes just stop my battalion right there, have them connect in with the firing battery to get the range and deflection, and they'd fire in turn. That was always an incredible sight, to see a battalion of M-7s suddenly slam to a halt in the middle of the road, gunners leaping to position, orders echoing, gun tubes elevating, the sound of breech blocks opening and slamming shut, and then *wham*, one piece after another opening up, firing up to six rounds a minute while my radio would be crackling with reports from the forward observers. In more than one instance I watched the impacts with my own eyes.

Unless you have seen it with your own eyes, you can have no real conception of what a battalion of M-7s could do to the landscape in a matter of minutes. Fifteen to twenty 105 rounds loaded with high explosives could devastate an acre or more of ground in one salvo, tearing apart trees, collapsing small buildings, kicking plumes of dust and smoke to the heavens. If close enough, the concussive waves would come washing back to you. If the target didn't budge, "fire for effect" would be called in, and then the trees near you would shiver and rustle from the shock wave of the guns going off, the ear-shattering crack of guns filling your world, the smell of cordite pervading everything around you. Even the calmest and best-trained observers would get caught up in the fury at times when the firing was coming in hot and heavy and on target, and the radio would crackle with their reports urging us on, to pour it in. If close enough, we'd see an entire hillside or woods wrapped in smoke and flames, well-timed air bursts slashing down into the ground, standard HE bursting on impact, and then, finally, the order to cease fire would come in.

The old saying about the silence being shattering is true. After a sustained barrage, even of just five minutes' duration, the silence was strange, unreal. For a moment the men would look at each other, nodding, most of them pulling out cigarettes and lighting up. You'd hear the last of distant explosions rumbling away into silence. Strange, I do wonder at times where does all the sound of war eventually go. Are there molecules still subtly vibrating from the salvos I fired nearly sixty years ago?

Soon the order would go out to pick up the march, and again we'd be racing forward, maintaining our position at the head of the column, lead battery deploying out, battery to the rear falling back in, Piper Cubs swooping far forward and circling about, innocent unarmed toy planes that could call down hell, forward observers pushing ahead. At times we'd pass what we had done.

There was no gloating, no glory. A professional judgment, yes, I'll agree to that, wondering who was firing short or long, or noting how tightly bunched our impacts were on the target and passing back to my men a compliment when it was obvious that we had done it right.

What it did, the blood, the dead Germans, the dazed and shell-shocked wounded, the burning trucks, the dead horses, the dead civilians caught in the middle—those things we had to block out or we would have gone mad. The images seeped in nevertheless.

And thus we advanced, day after day, following a column of smoke by day, a pillar of fire by night, like something out of the Bible, moving so hard and relentlessly that across the next two months I don't think I got more than two or three hours' sleep at a stretch and went days without changing or washing, other than a quick shave and scrubbed face and hands.

It was one of the most challenging and memorable events of my life, and again that paradox: though horrible and heartbreak-ing, it was also the most exhilarating and one that I would have not missed even if offered a million dollars. It was a moment that we, the aging veterans of a long ago war, will carry in our memory with pride till our dying day.

This rapid advance against a totally routed enemy did not un-fold all at once. Though we were breaking out of the Normandy pocket in those last days of July 1944, the initial thrust was a tough, bitter fight. A moment early into the breakout stands clear in memory. We were advancing in column along a road when a startled observer called in a warning, that a German battery ap-peared to be on a parallel road less than a mile away. I ordered my driver to pull over, got out of my jeep, and went up to the top of the low berm that flanked the road. I trained my binoc-ulars on where my FO was calling in, caught a glimpse of the Germans, and then the impacts hit, at least one shell, maybe two or three, striking the berm directly in front of me. If the incom-ing had been a couple of feet higher, it would have cut me in half.

The detonations howled past me like a hurricane. All that saved me was that I was literally at the point of impact and the blast expanded outward. Anyone standing a couple of feet to either side of me would have been shredded.

One of my sergeants to this day recalls seeing me a couple of minutes later and still laughs at how white I was and still in shock. Human nature is fascinating, how we so quickly laugh about such a moment, which if it had played out ever so slightly differently, would have been a tragedy to haunt our friends for the rest of their lives.

The moment was a classic example of what happens to "he who fires second." The Krauts had the moment; they were deployed and fired first, and it instantly developed into a hell of a brawl at near point-blank range—until they broke and ran. Though they had the advantage of the first shot, our firepower was overwhelming and shattered them.

I think too many picture the breakout as the beginning of the "picnic," that it was easy rolling from there right up to Market-Garden in September.

It wasn't.

Though beaten strategically and operationally, the Germans still had a punch in them. When cornered, they fought viciously because they were retreating, and scared, and just wanted to get the hell out of the trap and God save anyone who got in their way.

We had one very bad twenty-four hours at the very start of the breakout when our rapid advance literally plowed us into a retreating German column. It was so well concealed that we didn't know about them until they suddenly started popping up on all sides. We were caught in the middle of a tidal wave of Krauts trying to get out of the pocket, we were swinging around them. At that moment it was a question of who had who.

It turned into one of the ugliest fights of the war for me. Our infantry support was nowhere to be found. It was cut off from the rest of us, other than some panic-stricken men who came running back into the bastion position I was frantically setting up. Another officer and I literally were knocking these men down with our bare hands and dragging them in, yelling at them to grab a weapon and get back into the fight.

As the fight opened up, I pulled my battalion off the road and into formation. Across the road and a quarter mile or more away was one of our infantry units digging in as well.

Yet again one of the smart design points of the M-7 came into play—the pulpit with the .50 machine gun. Hundreds of Germans were swarming around us. Air support was out of the question. We'd have been nailed as well, so it was fight it out on our own.

We had Germans coming in from every direction, and if they had been better coordinated and had had heavier weapons, they might have had us. The Germans were in so close there were points where we couldn't even use our artillery. Every man, from cook to truck driver up to the battalion CO, had gun in hand as I circled the battalion in, like we were a wagon train in an old Western about to be overrun by the Indians. At places it was a grenade-pitching fight. Though my men were trained as artillerymen and not assault infantry, they fought with skill and courage and didn't give an inch.

At one point the fight simmered down. I heard movement on the road and thought it might be some of our armor coming up to support us. I headed down to the road to flag them down. How I mistook the sound is beyond me, perhaps my hearing was already going bad by that point because any vet will tell you that a German tank has a distinctive grinding metallic sound unlike our Shermans.

So there I was crouched by the side of the road, waiting for a relief force to arrive, when around the bend I saw them— German tanks, and coming on fast. The field behind me was open; if I had bolted, they would have gunned me down. They had yet to spot me crouched down by the side of the road. So I played dead, slipping into the drainage ditch and sprawling out. The tanks screamed by, only feet away from me, the ground shaking. Fortunately, no one aboard decided to take a potshot at me just to make sure I was dead, nor did they notice my rank and decide to check my body.

For that matter, if the Germans had spotted my guns at such a short range, the tanks could have taken them apart. We were capable of taking on German armor when they were a half mile or more out, plastering them with "willie pete." White phosphorus was a ghastly weapon that I would have refused to use in a concentrated barrage on infantry if ordered to do so, but it was deadly against tanks. If you burst a round near them, the burning phosphorus was sucked into the engine, triggering a fire.

No one back with the battalion decided to venture a fight with the retreating tanks, which I was damn glad of as I slipped back into the perimeter, the German armor disappearing down a canopied lane.

The battle continued through the night.

We nailed somewhere around a hundred enemy vehicles, tanks, trucks, towed artillery pieces and killed, wounded, or captured hundreds of Germans from a wide assortment of enemy units that were all mingled together.

I lost three drivers in the fight, one of them lasting in his assignment not much more than fifteen minutes before a sniper took him out when he crawled under a vehicle to get a few minutes' sleep—from which he never awoke. The look on my newly assigned fourth driver's face when he got called over and was told to get in the jeep said everything. He manfully did his job, but clearly he thought it was his last day.

Come dawn, we had over a hundred Germans down on the ground inside our perimeter and under guard as prisoners. That is another point of pride for me. We fought all our fights with a sense of honor. If a man surrendered, he was a prisoner, and was treated as such. I have been disturbed by recent films that portray American GIs of World War II as dispatching surrendering enemy soldiers as if they themselves had become like the SS. Maybe it did happen in other units. I did witness a moment like that in the heat of battle in North Africa, when some of our GIs began to shoot surrendering Germans, but it never happened in my unit.

The slugging match continued into the morning of July 31, when a relief column finally came up and we reestablished contact with the rest of the army.

We were pulled from the advance for a day for maintenance and resupply, and then we resumed the march on August 2, with Combat Command B in support of the 2d Armored Division. The next week was a frustrating one. First we advanced in one direction and then in the other. Priority to the few good roads in the region was given to armor and then to infantry. Yet again high command did not see us as an integral part of this attack. In response, I ordered up another bulldozer, and it simply plowed us a road through the fields and hills. I'd be damned if we were going to be left behind.

The German pocket continued to collapse as we cut around to their south and then drove east. At the start of the second week of our breakthrough, we were assigned to the Barentan-Domfront sector in an effort to seal off the route of retreat of the German Seventh Army, which was moving hell-bent toward Germany, with us cutting north to stop them.

A vicious fight ensued for several days, part of the greater battle of the Falaise pocket. To our chagrin the Germans managed to shoulder their way through, while we provided intense fire support as our infantry attempted to seize the town of Ger.

I went up to the front with one of my FOs to check with the infantry we were supporting. Mission accomplished, we started back to our jeep, parked a mile to the rear, and ran smack into some German tanks that had cut into our lines. They opened up with my FO and I out there naked, no cover in sight in that broad open pasture. We ran like two football players gone berserk, zigzagging like crazy, the 88 shells zipping across the field. At least the tanks didn't start chasing us, they'd learned not to go wandering out into the middle of open fields, and thank God for that, for we'd have been crushed like bugs. I actually wondered if those Germans were playing with us, or trading bets on who could hit us. We must have run three miles total to get the one mile back. Our driver, being sensible, had simply hunkered down with the jeep, which was parked in a lane out of sight. Not a word was said as we piled in. He threw the jeep into reverse and got us the hell out of there. I think it was a half hour or more before I finally stopped shaking and caught my breath.

Behind us the Third Army raced eastward in its brilliant charge, led by George Patton, in a vast end run across the length of France. (A football analogy is best here; we were the blockers who allowed the running back to break around the flank and into a clear field.) Across all these years I wish we had been with Patton. There was a sense of frustration that, though we were moving, we were not moving fast enough. George knew the way. I am still convinced, sixty years later, that if he had been given carte blanche, or better yet, if he had been in command, we would have been on the banks of the Rhine by the end of September, and perhaps at the gates of Berlin before winter, with the ghastly waste and destruction of 1945, and all the long twilight years afterward, avoided.

Here again is another paradox of war, that relentless aggressiveness can, in many cases, actually avert tragic waste and losses by overwhelming an enemy before he has time to regroup and continue the struggle. By striking hard, one ultimately avoids the terrible cost that timid souls too often create.

On August 18 we were pulled from the field for seven days, relieved of our attachment to the 2d Armored for a much needed refit and overhaul, the first true top-to-bottom check since the landing.

Every gun, truck, tank, and plane was taken apart and rebuilt, and the men were allowed a few days' rest after two months of nearly continuous combat. For the first time since June 6 we slept beyond the range of gunfire.

We also got to see Dinah Shore perform. She was obviously sick as hell. The weather was crummy and she barely had the strength to sit under cover in the back of a truck, but she still kept on performing for her boys in uniform even though it was pouring rain. She was remarkable. We all knew she was putting every ounce of strength into trying to give us a few minutes' respite and the affection we felt for her was a tonic that lifted all our spirits. My men were telling her to stand down and get some rest, but she kept insisting on doing "just one more for you guys."

After the show, I ordered her into the hands of my battalion surgeon. He checked her over, she had a raging fever, and got some pills into her. After she left my "doc" grinned and thanked me, saying it was a real morale boost to have given that physical. After months in the field, dealing with death, wounds, and GIs who stank, I can forgive his slight lapse of "professionalism."

Finally, after a week, we were given the order to head back up to the front lines, which had swept eastward. Word came back that Paris had fallen and the Seine breached. Long afterward I'd find out that my old M-7s with the 58th, which had been transferred to a French unit after Sicily, were some of the first weapons into the city, advancing down the Champs Elysées. If machines have souls, those M-7s truly deserved the reception given to them in that parade.

We pushed back up toward the front. This time we were briefly attached to the 30th Infantry Division, and within a day we were back in action, supporting the infantry as they pushed out of the Mantes Gascor front. The following day we were transferred again, the interesting fate of a fire brigade unit, and reassigned back to our old friends, the 2d Armored, now northeast of the Seine.

We raced eastward in a wild advance, leaping over the Seine. Our mission was to drive all the way to the Belgian border.

Here was mobility at its best, a combat command unit, a temporary, composite organization of armor, tank destroyers, mobile assault infantry, recon, and us. Often we simply roared cross-country, staying off the roads that the heavier tanks and the less mobile supply vehicles needed as we relentlessly drove the Germans back toward their homeland.

Hitting the Somme River, the tragic scene of the bloodiest battles of World War I, we were briefly delayed while bridging the river. The engineers threw a bridge across, and at dusk we drove forward, in the rain, advancing another ten miles into the northeast of France, tearing over ground where hundreds of thousands had died thirty years before, the evidence of their struggle still visible in a landscape littered with shell holes, collapsed trenches, and fields still marked off as minefields. And cemeteries. It is a minor point but one worth remembering: Throughout the four years of German occupation the cemeteries of French, British, and American dead on that field were treated with respect by the German conquerors. The German high command, in spite of their Nazi masters, still adhered to some of the conventions as a matter of honor.

It was during this stage of the advance that I took more direct control of my lilliputian air force. Division had insisted that my planes operate out of a division airfield, which at times was dozens of miles behind the line. It was here that I finally put into place the system of keeping a supply vehicle loaded with aviation gas, oil, and spare parts with my battalion command. The pilot simply put the plane down in the closest field nearby, and the second plane went up to take his place.

We were rapidly pushing toward the Belgian border when the great vexation of modern warfare finally hit us . . . gasoline.

We'd run hundreds of miles from Normandy over the previous month, and every bullet, shell, ration, and gallon of gas had to come up from the beachhead. Though Cherbourg had been taken, it was useless and would remain so until after the war. We had laid a gas pipeline across the Channel, but it was not large enough to keep a modern fighting machine of millions of men and hundreds of thousands of vehicles moving rapidly.

Here again, I agree with Patton.

The precious gas should have been diverted to the Third Army, and that spearhead kept moving; instead, Ike insisted on advancing on a broad front. Though we did not know it then, plans were already afoot for Market-Garden, the attempt to make an airborne assault across Holland to the Rhine and beyond, and thus Montgomery was already getting more than his share of the precious fuel in preparation for that offensive.

We were within spitting distance of the Belgian frontier when the fuel tanks ran dry. Reluctantly, I doled out the last of my reserves to an antiaircraft battery in the line of march with us, and on September 2 we all ran dry near Cambrai, France, another battlefield of World War I. It was maddening, for the Germans were on the run. We watched, frustrated, as they simply pulled away. Crippled as they were, they still had some fuel, and we had none. A wounded prey would now get a chance to reform, refit, and dig in. We all knew that the handful of casualties we were suffering each day would soon be hundreds if the Germans were allowed to catch a second wind.

Thus we sat for several days. Some British soldiers stopped by for a visit, many of them vets who had crossed that ground in the retreat of 1940. Finally, we were refueled and crossed into Belgium.

In three months we'd engaged in hundreds of fire missions, destroyed hundreds of enemy vehicles, and inflicted thousands of casualties in one of the greatest feats of arms in American history. I was proud of the 62d Armored Artillery Battalion beyond my ability ever to express it.

The battle for France was over. The battle for Belgium, Holland, and Luxembourg was about to begin.

13

Stalled

In the second week of September we cut across southeastern Belgium and pushed toward the narrow finger of Holland that extends down along the border of Germany.

I have to make a personal observation here that I know some vets will fully agree with and others will question. I guess it is simply a matter of where you were on the front lines.

As we raced across France the reception by the civilian populace had varied, and in some cases it was downright chilly. Part of it might have been the nature of the fight and the German retreat. We encountered one ghastly incident coming into a town on the heels of the retreating Germans. There, in the village square, we found dozens of dead civilians, shot only minutes before. The survivors of the massacre told us that a retreating unit of Krauts simply machine-gunned the town as they drove through, and then announced that it was their way of saying farewell. Incidents like that forced ever more strongly upon us the reason we were fighting.

As we crossed into Belgium, however, the attitude of the civilians changed to outright celebration, and when we finally reached Holland it was a genuine frenzy.

During this advance I somehow wound up in the middle of

a tank battle. I was riding in my jeep at the forward edge of our column. An open field was before us, and I told my driver to keep on going. Next thing I knew I was ahead of everyone else, literally the point man of the advance. Behind me was a company of Sherman tanks, and there, on the other side of the field, were German tanks. I remember them as Mark V Panthers.

All hell broke loose, the Panthers and Shermans trading shots, with me out in the middle of that field, like one of those tin ducks going back and forth in a shooting gallery. I think the Germans were hunting for bigger game, keeping their aim on the Shermans, but still, every armor-piercing bolt, ours and theirs, was tearing across that field. We started to zigzag frantically. When an 88 zips past you only a few feet away, you know you've had a close encounter of the worst kind. It tears the air. You feel the turbulence, and right after the shell passes, that strange crack of something going past you at supersonic speed is followed an instant later by the report of the gun going off. If the shell passes close enough, it can knock you over, and many claim the shock wave alone can kill you.

We cut across that field like frightened rabbits, gunning the jeep one way, then the other, trying to stay out of the sights of the Germans and of our own tanks as well. A tank gunner only has limited forward vision, and if we popped into view at the last second, just as our side was firing . . . well, getting killed is the same, whether it's by one of ours or by one of theirs.

We sprinted back out of that field. The entire incident must have lasted only a minute or two, but it definitely took a couple of years off my life, one of those moments when your knees are jelly afterward and you have that stupid sort of grin on your face that conceals the fact that you are shaking inside.

When we got back to my battalion, the story got spread around by my driver, and it gave the men a good laugh.

There are two incidents of that advance into Holland I will never forget.

Just as we reached the border and crossed into the narrow strip of Holland, pushing toward the Albert Canal, our column halted before a house. I saw a flutter of a curtain in a home facing the street, a wizened old lady peeking out at us. The curtain was drawn back down and then, a minute later, the door opened and she came tottering out, approaching me. Without saying a word she opened her hand. She was holding an egg, which she pressed into my hand. She patted me the way old ladies do, and then without a word went back into her house.

I was stunned. That simple gesture spoke volumes. In a country stripped of all its food by the retreating Germans, that egg was a gift worth millions. She has lingered in my thoughts for sixty years.

The second incident was far more traumatic and revealing of all that we were fighting against.

We had crossed into Holland around the tenth of September. We faced sporadic resistance, the countryside flat, open, dotted with small towns and villages, some of which were burning, plumes of smoke rising in the distance.

We were at the forward edge of the advance. A long sinuous column of troops, tanks, vehicles stretched behind us to the horizon.

Our column stopped for a moment, the forward recon units ahead of us probing. On the road beside us was a small home, typical of the Dutch, well organized and neat.

The front door cracked open, a middle-aged man looking out at us, wide-eyed. Hesitantly he came out and approached me.

"Are you Americans?" he asked nervously.

Smiling, I nodded.

"Are you here to stay?"

Proudly I pointed back behind me. "The entire American Army is coming this way. We're here to stay."

Tears were in his eyes as he turned and ran back to the house. I didn't take any further notice of him as we waited for orders to press forward, my men taking a break for a few minutes, wolfing down some K rations, or grabbing a quick smoke.

The door to the house opened again and the man and his wife stood there, gathered around them several gaunt children and another couple, who were pale, almost ghostly white. It was obvious they were frightened as the Dutch couple gently led them out into the sunlight. The youngest child was maybe three or four years old and she looked up at the sky in wonder.

All of us fell silent, looking at them, the Dutch couple approaching me, leading their companions. I had a gut sense of what I was witnessing but it still wasn't sinking in.

The pale, fragile-looking children clung to their parents, and the Dutchman approached me again.

He looked back at his frightened friends.

"They're Jews," he said. "We've been hiding them in our attic since 1940."

As my comrades and I looked at those frightened children, the youngest obviously standing beneath the sun and looking at the open sky for the first time, all that we had endured, all that we had been fighting for came into focus.

I think every one of my men saw their own children standing their, their own families caught in this universe of suffering created by a monstrous cult gone mad. Many of my men, hardened as they were, filled up with tears, and then they did something wondrous, something so American, something that I will always believe defined who and what we are as a nation, as a people.

The men around me began to reach into their pockets. Some drew out packs of gum, others money, or K rations, candy, cigarettes that could be used for barter, anything and everything. A pile of offerings were laid before the sufferers. They stood there, still clutching each other, the parents nodding their thanks, the children gazing at us in confusion, for, after all, were not soldiers someone to fear?

Orders came over the radio to mount up and move forward. My men scrambled back to their vehicles, engines roared to life, the thunder of our might echoing across the open fields. The family stood there, the simple gifts of gum, food, and cigarettes a treasure trove in a world of starvation, their life and freedom a gift we had brought to their doorstep.

We rolled forward, leaving them there. The face of that young child has haunted me ever since, for she is the true face of war and all the brutality it can bring when evil is allowed to flourish. I have often prayed for her across the years, hoping that the trauma of her childhood would be left behind, that she would grow strong and live her life in happiness. She must be sixty years old now, and perhaps she has grandchildren who will never know all that she endured, which I am grateful for as well.

As for the Dutch couple who hid them, I believe there must be a special place in heaven for them, for they were the true heroes of the war. They fought in silence, alone, without glory or fanfare, placing their own lives in mortal peril to save another.

If ever there was a moment when I was proud to be an American, it was there, on that road into Holland. The strength of America was behind me, all the way back to the coast of France, a relentless tide that would not be stopped. Never again did any of us doubt what it was that we were fighting for.

On September 12 we pushed up to the Albert Canal, on the flank of Fort Eben Emael, that great monument to the folly of fixed positions. It was Eben Emael that had fallen to a brilliant glider-borne attack in 1940. The entire region was a giant interlocking area of fortresses and concrete pillboxes. Just to the east was the border with Germany and the Siegfried Line.

First the canal had to be bridged, against intense German resistance, my battalion laying down suppressive fire on the opposite shore.

The combat engineers of our army were men with guts. They had to do a job that in and of itself was dangerous, such as throwing a pontoon bridge across a river or canal with the utmost speed, and the usual routine be damned. To this was added that they were being shot at and the work had to continue regardless of danger or loss. Their efforts never ceased to amaze me.

The canal was bridged, and we raced across. That was an ex-

perience. The pontoon bridges were usually made of twin layers
of corrugated steel, troughs several feet wide and designed to
handle the tread of a tank or the wheels of a deuce-and-a-half.
Supporting the bridge were rubber boats. Driving an M-7 over
such a bridge was always a heart-stopper. You could feel the
bridge sagging beneath you, and the slight touch on the steering
handles would put the M-7 right over the side, destroying the
bridge as well. For effect, add in some harassing fire from
German 88s. My stomach was in a knot as I watched my battalion make the crossing.

We deployed out east of Maastricht and faced the legendary
Siegfried Line. We were a long way from Casablanca and North
Africa, for we were staring at last into Germany.

For years the German propaganda machine had been warning
us of this moment. It was one thing to wipe them out in Tunisia
or in France, but now we were at the front door of their territory, and they would fight to the death to stop us. Rumors
were that every last German would have a gun, a knife, a pitchfork.
We were already seeing evidence of this with their Volksturm units,
scratch combat formations made up of sixteen-year-old boys and
sixty-year-old men, armed with old bolt-action Mausers, grenades,
and an occasional panzerfaust. They were tragic victims but could
kill us even as we took them out.

For the next week the plan of assault developed, while at the
same time, to the north, the debacle of Operation Market-
Garden unfolded. I've always felt it was a mad scheme, a situation
of the tail wagging the dog. A full airborne corps was loitering
in England, having been out of the fight since Normandy. They
wanted a mission and finally got one after more than a dozen
cancellations due to either our rapid advance or the weather. The
plan was to lay an airborne carpet across fifty miles of Holland,
seizing three key bridges and dozens of minor ones, the last
bridge at Arnhem taking us across the Rhine. The logistical support involved was astronomical. The fatal flaws, as pointed out by
so many others, were that, it was all pegged to one road—and

to the assumption that the Germans were all but beaten.

I was required to detail off a couple of my FO's to this offensive in anticipation of a breakthrough that might result in our being reassigned. Their training was straightforward and finished within minutes. They were put into the back of a deuce-and-a-half, which drove across a field at ten miles an hour, and then told to jump off the back and roll. They did that several times and were checked-off as certified to jump. They went in with the airborne, and when they finally reported back to me weeks later, they swore up and down that they'd rather do another Omaha than go through another jump.

It was at this time, while preparing to push from Holland into Germany, that a moment came in my life that across all the years I've tried to push aside, one that I've spoken of only to a few. Even the thought of writing of it now produced an intense inner debate. Perhaps it's because there must be others out there who have endured it, and never spoke about it afterward, that I'm writing about it now.

I lost my nerve.

In World War I they called it shell shock, trying to logic it away with the belief that the actual concussion of a near miss did you in. Later generations called it "combat fatigue" or "post-traumatic stress disorder." I don't care what others have called it; for me it was a full-blown case of the jitters and an inward sense that I had turned coward.

It came on without warning.

I just awoke somewhere in Holland—I'm not even sure where anymore—and I was in its clutches. I was petrified that that day would be the day I got hit. Death itself wasn't too terrifying anymore, not after all that I had seen, but the process of dying, that was the terror, for I had seen more than one man die in terrible agony.

There was all the rest as well that suddenly piled into me. The endless decisions, each fraught with the prospect that my choice might send a man to his death, or far worse, that my mistake might kill someone.

Everyone seemed to want something out of me. All those below were looking for orders, for advice, for leadership, while those above demanded results and too often expected the impossible, or, worse yet, made decisions that I knew would needlessly kill men on our side.

Then there was the endless destruction. It sickens you and eventually leaves you numb, because if you don't go numb, you go mad, and yet each new day brought with it an unrelenting sameness of brutality.

Finally, there was simple physical exhaustion. Since the invasion I could not recall a single night of unbroken sleep. True unbroken sleep, eight to ten hours of sweet oblivion, was made even more poignant because in those rare moments when I could get an hour or two, I did so alone. My beloved Bets was four thousand miles away.

I remember reading once about how, in war, it is ultimately the memory of the simplest things that drives a man mad, a walk with a wife on an autumn day, the smell of bacon and eggs in the morning, in a world at peace.

And so I awoke one morning, somewhere in Holland, and I had cracked. I felt paralyzed. The sheer effort of getting out of my sleeping bag was almost more than I could manage. I just wanted to crawl into a hole and hide.

And yet I was "the old man," the battalion CO, the twenty-nine-year-old colonel that over five hundred men turned to.

That made it worse. If I had been a private or even a second lieutenant, I might very well have gone all the way over, just broken down, shaking, crying, and waiting then for an ambulance to take me to the rear.

You will recall that I showed no sympathy for the private that George Patton slapped in Sicily. I still don't. The difference here was simply one of time, the difference of two or three days in combat versus four months, and then four months more preceding that in Sicily and North Africa. I offer that not as an excuse, but merely as a way to try and explain it all, especially to myself. I guess that after eight months of warfare, I was used up. The problem was, I couldn't admit it. Yet how was I to continue to function, feeling as I did?

I recall the next few days vaguely. If anything, I was simply an actor at this point. I got into my jeep, nodded, stared straight ahead, and hoped that no one looked too closely at me. All the time my stomach was knotting up, waiting for the blow to hit. Inside, I was shaking like a scared rabbit.

I wonder now just how many of us were actors out there, how many were terrified to the point of numbness and yet somehow continued to function. I don't think I did function those four days, though across the years no one in my unit ever spoke a word to me about it. I wonder even now if some of the men knew, but have yet to speak of it and thus my discomfort, even now, with writing about it.

At night, in the few minutes when everyone thought I was asleep, I was lost in my own terror.

So it went for four horrible days, some of the worst of my life. I thank God that we did not face any major actions then, just routine movement and maneuver, the firing missions easy ones that my subordinates could handle while I went through the motions. I knew, though, that the charade could not last much longer, that soon they'd start whispering that "there's something wrong with the old man."

Then it hit. I was wounded.

I was in my jeep after a meeting at corps headquarters, my driver taking us down a narrow street in a Dutch village, typical of the area, with houses side by side, the street itself just wide enough for two medieval wagons to pass.

I was sitting there, numb to all the world. My driver had survived with me ever since that breakout fight back in France. Suddenly he slammed on the brakes.

"Plane!"

I looked up, and the analogy of the rabbit was a fitting one . . . a rabbit with a hawk swooping in for the kill. Coming in was a German plane, and it was obvious we were his prey. I was looking straight up at a head-on silhouette, not the slightest deviation to one side or the other. He was coming straight at me. I just sat there, unable to react. I don't remember much of the moment now, whether or not I assumed "This is it." My driver was out of the jeep, around to my side of the vehicle—how the hell he did it so fast I'll never know—I fell out of the jeep alongside him, slamming up against a doorway. The German plane let go a small bomb that blew against a nearby building, pulled out of his dive, and was gone.

I was alive. A small fragment had torn through my wrist, near the small spot where I'd been hit on Omaha. That was it.

I was alive.

And then the doorway we'd been huddled in opened, a Dutch civilian peeking out at us and the destruction.

"Get in here," he hissed.

We followed him and he quickly pulled open a trapdoor down into the basement of his shop. We followed him down and in the gloom we saw his family, and a crowd of neighbors looking at us wide-eyed.

Then something wondrous happened. We were Americans, the liberators, and they gathered round the two of us. One of the women saw that I was hurt, blood dripping from my hand, and she scurried up the ladder, coming down a moment latter with antiseptic and bandages. She set to work on me like a mother over a boy with a scrape. Her loving attention struck straight into my heart, nearly moving me to tears. They peppered us with questions, how was the war going, where were the Germans, was a safe to go outside now.

It was balm upon my soul, a reaffirming of why I was there, of what we were fighting for, and the fear fell away, the motherly touch as reassuring as if my own mother were there before me.

Surviving the hit, falling in with that family . . . well, it saved me and as I walked out of their humble shop and dwelling I did so with a sense that I had reconnected to all that I had been before. It was, as the psychologists say, a catharsis, a reemerging out of the darkness of hell into the light.

Yes, I would continue to be haunted, I still am haunted sixty years later, but never again did the nightmares gain mastery over my soul. I had a job to do and defending that wonderful family, my family, gave me the strength to continue.

The terror, the self-prophecy of death had been met, the dark angel had lightly tapped me on the wrist and moved on, its schedule filled with others that day.

As I stepped back out I looked at my jeep. The vehicle was shredded. Bomb fragments had turned every piece of sheet metal, the seat where I'd been sitting seconds before, everything, into a sieve. All four tires and the rear-mounted spare were flat, and yet, miraculously, the engine still turned over, and the radiator was intact.

That jeep became a source of wonder and admiration. Someone called back to the rear and ordered up five replacement tires. They were mounted, and in a couple of hours I was rolling again.

It was a strange, euphoric moment as I rolled along in my sieve. I'll admit there was almost a boyish desire to show it off. As we rode along, I could see GIs checking it out. More than one shouted, "Hey, what the hell happened to you?"

That as well was my therapy. That was how I somehow got cured of my shakes, my thousand-yard stare.

I guess, too, that inside there came a cold realization: either I had to break completely and be taken away, or I had to find a way out of it and continue with my job. The near miss, the wound, the Dutch family, all allowed that inner voice to say to me, "You got hit. You lived. Now you're safe again for a while."

Courage is not boundless, like the ocean; rather it is a well, and if drawn upon too often, it goes dry—in all men. I was fortunate that I found a way to put a little water back into that well, and thus I could keep on going. More than one of my friends could not. Only those who have been through what they went through can truly understand it.

The German propaganda machine had been pumping up the image of the Siegfried Line into a behemoth that would stop us cold and, frankly, at first look, from a distance through field glasses it did look foreboding.

There were the standard rows of dragon's teeth and barbed wire out front to stop any tank or infantry assaults, and well dug in were numerous pillboxes, along with heavy bunkers concealed in the woods and inside buildings. All of the positions offered what is called "interlocking fields of fire," meaning that each protected the other, and even if several were knocked out, positions to either flank still blocked the way.

But it was a damn sight different than Omaha. The ground was flat, we had plenty of time to do a close-up look, we had four tough months of experience, and momentum was on our side.

The firing plan was well thought out and aggressive, based on experience. Every pillbox was marked out, ranging shots laid in, and then during the night we moved our batteries up to within a quarter mile of the line. With us were antiaircraft batteries, direct fire support from armor, and air cover.

At first light we plowed into them. We tried some direct fire from my M-7s but the shots simply bounced off. Here is where the antiaircraft batteries came in, quad-mounted .50 caliber guns. They zeroed in on the pillboxes, pouring a steady stream of fire straight into the embrasures of the pillboxes, while armor plastered them with armor-piercing rounds.

We knew the German counterresponse as well, and before fifteen minutes were out, we jumped positions to avoid their counterbattery fire. Here again is where speed in artillery is such a crucial factor. We had them figured out by this point, and how long it would take for FO's to call in, range to be set, and fire sent out. With the M-7s and mounted quad-fifties we kept shifting on that flat open ground.

It was a firepower display unimaginable to me only a year or two earlier. It might take time to dig them out but ultimately the Germans in those pillboxes didn't stand a chance.

Thus it went for over a week. The pillboxes were well constructed. We counted thirty direct hits from our battalion on just one box with us darn near sighting down the barrel at ranges of less than a mile, which for a 105 howitzer is nearly point-blank range. At least half of our shells simply bounced off, just gouging a shallow chip into the reinforced concrete.

Gradually though, we started to peel them open with a combination of our suppressive fire, direct fire from the flak guns into the pillbox firing ports, air strikes, and direct fire from tanks.

As we started to crack them open, my air observers kept a careful watch for the German crews bailing out and heading to the rear. It might seem hard today, but this was war. As soon as they started to run, my airborne observers called in the coordinates and we laid down a curtain of fire that cut them apart.

The assault troops went in next, dismounting from their vehicles just short of the dragon's teeth and pushing in, advancing under our curtain of fire.

Once a piece of ground was secured the combat engineers came in, blowing lanes through the dragon's teeth and the minefields, while we continued to hammer the secondary line, sending the Germans fleeing.

The battle was a tough-fought affair for over a week. We were in direct support of the 30th Infantry Division. The Germans fought back with tenacity, a marked change from the rout of only weeks earlier, a direct result of their having some breathing space when we ran out of gas at the start of September.

A number of counterattacks were launched, sometimes with tanks in support. We poured out a curtain of fire on them, with prisoners reporting casualties of up to 50 percent just from artillery. A grim harvest, but far better that than our infantry having to deal with them instead.

Gradually we slugged our way into Germany, yard by yard, crossing the Wurm River on October 2, 1944 and advancing just under half a mile. We were just north of Palenburg and on the following morning threw back a concentrated German counter-attack and then had a day-long slugging match pushing back or destroying their infantry, mortars, and artillery. Our infantry seized the town.

It was during this time as well that I lost my experienced pilots through tragedy and asinine army bureaucracy. I received orders that the army had decided in its infinite wisdom that my two pilots were not qualified to fly, this after each of them had logged well over two thousand hours of air time, a good bit of it under fire, dodging small arms, antiaircraft, and even some fighters, while all the time providing absolutely top-notch spotting.

I had gone up with them once and that was enough for my blood as my pilot wrung out every ounce of performance, most likely with the secret intent of getting "the old man," to throw up. We dodged around trees, flew under power lines, and I finally wound up just closing my eyes and hanging on. He wasn't just showing off though, his split-second timing kept us alive as we droned over the German lines at eighty miles per hour.

That skill wasn't good enough for the paper pushers; my two pilots were detailed to report stateside to be properly trained as pilots. On the one hand I was personally delighted for these two men, they had served with valor and if anyone needed a break they did. Yet, as the commander of a battalion in action, I was furious, because I was losing two of the best members of my team, with two replacements coming in who I now had to break in.

The following day, flying what was to be one of his last mis-sions, one of my pilots was shot down and killed along with his observer. Some men think that there's a jinx about getting good news, that the gods of battle will play with a man just before slaying him. Or it's simply that a man's edge is off, he's either a little too cautious, or a little too reckless and makes that decision to turn, to duck, or to hit the ground a split second too late. Right at the end of the war I lost a man who foolishly stepped out into an open field to cut across, rather than keep to the woods and walk around it. A sniper nailed him halfway across. The war was all but over and his combat instinct disconnected for a few fatal seconds.

My other pilot survived and was shipped back stateside for "training." Fortunately his instructors knew the game, and that this supposedly untrained pilot had more combat experience than every instructor and student at the base combined. In fact, they turned him into an instructor even as he went through the motions. He was finally awarded his wings and thus officially allowed to risk his life in combat.

On October 7 we were reassigned yet again, pulled from the 30th Infantry and back with our old comrades, the 2d Armor. Yet again I felt that they weren't quite sure what to do with us. The battle of Aachen was unfolding to the south of us, with the 30th Infantry turning to try to close the pocket on this, our first major target inside of Germany, and thus a battle with great symbolic weight. To the north, Market-Garden had collapsed into a stalemate. The ground directly ahead was so heavily congested with a variety of units that we were ordered to hold in position, the logic were that our guns could range across the front line, but I'd have preferred us closer in and on the move.

That was not to be, and for the next two weeks, frustratingly, we were locked in place near Palenburg. For that matter it seemed like everyone was locked in place, crawling forward by yards.

This stalemate, at least for me personally, ended on October 24. I received orders that we were being relieved of our attachment to the 2d Armor and shifted over to control of V Corps and pulled back down into Belgium.

I mounted up my battalion and left Holland behind. My case

of broken nerves, the old woman and that Jewish family, the Siegfried Line, and the slugging match in support of the 30th Infantry and 2d Armor. What was to come was one of the most dramatic and challenging assignments of my career. We were being assigned to the 102d Cavalry Group, to be known as Dolph's Light Armor Division, a command that would set the pace when it came to mobility and élan.

14

To the Ardennes

Col. Cyrus Dolph was the kind of commander I'd been looking for across three years of war. He was tough, agile, aggressive, and had iron nerves. One of my favorite decrees from head-quarters—I still have the original in my collection—was dated shortly after I joined his unit. It simply stated that if Kraut tanks broke through our lines, "Don't worry." Someone in the rear would take care of them, and we should keep going forward. No whining, no hand-wringing, and no worrying about the flanks. Our job was to be the point team for the Corps or as a hinge between V Corps and units to either flank, and to relent-lessly drive the Germans back.

The 62d was a fire-brigade unit assigned to what was the fire brigade for all of V Corps. Our job was to spearhead the ad-vance. Strange as it may sound, that was exactly what my men and I wanted. We were sick to death of squatting, of being employed like standard towed artillery under the control of of-ficers who still thought it was World War I. Our job was to get to the hot spot, blast a way through, mount up, and then keep on moving. Firepower and agility—that was what we wanted, and that is what Colonel Dolph expected of us.

What became known as the Light Division was a composite

unit made up of mobile armored artillery, including my 62d, a ranger battalion as assault troops, two cavalry recon squadrons, some armor, engineers, and a battery of AA.

Dolph's modus operandi was straightforward and as aggressive as all hell. He saw the advantage of mobile firepower that could quickly overwhelm. We advanced ready for a fight, and my battalion was often in the lead. We hit a strong point, and my guns immediately went into play, while the infantry, especially ranger and engineer units, would dash for the flank, cutting a straight line at a right angle to the axis of advance, sometimes a few hundred yards, other times a couple of miles, still mounted in trucks or half-tracks, then drive straight into either flank. If the enemy was still holding on, they were quickly outflanked and the pocket closed. If they still held out, well, frankly, we just blew them apart.

This was a man I was proud to take orders from. Morale soared.

In spite of the mobility and aggressiveness of our unit, the overall advance had lurched to a crawl.

Once assigned to Dolph's unit the 62d shifted to the south, covering over fifteen thousand yards of front between Lammersdorf in the north and Monschau to the south. Even as we joined Dolph, all thought of offensive action was essentially gone. The first tip-off was the extent of the front we were covering, over nine miles for one artillery battalion, with a skeleton crew of several troops of recon cavalry out front. In short, it was a clear sign to me that we had run out of steam after our brilliant breakout of midsummer.

A number of factors were coming into play to create this. First, the available number of combat troops was down, way down. Since June 6, United States military forces in Europe had sustained nearly a quarter of a million casualties.

Our long-term development plan, laid out at the start of the war, envisioned an army of a hundred divisions, well supported, with a heavy emphasis on armor and artillery. We never made it, while the Russians, without much more overall manpower, put hundreds of divisions in the field and thought nothing of the millions lost.

The difference between the Russians and us was our support and logistical tail and our huge commitment to our Army Air Force and the Pacific war. A lot of the supplies, medical support, and just plain luxuries we thought were essential the Russians did without, and thus their ratio of men actually on the front line was far greater.

To support our massive air fleets, it wasn't just pilots, but millions more serving in the complex array of construction, maintenance, and supply needed to keep our tens of thousands of planes flying.

In the Pacific millions more were in the fleet, in the marine assault units, and army troops under MacArthur and serving in China, Burma, and India. In northern Europe for every man toting a rifle on the front line eight to ten men were behind him driving trucks and hauling supplies and crewing ships, all the way back to New York and Chicago. What it boiled down to was that we were running out of combat infantrymen. If seasoned combat divisions, like the 1st and the 4th, took two or three thousand casualties, they were essentially fought out and needed time to rebuild.

The army system of making up those losses was ill conceived and hated by all of us.

Draftees, eighteen-year-old kids, and twenty-five- to thirty-five-year-old men who had been deferred earlier, were now being shipped straight from basic training to Europe and routed through the infamous repple depples. These replacement depots were nightmare places, great morale crushers in which the men were herded like cattle, complete with MPs keeping an eye on them, ramrodding them along. A division would call for five hundred replacements, and they might get two hundred; the names of the replacements would be called off, and they would be loaded up and shipped to the front. A day later they were on the front line, without any orientation or time to integrate.

It was ghastly.

The hardened survivors of most units looked at these replacements as sheep being sent to the slaughter, and these old hands did not usually want to get involved with them and pull them physically and emotionally into a tightly knit bond on the squad and platoon level. That bonding was essential for survival. They'd seen too many comrades killed, and these replacements died so damn quick, often on their first patrol, that the old hands didn't have the emotional reserves to try and get involved. So the replacements got hit, and then another call went out to try and refill the ranks. Thus, riflemen on the line were always in short supply.

If an old vet got hit and was sent back beyond battalion aid, he ran the risk of being sent to a repple depple once he was declared fit for duty and reassigned to another unit, not his old unit. It was common for such men to desert from the depot and light out on their own to get back to their buddies. A system that forced men to desert in order to get back to their combat units was flawed and a serious drain on morale.

I tried to work my way around this system. I had a darn good personnel sergeant who knew how to pull the strings and slip around the system. If we needed replacements, he'd go "scrounging," looking for experienced vets who had become detached from their unit or for men who had been wounded but were out of the loop and ready to go back to the line. He'd make them "an offer they couldn't refuse": a chance to become an artilleryman in a good battalion rather than a rifleman on the forward edge, a chance to get in with a unit that was close-knit and took care of its own.

When replacements did come in, I made a point of integrating them quickly, with the right old hand keeping an eye on them. I knew that the first week was crucial if these new men were to survive.

Some units did this, and it showed in a lot of ways, in their morale, in their casualty reports, and in the way they handled the crisis that was about to hit us.

Others did not, and the results showed.

Regardless of how we and other units handled the problem on the platoon, company, and battalion level, overall our army was in a bad way by the end of November. Everyone knew it. We were fought out and poorly supplied; morale was down, and our fighting edge was off.

In contrast, though I might have had some complaints about how the British high command worked at times, I always held their fighting men in the highest regard and admired the way they were organized at the regimental level. They still tended toward the old system of the training battalion, a formation that would take in the new recruits out of basic, model them into a fighting unit, inculcate in them the traditions of the unit, and then move them together into the front lines, while rotating out a unit that was fought out and needed to be refitted.

If there was an overall problem for our British allies on line to the north of us, it was that they were now beginning the sixth year of their war. They were exhausted physically, emotionally, and financially, and so they were overly cautious as well, all sense of dash and offensive spirit gone.

Across the front morale was down. Actual combat units were stretched thin; the density of men on the front line was dangerously low. Crucial supplies were in short supply, and the heady days of August and early September were replaced with slogging through the dismal fall and early winter, a time when many of us believed we could have already been to the Rhine or even the Elbe.

The weather was another factor. It was cold and rainy, conditions absolutely miserable, which was yet another drain on the morale and on the physical condition of the men. Illnesses were soaring, along with plain physical collapse after months of living on rations, sleeping in the rain and mud, and never getting enough sleep.

Winter clothing was in short supply as well. It seemed that the rear echelon and supply troops had an abundance of heavy winter boots, overcoats, and white camo pullovers, while many of our men were still in summer gear, soaked and freezing. On the front line many of our troops looked like veterans of Valley Forge rather than a modern army. Men stuffed burlap bags with newspapers and wrapped them around their feet. They wore tattered blankets as capes, and mittens with bare fingers sticking out. If a dead man had a good pair of boots, they were taken. It was a horrible sight to see American dead with bare feet, like something out of an old Matthew Brady photograph of Confederate soldiers.

My battalion was a classic example of this problem, and I'm willing to bet that many an old frontline vet will nod his head in agreement with my experience. We finally got our issue of winter clothing, boots, and whitewash paint for our vehicles . . . in March, just as the spring thaw was hitting.

It seemed as if the war would drag on forever.

As the campaign limped into the middle of December the confusion about our own position, of who we answered to as a battalion, surfaced again. It would dog us for the next couple of weeks. We were a "hinge" unit, covering the front between V Corps and XIX Corps near Monschau. The 78th Infantry, with XIX Corps, claimed we were supposed to support them, while V Corps tasked us to provide covering support for the thin screen of cavalry recon that was holding our front.

I started to receive conflicting orders. That indicated to me that things were indeed shaky along our front. I had a general officer from corps, who shall remain nameless, visit my unit. He looked at my deployment, with my guns positioned on a reverse slope for protection from incoming, but still capable of shooting out to the front line, and he couldn't figure it out. He kept asking how we were supposed to shoot from behind the hill. Then he left. We all stood there incredulous at his stupidity, wondering how the hell he had risen to such a lofty rank. I'd like to think that he is typical of all armies, and not just America's, but at that moment it did make us wonder how the hell we were winning.

The men, especially my forward observers and liaison officers working with the cavalry squadrons, began to get that "bad feeling": Something was definitely heading our way, and it wasn't going to be good.

The infamous bad weather of that December began to take hold, with snow, fog, and low visibility. My FOs in front of Monschau could see deep into enemy territory, when weather permitted, and they were catching glimpses of one hell of a lot of movement, often too far away for us to engage it, of clearly visible troops, armor, and trucks. These reinforcements were moving up close, then going into concealment in the forests.

Something was building up, and it was damn big.

There seems to be a myth that the opening of the Battle of the Bulge was a complete and total surprise. That's ridiculous. Warnings were coming back for days. Any savvy company commander was getting the information from his troops and then passing the word up the chain, but with no results. Not to worry was the usual reply.

My FOs and even my little air force (and cavalry scouts) were telling me that something big was afoot. We knew something was coming, and in our own way we began to get ready, stockpiling ammunition and keeping a careful watch.

If there was a surprise, it was in the rear, starting with division headquarters and extending from there up the line all the way back to SHAEF. The reports coming in from the front line simply did not fit their vision, or to phrase it in more modern jargon their "paradigm." To their thinking the Germans were finished, reduced to throwing old men and boys into the lines.

I think part of that paradigm was formed by our own condition. If we were fought out, than most definitely the Germans *had* to be fought out as well. So to the rear echelon the reports coming in were simply those of men who were getting jumpy over nothing.

As has so often happened in the history of American arms, the information was there before us, but the higher-ups simply were not listening, and instead were projecting back down the line their own fantasies. While they stared at maps and charts, rather than crawling up to the line to see for themselves, their wishes turned into facts.

I'd have given one hell of a lot, in those first two weeks of December, to have seen someone with a couple of stars on his shoulder on the front line, the real front line, the way German generals did it, talking directly with the men who knew what the hell was happening just a mile or two to the east, rather than sitting in a chateau all the way back in France dictating orders that we were overreacting.

For most of us the Bulge was no surprise. We knew it was coming and sensed it was going to be the worst fight since Normandy.

I started calling back for support, and though Colonel Dolph agreed, the higher-ups back with corps ignored our pleas. Finally, on December 15, just before everything went to pieces, I was told that a couple of battalions of infantry would be moved up to support us. Meanwhile, down at our level, we decided to set up our own firing plan, to tear loose with a disruptive strike (an intense bombardment designed to hit into what we suspected were concentration points and throw them off balance).

Throughout the sixteenth of December we prepared, knowing that something was coming our way. Some other units did this as well, but far too many did not, deferring to high command, sitting back and relaxing. The weather was terrible, Christmas was only a week away, and next year, once we built back up, we'd finally steamroll forward through the old men and boys and take Berlin.

As darkness fell—and it comes early in northern Europe in December—we began to fire interdiction strikes on suspected points of concentration.

I was up all night, monitoring reports from our FOs, who were getting increasingly concerned that something big was rolling our way.

It's strange how after a couple of years of combat you develop a remarkable sense for the battlefield. Subtle indicators that the rest of the world misses go off like alarm bells in your head. It's as if you can actually smell battle coming. I think that was the big problem for the unit directly to our south, the 99th Infantry Division, which was about to get bowled over. They were new and just didn't have that feel.

On the night of December 16–17 it hit. German transport planes swept over our lines, and almost immediately we started getting reports of paratroopers and commandos in our rear. Mixed in would be the infamous troops in American uniforms who, though only a handful, would sow chaos.

Dolph's standing orders to ignore what was going on to our rear and to fight to the front stood, though we had every man from cook to mechanic to gunner ready and armed.

The FOs started calling in missions, and soon the entire front line exploded. German infantry at battalion strength began to assault directly into our forward screen of cavalry.

My headquarters was on the northern flank of our battalion front, which was nearly nine miles wide, but the bulk of my guns were to the south end of that, almost adjoining the 99th Infantry Division, which was rapidly disintegrating under the enemy's hammer blows. I decided to shift down, but it wasn't simply a lateral move, since there were no direct roads running north and south. I had to drive back a half dozen miles, then turn south then finally east again, a drive of twenty miles or so to get to my batteries at the south end of our sector.

It was a journey through utter chaos.

Fortunately, I brought along one of the battalion's Sherman tanks, and in fairly short order I had to use it as a bulldozer, literally, to push my way through the disorganized units, primarily infantry, running for the rear. All of them screaming that the Krauts were closing in. It was one of the most heartbreaking and humiliating sights I had witnessed since driving through the wreckage at Kasserine Pass two years earlier.

It was senseless to try to halt this rout. I was a colonel from an artillery battalion, and these men had but one desire, to get the hell out of the way. I simply pushed forward, ignoring their hysterical warnings as my jeep followed behind the tank as it cleared the way.

It took me several hours to regain position with my batteries and a hell of a lot was happening quickly. At around nine-thirty in the morning a full battalion of German troops punched through the cavalry screen. The pressure was so intense that the screen pulled back and parted, letting the Germans through. My own batteries were dug in hard, and the Germans flowed around them into mobile reserves Dolph had positioned to the rear, along with those two precious battalions of infantry that corps had released to our sector the day before.

Firing missions piled up while, to the south of us, the break-through blew wide open as the 99th Infantry disintegrated, with a couple of thousand men in that unit surrendering.

You could hear the battle widening. Gunfire that was to my front before, was expanding around to my right and into my rear.

I started patching my FO reports back up to V Corps, and more and more artillery battalions came into the fight with the 62d directing the fire.

We soon had fifteen or more battalions responding to our calls for support. That is roughly three hundred guns, a mass of fire-power undreamed of.

It was a virtual hurricane of steel and fire as batteries of 105s, 155s, and, far to the rear, the big eight-inchers responded to our calls. The targets were swarming everywhere. Battalions of Krauts were on the move, columns of armor, vehicles, towed and mobile artillery. The firestorm would come down on them, and acres of ground would disappear in a blinding flash.

Where we were positioned there were some dragon's teeth made by the Germans for the defensive Siegfried Line. On the morning of the second day of the offensive, a battalion or more of German infantry swarmed through the dragon's teeth in a full frontal attack on our position.

It was little less than murder as my men and I unleashed a firestorm.

This was the last major push into our sector after repeated attacks. But we had held, and by holding became the northern shoulder of the Bulge. To our south the Germans continued to storm due west, but we were the upper end of the funnel, able to call down fire on what had become the German rear.

As the German penetration went in deeper, American units were rapidly played off to the northern flank to contain and funnel the breach. At one point I had fire missions going out in an arc of 270 degrees, which meant that there was only a small corridor back to our rear lines.

There was confusion as well back at headquarters, with conflicting orders still coming down as to who we were supporting and when. I tried to ignore it as much as possible and simply put down fire when and where it was called for.

My greatest fear, that we'd be overrun, that our cavalry, engineer, and infantry supports would give way, had not been realized. Thus we were able to hold our ground and play hell on the German flank.

We received a new and deadly weapon at this time, the proximity fuse. It was a remarkable weapon, a tiny vacuum-tube radar transmitter mounted in the nose of an artillery shell. When it detected an object, it detonated. It was originally designed for antiaircraft use in the Pacific, and starting in the summer it was used to knock down V-1s over England. The high command was fearful of its release into the mainland fighting, concerned that a dud shell might be recovered and that the device then would be replicated by the Germans.

The crisis of the Bulge triggered its release, and the results were deadly. The detector would set the shell off roughly thirty yards above the ground, ideal burst height for laying down a spray of shrapnel across a quarter acre of ground, killing anything underneath. In short order the Germans noticed the difference, but couldn't figure out why our air bursts were so deadly accurate. They were terrified. The only problem I noted and reported back on, since ours were among the first batteries to receive the shells, was their tendency to detonate above the battery if there was a salvo firing. One shell was detecting another as it cleared the barrel. Fortunately, the upward velocity caused the shrapnel to disperse harmlessly, but it rattled us all until we quickly came on the solution of just firing in sequence.

By the first week in January the steam was out of the German offensive, and once again we were champing at the bit. Patton saw it correctly. The Bulge was not a threat to our line, rather it was the golden opportunity of the war to pincer off an entire German army and put it in the bag for good. Unfortunately, high command, both Monty, who was in control on the northern flank, and SHAEF continued to call for the slow steady push rather than a daring pincer attack. As a result, hundreds of thousands of Germans escaped, along with many of their elite units, which were then shifted down to Hungary to stave off the Soviet winter offensive.

The Bulge, the greatest single action in American military history, cost us close to a hundred thousand casualties with tens of thousands more permanently disabled by frostbite, exposure, shock, and disease.

It was the battle in which we stood up against the best and held fast. Even when the front line was temporarily broken, those farther back dug in and held on against the elite SS and panzer divisions. After the Bulge I don't think any one would ever dare to question again the combat worthiness of the typical GI. It wasn't about supplies, air cover, equipment, rations, or luxuries. It was about guts. Our men showed it.

So passed my Christmas and New Year's. It wasn't until a month afterward that I learned just how horrible the holidays were . . . for my wife at home.

Shortly before Bets passed away in June 2001, she shared the following story with a family friend. I feel it is worth including, since any narrative of this war is not just about those on the front line, it is about what an entire family had to endure.

From an interview with Betty Bennett
The Battle of the Bulge was on and we were starting to get the first reports back in the States about how tough the fighting was. And then the telegram came to Don's father.

I had gone home to live with my parents that winter, and I guess that's why the telegram didn't come straight to me since I had been staying with Don's family just before this happened.

I got the phone call from Don's father. Sixty years later it's hard to actually remember it. I know I blanked it out of my mind, that moment, his father crying, telling me that Don was dead.

I'd shared that moment with more than one wife during the war, and afterwards when someone in Don's unit was killed and I went over to see the widow. The girl sits there stunned, trying to put on the brave front. I've seen them make tea and coffee, not a tear, just a vague distant smile, more than one saying that maybe it was all a mistake, that something in their heart told them that their husband was still alive and it was all a mistake.

I would sit there, listening, nodding, holding their hand, and inside I'd be in anguish, knowing that their husband was dead, and the girl was still dreaming, not ready to accept the truth.

From what I can actually remember of that month after the news came, I guess I was in the same state. My heart couldn't believe it. I kept picturing Don alive, I'd dream of him being alive, not dead.

I went through Christmas like that, and it was made worse when on Christmas Eve the florist sent over a bouquet of gardenias, my favorite flowers. There was a card on it addressed from Don, saying that he loved me, and wishing me a Merry Christmas.

I stood there holding the flowers, crying, not sure what to

believe anymore, as if they had somehow come to me from beyond the grave.

Then I finally realized that maybe Don had made some arrangement for them to be sent months before. At last it came
out that before he shipped out Don had asked his father to send
me gardenias on my birthday and Christmas and to put his name
on the tag. Poor Dad had placed the order just before the telegram came, and then forgot to cancel it. When he found out, he
felt just horrible, and blurted out the truth, which made it even
worse for both of us.

Finally two strange things happened. A letter came from Don.
It was a V-mail, one of those small letters where you were only
allowed enough space for a few lines. The letter was dated after
Don was reported killed.

That hit hard.

I had heard of things like that happening before, a girl getting
a letter from her husband and it was dated after his reported
death. Usually it was the War Department that made a mistake
in the telegram with the wrong information about the date of
death, sometimes the letter was written before the man died, left
on a desk, and then mailed the following day by a buddy.

I didn't know what to believe.

Next came a phone call, and this was when I started to think
maybe there was a mistake, even though the phone call was heartbreaking. The call was from the parents of a soldier named Donald K. Bennett. The difference in name between their son and
my Don was the middle initial. Next, their serial numbers were
only one digit apart. Finally, their son and Don had been classmates together at the Point. Their boy had gone on to the Air
Corps while Don went into Artillery.

They had received my Don's footlocker, which had been in
storage somewhere on the East Coast. It was a horrible shock for
them, the locker arriving without warning, a note attached saying
it contained the personal effects of their dead son. They had not
heard a word about any of this, assumed their boy was alive, and

then this locker shows up, shipped over from some warehouse where the men had packed up their personal possessions before going overseas.

They open it up, but nothing inside belongs to their son, its old clothing, a few books, some personal things, belonging to my Don.

This was the horrible part for them. They had called me, believing that they were helping to return some personal effects that had been accidentally shipped to them. I can imagine their terror and shock when there was a knock at the door and there was a box.

We all lived in fear of that.

You'd see the Western Union boy coming down the street on his bicycle and the entire neighborhood would fall silent. He was the messenger of death, and where he stopped the world for that family came to an end. A shipping company would arrive with a footlocker, and that was another message from the war delivered to your doorstep.

This frightened couple opens the box and there was the confusion and then, most likely, tears of relief. It wasn't their boy who was dead, it was a mistake, it was someone else. They find Don's home address and make a long-distance call, figuring that was best since the one who died had been a classmate of their son.

As we talked, though, their consoling started to change and the terror returned for them, while hope grew for me.

What set it moving that way was my mentioning that though I had received the telegram from the War Department, I had just received a V-mail from my Don dated after his reported death. They fell silent. It had been over a month since a letter had come from their son, and he used to write almost every day.

It was a heartbreaking moment. Down deep I wanted to change everything around, that it would be their son who was dead and not my Don. And yet I was talking to them, they were frightened, and of course they wanted it to be my Don who was dead and their son who was safe and alive.

As I try to remember the numbed shock of those weeks, I think it was at that moment it was no longer just a dream, that I actually could cling to a hope that Don was alive.

They said they would ship the box up to me, try to reach their son, and find out what happened. I tried to get an answer from the War Department, but you have to understand it was next to impossible for the Pentagon to figure things out and that was not because the people working in the office that handled casualty reports didn't care. The Battle of the Bulge was still on, and tens of thousands of men were dead, wounded, and missing. Trying to backtrack one mistake was all but impossible.

Of course I had stopped writing to Don, but that night a V-mail went out.

And then I waited. Given that Don was up on the front line, and the way the Bulge was being fought, it was taking a couple of months for a message to reach him and for him to reply. Then another letter came in from him. There was no mention of being hurt, though I later found out he had been wounded just before the Bulge started. It was just Don's way not to tell me since he didn't want me to worry.

Finally I got a letter from the parents of Donald K. Bennett. Their son was dead, shot down over Germany. Their son was dead, and in his death, I knew my Don was alive. Their son no longer wrote. The letters from Don kept coming.

I never met them. I've wondered since who they were, what their son was like, how did they continue to live after he was gone. I felt, in a way, that his life was traded for the life of my husband. I still feel guilty, that when I talked with them I was praying that it would be my husband who was safe, but that then meant it was their boy who was lost. That thought has haunted me. I think it's one of the reasons it is so hard to remember it now. I've spent sixty years wanting to forget.

I know without a doubt that the Christmas of 1944 was far worse for Bets and for millions of other wives stateside than it was for any of us on the front line.

15

To the Elbe

January was a cold and terrible month of that war. Temperatures often plummeted to zero, the grim task of cleaning up after the Bulge continued, and it seemed at times that we'd still be there come 1946. It continued to snow, the locals telling us it was the worst they had seen in decades, with drifts piled four feet deep and the ground frozen solid. In wartime that means digging a foxhole is like chipping through concrete.

I had maintained a hard and fast rule with myself that I ate what my men ate, and slept as my men slept, so if they were out in the open, or dug in under an M-7, I did the same.

One night some of the men finally convinced me that I needed at least one night under a solid roof in a warm bed. I guess they just saw that I was completely worn out. Their concern for me was touching. So I relented. There was an abandoned house nearby, and some of the men even made up a bed in it and laid a fire.

It was strange. After months out in the field I actually felt a bit claustrophobic and creepy being under a solid roof again. I guess my reaction shows that a man can get used to almost anything, and once he is into that routine, to try to turn back to a softer way of life is disturbing.

I couldn't get to sleep. Something just didn't feel right. Up there on the second floor of that house I felt absolutely naked and exposed.

I finally grabbed my sleeping bag and went down into the basement. Maybe it was that angel, that sixth sense that had been with me all the way back to North Africa, that whispered a warning.

I'd barely settled in and *wham!* a German shell blew the house in with a direct hit. The building collapsed. My men, in a mad panic, scrambled into the wreckage and pulled me out of the basement.

Again that moment where everyone kind of laughs even as we were all shaking.

It was one of those one-in-a-thousand shots, the type of harassing fire that kills randomly and is always stalking the front.

We were also catching occasional shells from a huge railroad gun that must have been firing a 240mm shell. One night the entire eastern sky lit up with a flash, and all of us wondered just what the hell had happened: Had a fully loaded plane gone down? Was a town being bombed?

We didn't know.

And then, thirty seconds or so later, we heard it coming in. Everyone dived for cover, the shell detonating a quarter mile or so away with a terrifying impact.

Thus it went for several nights. After the first shock, it became a part of our routine. We'd spot the flash, a warning would be shouted, and then we'd take a leisurely thirty seconds getting under something. It never did any real damage and almost became a form of entertainment, but if they had ever managed to get a good FO into our lines, a single impact could have wiped out most of a battery.

It was evident that the Germans were beaten, but they were not going to give up without one final, desperate struggle. Occasionally we'd see high-flying formations of heavy bombers heading for the heart of the Reich, and their battered formations coming back. The sight was always a powerful one, and all of us thanked God that they were ours, and that it was not our homes and families under such a terrifying bombardment.

In their last gasp the Germans were throwing anything and everything back. We caught some glimpses of their new ME-262 jet fighter, and it was a frightening sight, like something out of a Flash Gordon movie, which was the *Stars Wars* of my generation.

One morning they even fired off some V-1s from in front of our lines, most likely aimed at Antwerp. You could hear the popping drone of its engine as it winged in. The sight of the darn thing set me off, and I actually pulled out my .45 and emptied a clip at it. It was low enough that if I had hit it, we'd have all been wiped out.

We slowly resumed the push, my battalion acting as part of the hinge between V Corps and XIX Corps, with both of those units squabbling over who had control of my firing missions. It did make me wonder at times whether we were all on the same team and just how ridiculous egos get when somebody gets a star or two on his shoulder. It was a lesson I hoped I learned well, and tried to keep close to my heart as the stars gathered on my own shoulders in the years after the war.

We now pushed up toward the Roer River. There our advance slowed again as we prepared to jump that river toward the end of February.

On March 2, 1945, we crossed the Roer and from there drove toward the Rhine. We were now moving into the heart of Germany.

Our sector between the two corps got impossibly wide, at times fifteen miles or more, with nothing in between, and Dolph driving hell-bent for leather, telling us to forget about the flanks, just keep going forward.

We were moving into a part of Germany heavily hit by air attacks since 1942. The civilians we encountered were scared but at the same time damn grateful that at last the war was over for them. If a house was empty, that usually meant it was owned by a Nazi or by someone who was still supporting them, and had fled. Those who stayed behind wanted the war to end.

I remember one house I set my CP up in, and the irony of it all. The owners were friendly, could even speak a few words of English, and there on the wall were some old photographs, taken in 1919, of World War I doughboys posing with the family. And now the sons of those doughboys were back.

The Germans were exhausted. All they wanted at this point was for the whole damn thing to be over with, even if it meant defeat. One thing that was clearly evident was that if they were going to surrender happily to anyone, it was to us. Rumors were already sweeping across Germany of the barbaric horrors the Soviets were perpetrating as they pushed in from the east, having reached the Oder River, less than a hundred miles east of Berlin, by the end of January. Millions of refugees from that front were heading west, bearing tales of a medieval-like storm of rape, pillage, and mass murder.

Something that still haunts me about that advance from the Roer to the Rhine was a city burning in the night. We were downwind, the scene before us apocalyptic, the town having been flattened in a pitched battle just before my unit arrived. Hardly a building was left standing, the dead littered the streets, everything was wrapped in flame and smoke, dazed survivors huddled in the wreckage.

For some reason, to this day I can't stomach the smell of burning leaves or rubbish. It flashes me back to that night, to that grim and terrible place of death. A scent on the wind that so many find pleasant, evocative of Indian-summer afternoons in the fall, still puts me inside my house, with windows shut, and the air filter running.

The crossing of the Rhine was the next barrier, and the leap across this great obstacle, both physical and psychological, happened near us when Remagen was taken in a valiant assault. To our north the Brits were preparing, in their usual systematic manner, a set-piece attack that took weeks to prepare and involved the last great airborne drop of the war.

I'm actually a bit saddened to admit that I missed this moment.

I got leave.

Omar Bradley decided that it was time to get a few of the combat officers at battalion level off the line for a weekend, and I, along with a handful of other battalion commanders, was given a three-day pass to London. I'll admit that when the order came through, I was relieved and delighted. A chance for a couple of days out of the madness was like an angel descending from heaven with an offer of a free pass to paradise. And yet I felt guilty as well for taking it, though my men were supportive, all of them telling me to get the hell out of there.

So I reported back behind the lines, where a C-47 was waiting. A couple of hours later I was in a jeep taking me to my hotel in downtown London. The sight of London shocked the hell out of me. The pounding Londoners had endured during the Blitz had been bad enough, but the rain of V-1s and V-2s had reduced a fair part of that once glorious city to rubble.

Entire city blocks were blown out, shattered windows on buildings still standing were covered over with newspapers and bits of plywood. It was a bleak and depressing sight.

Any fantasy images some might have of a group of officers, straight from the front, running amok in London are just that, fantasies.

My main goal was simply to sink into a warm tub and then a bed. I must have slept through most of the leave.

I did manage to get into Westminster Abbey for Sunday services, an experience I'll never forget. The uniforms of those gathered there were from around the world, a dazzling display of the dying vestiges of the British Empire, combined with those of us from the New World and the grim survivors of occupied Europe. The great stained-glass windows behind the altar had been blown out during the Blitz, and sandbags were still piled up around parts of the building. A replacement window that would go in after the war is one that I pray stands for a thousand years. Dedicated to those who gave their lives in the Battle of Britain, it is a memorial that, every time I've seen it in the long years afterward, moves me to tears.

When I returned to my command after that glorious leave, my battalion was across the Rhine and racing on the final drive to what we figured would be Berlin.

The back of German resistance was broken. At times we were charging fifty or more miles a day, and the method was simple. If a town hung out the white flag, and stuck by that flag, we just raced through and kept on going. If anyone put up resistance, we methodically started to flatten the place until they gave up. At this point, though, except for a few fanatics, the wind was at last out of their sails. Since we were usually on the point of the advance, we simply took the weapons of any surrendering troops, told their officers to start leading their men west, and pushed on.

It was here, however, that the underlying horror of all that Nazism stood for, became evident.

For those born long after the war, it must be hard to imagine a world in which the words, *concentration camp, holocaust,* and *final solution* were not part of the lexicon. Those words once held no meaning to my generation. Now the mere uttering of them instantly conjures up images of just how evil one man can be to another, one nation to another, one race to another.

There was a terrible distinction within the Nazi system. The camps for the mass eradication of the Jews were located primarily in the east, outside Germany proper. The region we were crossing through, part of the industrial heartland of Germany, the equivalent of our Pittsburgh, Cleveland, Toledo, and Chicago, lay along the Rhine. It was there that the Nazis established hundreds of slave-labor camps. Death might not be as swift for prisoners in these concentration camps, but it was there and waiting, through slow starvation, overwork, disease, exhaustion, and random violence.

Near Leipzig we took a town with a slave-labor camp on the outskirts. There were the usual denials, the averted eyes, the hand-wringing denunciations of the Nazis by the German residents. My men and I were furious. Word was already going through our entire army as to the nightmare being uncovered, and special units were rushing in to provide aid. Unknowingly, in some cases, our own compassion was killing the victims. We passed out concentrated K rations to men and women who had not eaten a decent meal in years; they'd overeat and die.

The visages of the liberated prisoners haunt me still, skeletal faces, children of fourteen, wizened and ancient, with skin like brittle parchment, all enveloped in a fetid stench of unwashed bodies, feces, and urine.

The rage is still in me when I remember the august burgomaster of the town we were occupying approaching me, all official and proper. He was concerned about lawlessness, for, after all, Germans respected the law. These walking dead, who were flooding into the town, were frightening the good citizens. Could Herr Colonel please arrange to place armed guards in the town for its own protection?

The impulsive desire to simply draw my .45 and shoot the son of a bitch still frightens me. I did manage to control myself, but barely. After all I had seen, all the thousands of dead, the bodies of my comrades rolling in the surf, frozen in the forest of the Ardennes, bloating under the Sicilian sun, of all the burning cities, the dead French civilians piled in the town square, that family back in Holland—after all of that the nightmare demons locked in my own soul came close to soaring out and taking possession.

I threw him out, grim, angry, snarling a wish that I just might arm the walking dead, staggering about in their striped prison uniforms, and then cut them loose on the town.

The devil walked the landscape of Germany in that spring of 1945, and it is a wonder that we as well did not embrace him at times and sink into the mire of mindless violence that was consuming the world.

Are we different?

I would like to think so.

I would like to think that some places in this world did, and still do, harbor a different kind of man and woman, ones that can transcend the darker demons and, as Lincoln said, answer instead to the better angels of our nature.

It is said that when Patton first walked through one of these camps he broke down and wept.

Eisenhower vomited.

I know, I understand, and I will never forget.

We reached the Elbe at the beginning of May 1945. To the east Berlin was in flames, the funeral pyre of the Thousand Year Reich. We had hoped to march into that city, to personally drive a stake through the heart of the beast, but perhaps, at least for us, it was best that we did not.

The Russians sustained well over a hundred thousand casualties in that Götterdämmerung.

Across the Elbe, Germans by the hundreds of thousands were swarming westward, desperate to escape the hordes unleashed in the east. And yes, there was some pity in our hearts, even after all we had seen, for we were only human, and there was within us a memory of what we were, the world we had known long ago. To look into the eyes of women who had been raped, of old men who had lost everything, including their children, the eyes of the terrified, innocent babies, touched our hearts, and in that moment we would still extend a hand, offer a K ration, and put a cigarette into trembling lips, even though they had been the enemy.

On May 7, 1945, we were in Czechoslovakia.

Patton's Third Army had sliced deep into Czechoslovakia, a couple of hundred miles to our south. With the order to halt on the Elbe, the assumption was that if there was to be any tough action ahead, it would be down there, where large German formations were still intact and rumors still abounded of an Eagle's Nest, a German redoubt in the mountainous region of south Germany and Austria. Our entire corps was transferred south. Third Army was poised and ready to drive in on the southern flank of that position.

We pulled back from the front line and motored south, passing through what were now the rear lines and the wreckage of the Third Reich.

Civilization had collapsed, and it had fallen upon us to restore it. Something that is often forgotten in such moments of high drama and history is that everyone must still go on with living and trying to stay alive. For the German people it meant finding food, shelter, and medical attention, and somehow restoring a civil society after a complete and total breakdown. For the vast numbers of slaves it meant trying to find a way home and a means of staying alive. The roads were clogged with refugees, a sea of humanity unlike anything seen before in modern history, passing through still-smoking cities, past blackened vehicles, tanks, cars, and trucks littering the sides of the road, and upturned earth, of German dead, and American dead yet to be recovered by graves registration.

Czechoslovakia was in chaos as well. There had been a war within a war. In that final week the Czech people had risen up against their Nazi occupiers, but the fight was far more complex and deadly than is discussed today.

Hitler's excuse for the first and second invasions of Czechoslovakia in the fall of 1938 and early in 1939 was that this was territory that had once been part of Germany, stripped away by the Versailles Treaty. On that technical point he was right, and there were indeed areas of Czechoslovakia that held a majority of Germans. The transfer of power was therefore greeted openly by some even while their Czech neighbors lamented. Czechs had been drafted into the German army and the German workforce during the war. In May 1945 the eastern part of the country was already occupied by the Soviets who were closing on Prague, and then the explosion hit, a violent uprising aimed not just at the occupying army but at their German neighbors as well. Part of the uprising was nationalist, the other communist, both factions vying for postwar control. The result was a bloodbath.

Tens of thousands of German civilians were murdered in the uprising, and tens of thousands of Czechs were arbitrarily executed by the Germans. Twenty-three years later, when I was positioned on that same border, now wearing three stars and in command of a corps, I could still sense that hostility between German and Czech.

We arrived in Czechoslovakia on May 7, 1945, and were poised to press east. Sporadic action was still flaring around us, most of it the vengeance fighting between German and Czech, but regardless of the motivation it could still kill any one of us, men who had survived for nearly three years and realized that there was a chance to actually get out of this war alive.

I can't emphasize that enough. On the day we shipped out, whether it was in 1942 or as a replacement in the winter of 1944, there was a certain gut sense that the trip was one-way. You were going into the greatest war in history, a conflict that at times was killing over a million people a month, and you, insignificant you, would never get out of it alive. On the day I said good-bye to Bets I walked out the door believing that my chances were slim, a belief I had carried even before the war, when I was a cadet at the Point, and we few on the Hudson saw the juggernaut coming at a nation that was dangerously ill prepared.

And now it was almost at an end, and all of us were jittery, wondering if that last sniper round, that last shell, or some lunatic in a plane firing a last shot might take us with them.

Behavior was strange. Some men turned into foxhole huggers; others, in a bizarre paradox, got reckless, taking dumb risks driving, or, as I mentioned earlier, cutting across an open field when two years of battle experience said always stay inside the wood line and go the long way around.

And indeed men were still dying, tripping over land mines, picking up a booby-trapped souvenir, getting shot by some crazed sixteen-year-old Hitler Youth who wanted to take one of us with him as an offering to his dead Führer.

So I gritted my teeth and tried to stay focused on what the next day would bring. Rumors were running riot that Germany had surrendered, would surrender, or that some damn Nazis were holed up in Bavaria and about to unleash their stockpile of chemical and biological weapons.

That was a part of the war that sounds chillingly modern to today's readers. Few remember that it was a serious element in the war of my generation as well.

The horror of chemical weapons used in World War I had triggered a universal revulsion in 1918, and all nations quickly swore they would never use them again. Yet, throughout World War II, the specter of their use was always present. All that stayed the hands of the belligerents was the fear of swift and certain retribution by their opponents.

In May 1945 the surviving Nazi fanatics, who knew they were dead if caught, had nothing more to lose. And scientists had been hard at work across the twenty-six years after 1919. Nerve agents were stockpiled in Germany and just behind our own front lines, almost as dangerous as the ones we fear today. After the war, evidence was released that the Germans and the Japanese had experimented with biological agents as well. Some of those Japanese experiments in the east were performed on American POWs.

Everyone was on edge, afraid that in its final gasp the Reich might exhale a deadly miasma of poison gas, anthrax, and plague that might consume the world. Though atomic research was still the most closely kept secret of the war, those of us with a bit of technical knowledge had heard the rumors about atomic weaponry. Goebbels in his propaganda broadcasts in those final months constantly droned on about the terror weapons that in a single day would reverse the tide of the war, and atomic weapons, though never spoken of, were in our darker thoughts as well.

Those days of May 1945 were not nearly as heady as many now think or even remember. They were days laden with fear, a terrible sense that after we had survived so much, the horror might just keep on going. We feared as well the first inklings of the long twilight struggle to come.

I had a photograph in my possession, now lost, taken on May 9, 1945, the day the fighting officially stopped. Someone snapped a shot of my headquarters unit. Word had come down that at midnight May 8, it was over.

It was over.

At least that is what high command said.

Like all other units, we aimed our weapons skyward, most with blank rounds, far too many with full loads, and at midnight a vast explosion ripped across the front line and, sadly, more than one more soldier was killed when all those tons of steel came back down.

It was over. We gathered in a tent and uncorked some bottles of liberated wine to celebrate.

I wish I had that photo now, for if you looked into our eyes, you would have seen that, in a way, it would never be over. It is so popular today to call us the greatest generation, an accolade that I will admit gives warmth to our waning years. Yet, as I remember that photograph, I think we could be called instead the weary generation, the old-in-our-youth generation. It was in our eyes. It always will be in our eyes and in our souls.

There was no glory, only relief, only a wish to lay down our tools of death and to rest.

On that day I turned thirty years old. I was never so old as I was on that night. All the years since then have been a gift.

16

The Ending

The tragedy was not ended. It still echoes today.

Of all the horrors endured, what came next was perhaps the worst and the most haunting, for supposedly it came in a time of peace.

It was, as well, a betrayal of what we were supposedly fighting for and the foundation in blood of the forty-five-year struggle to come, a struggle which at times took us again to the brink of annihilation.

The Soviets pushed westward, and we drew up to a demarcation line near Zatavi, just west of Prague. And then came an order that we were to seal our line. We were to continue rounding up any German military personnel that wandered in, but no displaced peoples, that is, refugees, were to be allowed to cross into our lines.

What ensued was like something out of stories of the ancient world.

Ever since the beginning of the German pullback on the eastern front in 1943, millions of civilians had retreated with them. They were not necessarily pro-Nazi, but they were decidedly anti-Stalin. Retreating behind the Germans were Ukrainians, anticommunist Russians, ethnic Germans who lived in Russia before the war, Tatars who were descendants of the medieval Mongols, millions upon millions.

Some might be defined as guilty. They had allied with the Germans for a variety of reasons, and some of those reasons were understandable to those who claimed to support freedom. But what of the children, of young women who like all young women fall in love, of old men and grandmothers? Millions of these innocents were fleeing as well, and they saw that behind the flag of America there might be a chance to survive.

We betrayed them.

It was simple enough at Yalta. Just a few words and a signature was all it took. It was an agreement declaring that in the postwar world all civilians should be returned to their place of origin. Bureaucratically, that seemed logical enough, a simple way to sort things out, to separate the sheep from the wolves, to bring justice, and then to rebuild. And yet the agreement was a death sentence for millions.

We were ordered to seal our lines, to let no one pass, and the tragedies played out before us tore our hearts out as these pitiful survivors, terrified of what was behind them, begged to be let through. Many of us turned a blind eye at first, and then orders, in the harshest of terms, came down from corps.

Then the Russians came.

I'll never forget my first sight of them, a vast sprawling horde coming up out of the east. Our allies yes, and yet still somehow alien to behold. On a road parallel to our position they came, a vast convoy made up of every kind of commandeered vehicle ever made, from civilian trucks and cars to the standard Studebaker deuce-and-a-half. One of these trucks broke down directly in front of us. The men piled out, popped the hood, stood around for a few minutes shaking their heads, then piled into another truck and left the abandoned vehicle behind. My men were incredulous. Hell, we would have had it back on the road, or if need be, we would have towed it along. They left it as junk in their wake.

Almost immediately the first confrontation came. A convoy started to roll straight for our line, and the next thing I knew, there I was in the middle of the road blocking their advance. I was polite, at first, but the tension was clear. The commander of the convoy demanded that we step aside, and I firmly conveyed that we were on the line of demarcation. They backed off. It was the first of numerous confrontations to come, all the way through my tenure as commander of the Defense Intelligence Agency.

Several days later the Soviets actually did infiltrate through our lines, moving into a town several miles to our rear, and started to run riot with the civilian population.

There are numerous stories, most of them apocryphal, that George Patton wanted to trigger World War III right there.

Well, I almost gave him that chance.

The Soviets had illegally cut behind our lines, seized a town, and then announced they were there to stay. Without waiting for high command to hem and haw, I mounted up my battalion, moved my M-7s in, ringing the town, and then at dawn sent in a polite message informing the local commander that it was best that he leave immediately.

If he had called my bluff, I think I might have fired. I was already getting fed up with them, but fortunately he backed down and retreated.

The true nightmare, however, unfolded a couple of weeks later.

Displaced persons camps were going into operation all along the front lines as refugees were herded in and sorted out to be shipped back to their old homes. In Czechoslovakia there were hundreds of thousands of DPs from the east . . . Hungary, Romania, all the way back to the Volga.

Orders came down for military police units to take these people and turn them over to the Soviets.

What unfolded before my eyes was a crime that history has turned away from, an act of shame that few speak of, and which my nation and our leaders were in part responsible for.

Within a couple of days after this transfer started, I received horrifying reports of massacres occurring right in front of our troops. Several commanders had protested and were summarily relieved of command and shipped back to the States.

I ordered one of my recon pilots to take me up. We took off and flew along the line of demarcation. It was a damned nightmare. Less than a mile away, on the Soviet side, I could see holding areas containing thousands of people, and they were being murdered. I could see bodies sprawled everywhere, columns of a dark, seething humanity marching east into the gulag, the weak, the old, the young, shot on the spot and left to rot.

I was sick with rage. To have fought for so long to end such madness and then to see the same ugly blot spreading again like a poisonous filth was more than I could bear.

I could not fly beyond that line. Soviet fighters were patrolling the front and would have dropped us, just as Nazi planes would have dropped us only weeks before. Our supposed allies had already established their curtain, and to this day I condemn any apologist who mouths platitudes about the Soviets and how wrong we were in 1945. Go and say those words to the forgotten dead, murdered in a time of peace, murdered for the solidarity of the working man.

To this day I wonder if I should have done more. Perhaps this book is in part an atonement for that, a reminder of what we fought for, and how across the years afterward far too many lies have been spoken about the confrontation with the Soviets and our supposed wrongs that created that confrontation.

I confronted them across thirty years of my career and never for a second did I doubt what we were facing, an evil every bit as evil as that of Hitler.

I do not condemn the ordinary Soviet soldier, so many of them died anonymously, heroes defending their motherland, and far too many were betrayed by Stalin and his henchmen, sent to the gulag along with the prisoners they were forced to escort.

I went to Corps and protested, but Corps command was not there, and not available. I was told that high command knew and would react, but it never did, and the shadow of those millions disappeared into the east to die . . . forgotten.

Should I have done more? That still haunts me. The rumors were circulating that any officer who voiced protest too loudly was on a plane back to the States, stripped of command. To hell with that. It didn't matter. What stayed me was the utter futility of protest. It was senseless to fall on a sword and change nothing. There was part of me that thought that before that month of May was out, the war would be on again, and if so, I wanted to be with my men.

War with Russia? Ask any veteran who was in Czechoslovakia that spring and he will agree. It was close, damn close, and for years afterward many of us wished it had simply been done and settled once and for all, rather than persisting for forty years of nuclear terror, which during that time seemed a path to mutual annihilation.

In the decade since the collapse of communism, maybe the staying of our hand can be seen as the right path, but that is little solace to the tens of millions who died and the hundreds of millions who lived in terror.

Patton fell, not because he was a madman bent on war and the lust for glory, but because he was a realist and a man of honor. I do not know how much he knew about the massacres, but I think he did know a good deal and protested what had been agreed upon at Yalta. Those souls, either naive or cunning in their support of Stalin, could not tolerate Patton's kind of truth, and so he had to be shut up and removed from command.

In the end a foolish accident stilled his voice.

If only he had lived long enough to tell all.

Those final months were a time of mingled hopes and fears. Of the fears I've only spoken a part. The Nazi specter that had consumed so many years of my life, and haunted so many nightmares since my days as a cadet, was dead. So many good people who had been seduced by it were awakening from the opiumlike dream and in that awakening were realizing at last the folly of their ways.

In the years afterward I have befriended a good many of my foes, including the son of Erwin Rommel, and many a general, one a survivor of Stalingrad and one of the last to leave Hitler's bunker. They are men of honor, devoted to country and family, and they will admit that they had been caught up in something that blinded them to where the path would ultimately lead. They stood the long watch against the Soviets with me, and they are an example of how even the best can be lured into darkness and then redeemed.

Of the evil men, far too many escaped justice, slipping through the cracks, crawling out of the slime and ruin they created. Justice must wait until they stand before the final Judge, and since we are all old men now, I wonder how many of them still lie awake at night, filled with fear for the sins they must answer for.

The war in that summer of 1945 was not yet over. It was a strange and confusing time. Within days of the official ending of the conflict in Europe, we started to behave again as we did before the war, even while the conflict with Japan was going on and an invasion that would have overshadowed the Normandy invasion was gearing up.

Our army demanded to be demobilized. If only the entire world could be like America, I think there would never be another war. Americans don't like war. We hate to get dragged in, but when aroused, we'll go out and do the job. But the moment it's done, the hell with the army, we want to go home.

Of course, as a professional officer in the regular army, this didn't hit me. If my orders were to keep me in Europe until 1950, I would have obeyed. But from the millions of draftees and volunteers, the men with old units such as the 1st Infantry

Division, the National Guard units like the 45th, or late-formed divisions like the ill-fated 99th, the universal cry went up: "We want to go home."

I could see why they felt that way. They'd done a magnificent job. They had accomplished what they set out to do, which was to kill Nazism and put Hitler in his grave, and so it was time to clean up, go home, and get back to normal life.

If only the world were that simple.

What was almost embarrassing was the response at home. Mothers started bombarding congressional offices with pleas for their darling boys, who while away had turned into men, wives for husbands, dads for sons, all of them voting constituents.

So Congress, with an eye toward the 1946 elections, put up a howl that the boys in Europe had done their job. By midsummer the country was in a political uproar.

What came out was a contemptible points system that pleased no one. For each month overseas a soldier got points, for each wound he got points, for each medal he got points—and those soldiers with the most points got home first.

It set off a mad scramble, men conning for bronze stars, men holding up scratched hands that in the point system equaled a leg or an arm blown off. Our combat units started to bleed out as the most experienced personnel were pulled out and shipped home. The greatest army in our nation's history began to shrivel up, even while the confrontation with the Soviets began to build and the war with Japan reached its horrifying climax.

I was, of course, out of this game, and my orders were already cut to take my battalion down to Italy and prepare to ship out for the invasion of Japan, but even as I prepared to do so, men were already rotating home.

On a very personal level, as I bid each man good-bye, I was delighted for him. He was a comrade, a companion from D day to the Elbe, and the fact that he had survived was a source of warmth and joy. And yet I was preparing for another fight, one

that promised to be every bit as frightful as what we had endured, and I was again facing new replacements, green eighteen-
year-old draftees.

That concern ended in a flash of light over Hiroshima and
Nagasaki.

It was yet another terrible step from that day so long ago, at
Fort Monmouth, New Jersey, when I watched a few pathetic
bombers attempt to simulate an attack on New York. We could
now annihilate an entire city with the push of a button.

Of all the implications of what those bombs meant, there was
little thought at the moment, though across the rest of my career
they would haunt me.

Not long would pass before I witnessed the detonation of an
atomic weapon. At that moment, in 1949, I saw what the end
of the world would look like.

In the 1950s I was directly responsible for what were already
being called tactical nuclear weapons, deployed in Germany.

In the 1960s and early 1970s, as head of the Defense Intelligence Agency, I was confronted daily with situation reports as
to the deployment and readiness of Soviet and Chinese ther-
monuclear weapons. I think that more than just about any other
living American I know the full horror of all that these weapons
imply.

But in the late summer of 1945 all that was yet to be. Six days
after Nagasaki the Japanese surrendered, and almost immediately
our orders to ship out to the Pacific were canceled.

Three months later, on a cold November morning, I landed in
Boston Harbor. It had been almost three years to the day since
I had left America outbound to war, part of a ramshackle convoy
of amateurs bent on freeing the world.

The welcoming celebrations were long past. Our boat arrived
without fanfare, though for those of us on board it was a moment of sweetness and unrestrained joy. I think that ship must
have listed ten degrees at the bow as we surged forward to catch
our first glimpse of home. Our tears washed the deck, taking

with them some of the pain, some of the darker memories of all that we had endured.

Bets was waiting for me, three days later in Chicago.

Her war was over, and mine as well.

It has been nearly sixty years since that day and as anyone who has lived to be my age will tell you . . . how swiftly it all passes. It seems but yesterday that I was there, walking down the gangplank, returning home, all my life before me, and Bets leaping into my arms.

It seems but yesterday that I said good-bye to her in the fall of 1942, stepping out the door into the unknown. It was but yesterday that I first saw her on the dance floor and but yesterday that I walked up the hill to the Point to join the Corps.

It is to the Point that I shall finally return and where I shall rest, with Bets by my side. Nearby will be the Chapel, where long ago I first heard the words that shaped my life:

O God, our Father, Thou Searcher of human hearts, help us to draw near to Thee in sincerity and truth. May our religion be filled with gladness and may our worship of Thee be natural.

Strengthen and increase our admiration for honest dealing and clean thinking, and suffer not our hatred of hypocrisy and pretence ever to diminish. Encourage us in our endeavor to live above the common level of life. Make us to choose the harder right instead of the easier wrong, and never to be content with a half truth when the whole truth can be won. Endow us with courage that is born of loyalty to all that is noble and worthy, that scorns to compromise with vice and injustice and knows no fear when truth and right are in jeopardy. Guard us against flippancy and irreverence in the sacred things of life. Grant us new ties of friendship and new opportunities of service. Kindle our hearts in fellowship with those of a cheerful countenance, and soften our hearts with sympathy for those who sorrow and suffer. Help us to maintain the honor of the Corps untarnished and unsullied and to show forth in our lives the ideals of West Point in doing our duty to Thee and to our Country. All of which we ask in the name of the Great Friend and Master of all. Amen.

As long as those words are spoken, acted upon, *and believed in,* I know that all the sacrifices of those who sleep the eternal sleep on the plains of West Point will not have been in vain.